The professions: roles and rules

The professions: roles and rules

Wilbert E. Moore
In collaboration with
Gerald W. Rosenblum

RUSSELL SAGE FOUNDATION
New York

*Printed in the United States of America
Standard Book Number 87154–604–3
Library of Congress Catalog Card Number: 78–104184*

DESIGNED BY BETTY BINNS

for Donald R. Young

A man of much eminence and
one much honored by the
intellectual and professional
community, who is also a close
friend of long standing and the
wisest man I ever knew.

Preface

IN September 1940, I took up my first post-doctoral college teaching position at Pennsylvania State College (now University), as an Instructor. Among my many initial assignments was a course on Sociology of the Professions, which had been recently introduced into the curriculum by Professor Kingsley Davis. Davis had two other points to his credit with me at that time (and several since) : He had been responsible for my appointment, when job-hunting was an assiduously pursued activity by potential candidates and head-hunting or body-snatching a responsibility not yet weighing down departmental chairmen. He also asked me to teach a course in Industrial Sociology, an assignment that affected my career as a teacher and writer for a considerable number of years.

Sociology of the Professions was taught by me for only a year or two, after which it was inherited by someone still more junior in the Sociology Department at Penn State.

This autobiographical note must have scant interest to persons other than my professional associates, except to establish a long record of considerable interest in the subject of this book. Meanwhile, a great many sociologists, both eminent and youthfully eager, have explored the professional sector of the labor force. Their distilled perspectives are represented here, to the best of my ability, in substantive allegations ; their scholarly contributions are recorded, sparsely, in footnoted citations and, more extensively, in the selected bibliography.

The autobiography continues a bit, however. When I was asked to join the staff of the Russell Sage Foundation I brought with me several continuing intellectual interests. Some were clearly consistent with the research and policy interests of the Foundation ; others, such as comparative analysis of social structure and change, required a little more mutual adaptation. But "the professions" were home base both for me and for the traditions of the Foundation, and the undertaking now presented was my original, high-priority intellectual assignment at the Foundation.

Owing to the Foundation's support, I have been able to muster other intellectual resources in getting access to the burgeoning literature on the professions. Several graduate assistants performed heroic labors in tracking, annotating, and classifying publications. Two doctoral students in Sociology at Princeton, Peter Stein and Michael Attalides, took basic notes and leads of mine and produced a bibliography, tentatively classified. Peter Nulty, a doctoral student at Columbia University working closely with Gerald Rosenblum, revised and amplified the bibliography, and undertook its classification according to a revised scheme of organization of the volume.

Professor Gerald Rosenblum of New York University, a former student of mine at Princeton, joined me for a few years at Russell Sage on this study. The original notions about a "scale of professionalism" were his, and their modifications, represented in the first chapter, have been developed with him. Rosenblum also served with me in tracking down information and scholarly references. He is the original author of Chapter 3 on the process of professionalization of occupations.

Professor Robin M. Williams, Jr., of Cornell University, a Visiting Scholar at Russell Sage Foundation during 1968–1969 and a long-time friend and one-time collaborator, provided a detailed and welcome commentary on an earlier version of the manuscript. Professor Robert K. Merton of Columbia University, a Visiting Scholar at Russell Sage during 1966–1967 and a former teacher of mine at Harvard, expressed extreme doubt about an earlier version of Chapter 1. I think he was wrong, but I appreciate this expression of the interest he shares with me in the subject.

Over the last ten years or so I have had many opportunities to discuss theoretical and practical issues relating to the professions with Robert B. Yegge, a former student of mine at Princeton and now Dean of the College of Law, University of Denver. Both in personal conversations and in several conferences in and around Denver organized by Dean Yegge, I have gained some insight and perspective on problems of the legal profession, and particularly the difficulties in making professional education relevant to professional practice. We expect a short collaborative study on paralegal occupations, undertaken during the summer of 1969 at the University of Denver, College of Law, to develop into further joint work in the near future.

To my colleagues and associates at Russell Sage Foundation I owe an unusual debt of collegial gratitude for suffering with me for so long on this project. To the President of the Foundation, Doctor Orville G. Brim, Jr., and to the Trustees, I owe a continuing debt of gratitude for according me the opportunity and resources for attending to what I regard as significant subjects.

Madeline Dalton Spitaleri, my secretary for several years who has left to become a full-time mother, saw this manuscript through various (sometimes weekly) revisions. This she did with unfailing good humor and exceptional competence, two traits that I often envied her.

A final autobiographical note: Doctor Donald Young, former President of Russell Sage Foundation, did not select me as a member of the Foundation staff; that was the decision of his successor, Doctor Brim, and on that I checked carefully before accepting the appointment. For Donald Young is a professional colleague and personal friend of long standing, and I wanted no taint of favoritism. Now that I am an almost free agent—despite a nearly coincident book written jointly with Doctor Young—I want by the dedication of this volume to represent in modest degree my continuing personal and intellectual debt to my friend and mentor.

Wilbert E. Moore

New York
Princeton
Denver
June 1969

Contents

The professions: roles and rules

Part one: The emergence of professionalism

Chapter one: The criteria
of professionalism*

TO have one's occupational status accepted as professional or to have one's occupational conduct judged as professional is highly regarded in all post-industrial societies and in at least the modernizing sectors of others. The qualities of what constitutes professionalism are not always constant and indeed not always clear. Nor is professionalism always positively valued. A person characterized as a "professional Southerner" or a "professional gossip" is held in low esteem. Even for approved performance, amateurism may be held in higher regard than the practice of some exceptional art or skill for pay. Such approval of amateurism is more likely in activities that we shall identify as quasi-professional than in those that require an extended period of fairly formal training. Amateur artists, performers, or athletes may not suffer very seriously by comparison with those who depend on such activities for their livelihood. The same cannot be said in the cases of physicians, lawyers, teachers, engineers, or airline pilots.

One outstanding difference between the "true" professional —a term we shall have reason to distrust in later discussion —and the quasi-professional is that the former typically deals with specific clients. And it should be added that the welfare of the professionals' clients is vitally affected by the competence and quality of the service performed; this is certainly not true in the same sense or same degree of esthetic and expressive activities. A poor performance may distress the beholder, but it scarcely threatens his vital interests.

Professionals represent the most rapidly growing occupational category in highly developed modern economies, and the end is by no means in sight. Meanwhile, countless (or at least uncounted) man-hours are devoted to the quest for en-

---

* This chapter was drafted and revised by Moore, on the basis of original ideas by Gerald Rosenblum.

hancement of occupational position and acceptance as members of the professional club. True, much of this hortatory and promotional activity is not carried on by regular practitioners but by teachers of the subject and especially by the salaried staffs of occupational associations and the editorial writers for associational house organs. Yet it must be assumed that these protagonists have the support or acquiescence of their constituencies.

Why professionalism should be held in such generally high regard is one question that will be explored later in this book. The meaning of professionalism itself, the criteria by which an occupation or an activity may be judged to be professional, are explored herewith.

Defining professionalism

Just as the representatives of occupations seeking enhancement of collective status have devoted much time and energy to the enterprise, so academic scholars have devoted uncounted hours to the definition and characterization of professions. Neither form of activity can be dismissed out of hand as entirely wasteful or inconsequential, though some of it undoubtedly is.

One difficulty in many scholarly approaches to the definition of professionalism is the attempt by one authority after another to identify the ideal-typical or quintessential characteristics of an occupational category, which can then be distinguished from all others with unfailing accuracy.[1]

The attempt to define professionalism in ideal-typical terms is of course methodologically tenable, if adequate operational

---

[1] Since our approach to the identification of professionalism is substantially different from that common in the literature, we do not at this point interrupt proceedings for an extensive review of the authorities. Principal citations appear in the selected bibliography (pp. 245–301).

The closest parallel to our approach that we have encountered is that of Sussman, who suggests a different set of criteria, but does select autonomy as the highest scale value. See Marvin B. Sussman, "Occupational Sociology and Rehabilitation," in Sussman (ed.), *Sociology and Rehabilitation* (Washington, D.C.: American Sociological Association, n.d.), Chap. 10, esp. pp. 181–189.

specifications are available for reliable identification of the selected characteristics. The difficulties with this approach are several: (1) the attributes so identified or the persons displaying them may have only an approximate and perhaps a very poor fit with attributes or persons identified as professional by other, not unreasonable tests. (2) The resulting division of occupations into professional and nonprofessional, the "true" professionals and all others, is a dichotomy that seems unnecessarily rigid in view of otherwise interesting ranges of variation. (3) By the same token, the process of professionalization, the strategies used to secure higher occupational status, are thereby dropped from view, except, perhaps, for the last step toward final success.

In short, we suggest that professionalism should properly be regarded as a scale rather than a cluster of attributes, and thus that attributes commonly noted have differing values. This approach does not exactly simplify the task of identification; on the contrary, since each of the scale points we are about to suggest has its own subset of scale values. We shall, nevertheless, put forward this set of suggestions, being convinced that only in this way can the wondrous array of technical occupations be put in some kind of order, and, importantly, can the process of status enhancement be understood.

A scale of professionalism

By way of preliminary specification, we may identify the professional by the following defining characteristics. The professional practices a full-time *occupation*, which comprises the principal source of his earned income. This sets the professional apart from the amateur, but not from a host of other full-time members of the stable labor force. It is a necessary but not sufficient condition for admission to higher ranks on the scale of professionalism. A more distinctively professional qualification is that of commitment to a *calling*, that is, the treatment of the occupation and all of its requirements as an enduring set of normative and behavioral expectations. Those who pursue occupations of relatively high rank in terms of criteria of professionalism are likely to be set apart from the laity by various signs and symbols, but by the same token are identified with their peers—often in formalized *organization*. Organization presupposes a distinctive occupation with a common commitment by those engaged in it to protect and enhance its interests.

An important next step in professionalism is the possession of esoteric but useful knowledge and skills, based on specialized training or *education* of exceptional duration and perhaps of exceptional difficulty. The qualification "useful" knowledge implies the next higher scale position of professionalism : in the practice of his occupation, the professional is expected to exhibit a *service orientation*, to perceive the needs of individual or collective clients that are relevant to his competence and to attend to those needs by competent performance. Finally, in the use of his exceptional knowledge, the professional proceeds by his own judgment and authority ; he thus enjoys *autonomy* restrained by responsibility.

Now these characteristics, we are suggesting, are not of equal value, and can be regarded as points—or, in view of subscales, as clusters—along a scale of professionalism. We shall discuss each one in turn.

OCCUPATION

In modern societies the specification that a profession is a full-time occupation might be regarded as of small significance, an example of things taken for granted. The stipulation obviously does not distinguish the professional from the majority of participants in the labor force. The chief point in such societies is simply to distinguish the professional from the amateur. And it is important to note that artists and entertainers may fail on this criterion, often by reason of insufficient demand for their services, which may or may not reflect their relative quality by other criteria. We should also note that it is unlikely that the professional who has a high score on subsequent scale points will have secondary occupations or income-producing activities radically unrelated to his primary occupation.

The very concept of occupation is relatively rare and on the whole relatively recent in the world's societies. There is no reliable way of distinguishing, among the many useful and essential activities for individual and collective survival, which constitute work or labor, except by use of some form of market test. Thus work is financially rewarded activity, and an occupation is a distinct and related set of activities in a system where some division of labor prevails.

That the professional or quasi-professional may be the first occupational type to emerge in social evolution, we shall suggest in the following chapter. Even so, neither the level of demand for specialized services nor the mechanism for their payment may be adequate in many societies for the full-fledged professional to exist.

In modern societies, the occupational qualification is commonly more nearly a ticket of admission to the game than a strategy for running up the score of professionalization. Even so, it is well to recall that many fields of service are not exempt from amateur competition. Lest it be thought that this is solely the situation of relatively high-ranking occupations only recently and incompletely professionalized, such as social work, we may note that medicine and law are by no means accorded the exclusive occupancy that practitioners in these fields claim. Part-time competition may also threaten, as in teaching at various educational levels. Such competition threatens both the claim to exceptional competence and the claim to a primary occupational commitment.

THE CALLING

It is the normal assumption that a young person undertaking the extensive training for a profession (or, for that matter, a skilled craft) intends to pursue a stable career in his chosen specialty. The idea of occupation of course may seem to imply some considerable measure of persistence, except at the very lowest level of skills represented by the casual laborer. Yet Wilensky finds more disorder than order in the careers of a majority of participants in the labor force.[2] And

<hr>

[2] Harold L. Wilensky, "Orderly Careers and Social Participation: The Impact of Work History on Social Integration in the Middle Mass," *American Sociological Review*, 26:521–539, August 1961.

persistence alone need not indicate commitment, for it may simply reflect lack of qualifications or opportunities to change occupation.

Commitment to a calling involves acceptance of the appropriate norms and standards, and identification with professional peers and the profession as a collectivity. For a youth to seek training in engineering or law with the specific intent of using that training as a steppingstone to a position in management is tolerated, but certainly not wholly approved by dedicated practitioners. Indeed, it may not even be tolerated if the candidate makes known his intention when he applies for admission to a professional school, any more than apprenticeship in a skilled trade is likely to be available to one known to have little or no intention to perform when fully qualified.

The peer loyalty associated with commitment to a calling may at times be inconsistent with the most effective service to clients. Goode has noted the common refusal of professionals to rank their fellows in terms of competence in any precise way when dealing with the laity. This author also observes that raising admission standards implies the probability that some current practitioners could not meet them. Yet disqualification is not enforced, nor is the implication mentioned to the laity.[3]

Other evidences of commitment share some of the ambiguity regarding a service orientation. The fact that professionals in private practice put in unusually long work hours[4] may signify either dedication or mere greed. The fact that

---

[3] William J. Goode, "Community Within a Community: The Professions," *American Sociological Review*, 22:194–200, April 1957.

[4] Harold L. Wilensky, "The Uneven Distribution of Leisure: The Impact of Economic Growth on 'Free Time,' " *Social Problems*, 9:32–56, Summer 1961. See also U.S. Bureau of the Census, *U.S. Census of Population, 1960; Subject Reports: Characteristics of Professional Workers*, Final Report PC(2)–7E (Washington, D.C.: Government Printing Office, 1964), Table 4. Almost half (47.5 per cent) of the salaried male lawyers and judges worked more than 40 hours per week, 58 per cent of the self-employed; the corresponding proportions for physicians and surgeons were 76 per cent and 86 per cent.

salaried professionals also work long hours undermines a
purely cynical interpretation, although the younger salaried
men might still stand accused of ambition. However this may
be, we do know that professionals attend primarily to the
good opinion of their peers, and that the legitimate practitioner feels in some sense damaged and resentful when a
member of the trade is discovered in some serious impropriety. The bond established by shared mysteries, exemplified in technical language and common styles of work and
often even common attire, bespeaks a consciousness of being
set apart, and insisting on it.

ORGANIZATION

Mutual identification of distinctly occupational interests, as
compared with and often in competition with common employee status interests, employer interests, or interest in the
entire sector of an economic system,[5] commonly leads to some
form of occupational organization.

The common occupational interests that animate the formation of a craft union or a self-styled professional association
include such mundane matters as the terms and conditions
of employment, but do not exclude such slightly more strategic considerations as criteria of access to the occupation,
the attempt therefore to exclude the allegedly incompetent,
and, to protect all this presumably honorable monopoly, the
maintenance of performance standards among accepted
practitioners.

It is extremely unlikely that an occupation will be able to set
itself apart from, and above, mere tasks set by the administrative wisdom of superiors without making common cause
in a formal organization. In the history of the Western
world, the craftsmen's guilds supervised standards of apprenticeship, competence, and performance. The distinction
between dextrous skills and somewhat more abstract learning developed only gradually, partly because some occupa-

---

[5] See Wilbert E. Moore, "Notes for a General Theory of Labor Organization," *Industrial and Labor Relations Review*, 13:387–397, April
1960.

tions managed to become affiliated with formal educational curricula. But in England surgeons were long denied formal professional status, since their skills were manual, and to this day English surgeons (with, now, a bit of inverted snobbery) are insistently called "Mister," and not "Doctor."

The subscale of organization with respect to achievement of, or approximation to, professional status appears to have the following order: (a) recognition of common occupational interests, with some priority over all other simultaneously competing interests; (b) some mechanism of control to maintain standards of performance; and (c) control of access to the occupation, so that qualifications for inclusion are essentially under the control and jurisdiction of current practitioners. (In temporal order, monopolizing a skill and determining criteria of admission may proceed concurrently. In fact, and especially as judged by both craft trades and semi-professional occupations, monopoly of the skill may well precede the setting of standards of performance for the fortunate ones admitted. Yet it remains true that control of access is crucial for setting the training standards for new recruits, and that is the only way to go on to the next point in the scale.)

EDUCATION

The occupations that have long been established as fully qualified professions—law, medicine, and the clergy, for example—are often referred to by the qualifier "learned." Yet at least until the emergence of universities and their gradual adoption of the responsibility for technical training in fields other than theology, the learning of a highly specialized branch of knowledge was more often by apprenticeship to a qualified practitioner than by classroom or laboratory instruction. It is still possible to read law and perhaps successfully qualify on a bar examination in some American states. Nevertheless, it is understandably rare, given the existence of law schools with formal curricula, and in many jurisdictions successful completion of formal legal training is a prior condition of eligibility for the qualifying examination. Law and even medicine have had a more tenuous relation to higher education in England, and the solicitor still prepares for his profession at the Inns of Court rather than in a university-based school.

Despite these relatively minor variations, formal educational qualifications are the general rule for many occupations in modern societies, and especially for those that claim and are accorded the status of professions. Some final, "finishing" part of the formal education is specifically designed as preparatory for the specialized occupation, and not simply as a general or liberal education (though the term "liberal profession" does imply that a person in such an occupation will also be broadly educated).

The precise length of training is variable in time and place, and among occupations. Thus we have once more the possibility of a scale-within-a-scale for the ranking of occupations. Some examples of differences in formal training for some professional and some other occupations in 1960 in the United States are presented in Table 1.1.

Owing to the almost uniform contemporary American training of the medical practitioner through internships and residencies beyond the M.D. degree, the strictly formal training represented in the 1960 Census surely understates the period of combined education and a form of apprenticeship.

It is also true that the educational standards for almost every technical occupation rise through time—and very rapidly in post-industrial societies. Thus, it is scarcely surprising that the educational attainments of young practitioners are well above those of their seniors. (Whether experience is an adequate substitute for rather more formalized training will engage our attention in Chapter 7.)

Since we are suggesting that a high educational attainment is a point along a scale of professionalism, some, perhaps somewhat arbitrary decision is necessary as to the precise definition of this criterion. We suggest that in the contemporary United States the minimum educational requirement be placed at the equivalent of the college baccalaureate degree. Since nearly all of the older and well-recognized learned professions in fact require training beyond the baccalaureate degree, this minimum may be too low.

Even postgraduate education may not be sufficient to estab-

Table 1.1: Educational levels of selected occupations, males, aged 14 and over, United States, 1960[a]

OCCUPATION	MEDIAN SCHOOL YEARS COMPLETED	PERCENTAGE OF THOSE WITH SOME COLLEGE EDUCATION	
		1 YEAR OR MORE	4 YEARS OR MORE
Accountants and auditors	15.3	72.1	43.6
Clergymen	17.1	83.6	70.9
College presidents, professors, and instructors	17.4	98.6	95.3
Civil engineers	16.1	74.3	53.8
Electrical engineers	16.2	78.9	58.4
Lawyers and judges	17.4	96.6	89.7
Natural scientists	16.8	87.1	76.0
Physicians and surgeons	17.5	99.1	98.2
Social scientists	16.9	84.3	70.5
Teachers (elementary schools)	17.0	96.8	86.0
Teachers (secondary schools)	17.2	97.4	92.7
Mgrs., officials, and props. ex. farm.	12.5	34.5	16.8
Clerical and kindred workers	12.3	25.0	7.8
Insurance agts., brkrs., and underwriters	12.9	47.0	23.1
Real estate agts. and brkrs.	12.7	42.5	18.5
Brickmasons, stonemasons, and tilesetters	9.7	5.2	0.6
Carpenters	9.3	5.0	0.8
Operatives and kindred workers	9.6	4.8	0.7
Laborers except farm and mine	8.7	2.9	0.6

[a] Source: U.S. Bureau of the Census, *U. S. Census of the Population, 1960*, Subject Reports PC (2)–7A, *Occupational Characteristics* (Washington, D.C.: U.S. Government Printing Office, 1963), Table 9.

lish a claim to professional standing, if its type and quality do not provide a clear distinction between the person with formal training and the person who is merely experienced. Thus, although a growing proportion of recruits to business management are products of graduate schools of business administration, the dominant curricula of those schools until very recently has comprised the analysis of "cases" of business organization and decisions. Until abstract analytical tools and theoretical principles were introduced, training in business administration merely substituted vicarious experience for real experience, and could not successfully distinguish between the professional and the layman.[6]

The suggestion of the baccalaureate cutting-off point is in part pragmatic, though we do not thereby abdicate any further interest in those cut off. We are attempting, in a very crude way, to suggest that there is a genuine scale of professionalism. Our criterion at this point is that we regard it as extremely improbable that technically trained persons with less than the equivalent of the American baccalaureate degree could manage to achieve the higher relative positions in any scale of professionalism.

SERVICE ORIENTATION

A distinctive feature of full-fledged professions, noted by most students of the subject, is a service orientation. Although this criterion, or scale point, can be defined (if not easily measured) rather narrowly, we may properly attend to three subsets of related norms: rules of *competence,* rules of conscientious *performance,* and rules of *loyalty* or *service.*

Competence refers not simply to standards for admission to a profession—assured by the control of access, including education and examining boards—but also to the maintenance and improvement of both individual and collective

---

[6] Barber rejects the claims of business management to professional status on several other counts, but accepts at face value the educational claims. See Bernard Barber, "Is American Business Becoming Professionalized? Analysis of a Social Ideology," in Edward A. Tiryakian (ed.), *Sociological Theory, Values, and Socio-Cultural Change* (New York: Free Press, 1963), pp. 121–145.

standards. Despite the patent difficulty of doing so in the contemporary world, the professional is supposed to keep current with developments in his field, so that his clients do not seriously suffer relative harm from his failure to do so.

Competence is for a purpose: conscientious performance. Once a professional-client relationship is formed, whether in private or salaried practice, the client's concerns are to be treated seriously, or at least as seriously as the case merits. Since the client is understandably prone to exaggerate his problems, his judgment is not necessarily binding on his professional adviser. Yet he may need protection against the casual or slovenly performer, and that protection can only come through a collectively enforced set of standards laid down by the profession itself.

To assure performance professionals are obliged to regulate their own conduct by adherence to ethical codes. Here we shall be rather general, as our detailed comparison of professional behavior in Part Two is in terms of types of role relationships, with the appropriate norms being intrinsic to the analysis. The general performance norms refer primarily to the professional's obligations to clients, but secondarily to peers, since incompetent or slovenly performance, or failure to protect a client's interests, necessarily reflects discredit on the professional collectivity. Indeed, the general functions of performance norms are, ideally, both to protect the ignorant client and the legitimate practitioner against the charlatan or the improper practitioner.

The norms of loyalty or service, which many authorities would regard as crucial criteria of professionalism, are also among the more difficult to verify. True, some normatively prescribed practices can be readily observed in practice—for example, preserving the confidentiality of the professional-client relationship. As Everett Hughes puts it, for the cautionary admonition of the marketplace, *caveat emptor*, professional practice substitutes the encouraging injunction *credat emptor*, let the buyer trust.[7] But the justification of

---

[7] Everett C. Hughes, "Professions," in Kenneth S. Lynn (ed.), *The Professions in America* (Boston: Houghton Mifflin Company, 1965), pp. 1–14.

that trust comprises the rules of competence and performance and also the expectation that the client will not suffer as a consequence of entrusting his personal affairs to another.

The service orientation as such, that the professional is supposed to serve the interests of clients and the community and not, in the first instance, his own, is the part of this normative complex that is difficult to verify. One difficulty is that professionals as an occupational category are among the more highly rewarded in modern societies. In principle, these are rewards for meritorious conduct, including the service orientation, but the circumstances are suspicious. If, in fact, all or most professionals rendered regular unpaid services for needy clients, one could give credence to the norm of service. Actually, such service is very rare, and may be unintended: a bill is rendered but goes unpaid.

We are not of course dealing here with altruism versus egoism. As Parsons has been at pains to point out,[8] it is the institutional setting of the professional that differs from the businessman, not necessarily his private motivation. Still, one should expect some attitudinal affinity with the norm, manifested in behavior, and that is precisely what is difficult to demonstrate. It should be added that some professional spokesmen are voicing concern about the availability and quality of professional services, particularly for underprivileged segments of the population. Thus, it is possible that the norm may be revived through collective professional action.

AUTONOMY[9]

The specialist in his field must be supreme, for who, other than another similarly qualified specialist, can challenge

---

[8] See Talcott Parsons, "The Professions and Social Structure," *Social Forces*, 17:457–467, May 1939; also in his *Essays in Sociological Theory: Pure and Applied* (New York: Free Press, 1949), pp. 185–199.

[9] Our use of the criterion of autonomy has a substantial congruence with Goode's characterization of a profession as a "community." See Goode, article cited in note 3.

him? The degree of specialization has gone on at such a pace that Wilensky could properly inquire, though answer negatively, "The Professionalization of Everyone?"[10]

Autonomy is in effect an ultimate value for self-identified members of an occupational category, and they are extremely unlikely to achieve that goal without having the prior qualifications that we have been specifying. Again, however, we are dealing with a scale-within-a-scale, and it is quite clear that the lower values of the scale do not require passing through the top values of the preceding scales. What householder could effectively challenge a plumber or electrician? But note that the well-trained engineer could at least engage the craftsman in conversation, and possibly make alternative suggestions.

The autonomy of the professional is not qualitatively distinct from that of other specialized and useful occupations, but rather builds upon his having passed previous selection points. The technical training of the electrician or the plumber or the carpenter is not trivial, but it is not outside the grasp of the do-it-yourself householder who spends a little time at the problem. The same allegation cannot be reasonably put forward with respect to medical diagnosis, the assessment of a case in legal litigation, or the discrimination among a set of experimentally verified but contradictory findings on an intellectual problem.

As technical specialization steadily increases, so must the relative autonomy of specialists. Yet if it is true as we claim that we are dealing here with a genuine scale, it must follow that the achievement of something like genuine autonomy depends upon such clear-cut criteria as avoidance of the self-service of the laity, commitment to a calling, organization to the effective point of controlling admission to the occupation, specialized education to the point and quality that one can readily distinguish the professional and the merely experienced layman, and effective norms to assure competent performance of services beyond the layman's grasp.

---

[10] Harold L. Wilensky, "The Professionalization of Everyone?" *American Journal of Sociology*, 70:137–158, September 1964.

Some methodological and theoretical problems

The discussion so far has centered primarily on the professions or near-professions, paying attention to ways of handling differences in degrees of professionalism, but implicitly treating occupations as if they were homogeneous with regard to the criteria we have set forth. This is clearly not the case, and we must attend to some problems that are presented if we wish to avoid naive generalization.

Perhaps the first methodological question to be asked is whether it is proper to treat professional and related occupations as a category with sufficient common features and sufficiently distinct from other occupational types to warrant the procedure. A negative view by Howard S. Becker[11] implies lack of comparability among occupations, but rests primarily on the lack of correspondence between professional criteria as symbols and the realities of occupational practice. Our objection to this view is that ideal values and norms are not made irrelevant by failures to achieve them. That could be argued only if a radical change or outright abandonment of professed ideals would have no consequences for behavior, and that we do not believe to be the case. There appears to be a sufficient consensus on the criteria of professionalism and sufficient prospect that the degree to which occupational status and practice meet those criteria can be objectively identified to justify dealing with that subset of all occupations for which the criteria are especially or peculiarly relevant. At the very least, we should argue that the proposed criteria of professionalism warrant the asking of common questions, even if the answers turn out to be different from one case to another.

The prospect that the common questions on, say, degree of professionalism will yield different answers as among occupations is not the least dismaying, as that is precisely what the suggested scale is all about. Yet how homogeneous is each occupation in its standards and patterned behavior? Al-

---

[11] Howard S. Becker, "The Nature of a Profession," in *Education for the Professions*, Sixty-first Yearbook of the National Society for the Study of Education, Part II (Chicago: University of Chicago Press for the Society, 1962), pp. 27–46.

though the answer, again, differs from one occupation to another, substantial inequality within a nominally uniform occupation is not uncommon. For example, the lawyer of record dealing with a client presumably enjoys autonomy in formulating his advice or pursuing litigation in the client's interests. But what of the salaried attorney in a law firm? He may never see a client, and perform legal tasks assigned by a partner in the firm. Were this subordinate position temporary, as it is for some, it could be regarded as an extension of apprenticeship. For those who stay in such positions throughout a career, the status is less than fully professional. Similar examples can be found within all of the established and high-ranking professions. The methodological moral is to avoid the unexamined assumption that the status of an occupation is to be properly judged by its ideal-typical representatives, who may not adequately reflect the range of skills and positions, and may not even constitute the majority.

A third issue is perhaps more one of definition than of methodology, but it deserves scrutiny in any case. Are clients necessary to professional status? The question is clearly relevant, since part of the norms and practices of professionalism are normally applicable to the context of service to clients' interests. In arguing an affirmative answer to the question, Wilensky[12] would exclude the scientist engaged solely in basic research or the nonteaching humanist scholar. Our view is that service without recipients is indeed a meaningless conception, but that the clients may be corporate or even communal, and that there is no necessity that the service be rendered in a face-to-face encounter. The scientist or scholar who does not teach or advise clearly lacks clients in the strict and proper sense of persons or collectivities dependent upon expert advice for their welfare. Freidson, on this basis, would draw a clear distinction, between "science" and "professions."[13] One can readily assent to the assertion

---

[12] Wilensky, article cited in note 10.
[13] Eliot Freidson, "The Impurity of Professional Authority," in Howard S. Becker and others (eds.), *Institutions and the Person* (Chicago: Aldine Publishing Company, 1968), Chap. 3, pp. 25–34.

that the absence of direct and immediate clients makes an important difference in occupational role relationships. Yet it does not follow that the scientist or scholar does not have a service orientation, even if the goal pursued is abstract and impersonal, and certainly does not follow that the "professional without clients" is not significantly oriented to other professional criteria and to the maintenance of high standards through the sanctions provided by peers (often formally constituted). It is to take account of differences in role relationships, without exaggerating their significance, that the designation "helping professions" is sometimes used to identify the high-level occupations oriented to serving clients.

For many analytical purposes, the notion of a scale of professionalism adds little if anything to the simple stipulation of the criteria here discussed, used as an enumerative definition of certain occupational groups. Aside from the disadvantage, earlier noted, that it may lead (even if implicitly) to a factually untenable dichotomy of professional and non-professional occupations, the tactic of attaching no relative values to the several criteria leads (again, often implicitly) to another untenable assumption. That assumption is that failure to meet one criterion has no implications for failure on others here posited to be of a higher order. This may be regarded as a merely empirical question, but that scarcely dismisses its importance.

There is a related question, and that is whether a scale of professionalism, taken as a tenable way of sorting occupations according to such criteria as responsible self-discipline, the enjoyment of confident trust, also constitutes a necessary *sequence* in the process of professionalization. That question will be explored in Chapter 3. Leik and Matthews have suggested a "developmental" scale,[14] with reference to other analytical problems, but that approach may have considerable utility in analyzing the competition for improved standing in the world of work.

---

[14] Robert K. Leik and Merlyn Matthews, "A Scale for Developmental Processes," *American Sociological Review*, 33:62–75, February 1968.

The dimensions of professionalism

The conceptual and methodological issues that we have been discussing provide an ample basis for caution in attempts to identify and compare the professions across space and time. The normal expedient in both international comparisons and in examining temporal trends is to develop lists of named occupations that are judged to be professional, and then to include all persons practicing those occupations. Even by such relatively primitive procedures, comparisons between countries probably approximate the more exact orders of magnitude. The data for 1950 are the most recent that are readily available. These show that the professions accounted then for 6 to 8 per cent of the economically active population in Western Europe, Canada, and the United States, and only 1 to 3 per cent in countries in South Asia and Latin America. The American trends are typical of economically advanced countries in their direction if not in their precise values. Professionals represented only some 4 per cent of the labor force in 1900, 8 per cent in 1950, 12 per cent in 1960, and a little over 13 per cent in 1966.[15]

The association between professionalism and economic development is clear from these and similar data. This is not the place to explore the question as to how much of this association is essential, such as the expansion of technologists in the strict sense, and how much one might simply call comfortable, made possible by the greater public and private prosperity that economic growth provides. Our present concern is simply to observe the rather small proportion of employed populations that are even approximately professional, and to note that these numbers do not begin to represent the

---

[15] The comparative figures in this paragraph were originally derived from official sources; they are presented in Wilbert E. Moore, "Changes in Occupational Structures," in Neil J. Smelser and Seymour Martin Lipset (eds.), *Social Structure and Social Mobility in Economic Development* (Chicago: Aldine Publishing Company, 1966), pp. 194–212. The proportions of the professional occupations in the United States are from U.S. Bureau of the Census, *Statistical Abstract of the United States, 1967* (Washington, D.C.: Government Printing Office, 1967), Table 328, p. 231.

strategic importance of professionalism in contemporary life.

Once more, however, we must be wary of assumed homogeneity. Not all professionals are equally valued in all situations. Clergymen may have a rather difficult time in some political regimes, and Protestant clergymen are, on the whole, relatively poorly rewarded in predominantly Protestant countries. The most conspicuous and proclaimed needs in newly developing areas are for medical and public health services and for engineers and related technicians. In some of these same areas people trained in law far exceed the demand for their services. Even in prosperous countries professional services are by no means equally distributed (or sometimes even sought) across various income groups. The notion of professional services as a social right is rather new, at least in Western democratic countries, and not widely established.

Whenever we discuss the professions collectively, as we shall continue to do on occasion, the comments will be limited to actions or problems that are legitimately common to the occupations that provide a high degree of professionalism for a major part of their recognized practitioners. Otherwise we shall have to note that similar questions yield different answers. Professions clearly differ in the primary service performed, but also in mode of payment, and the latter is not intrinsically determined by the former. Similarly, the modes of day-to-day organization in which professionals perform may have some relation to the special function and its appropriate technology, but need not do so. Hospitals make sense because many sick people need specialized care and because they may need ready access to drugs and to diagnostic and therapeutic equipment. But it is not at all clear that the practice of medicine for the ambulatory patient should commonly take place in the context of a group of specialists practicing together, whereas the fact of specialization within law firms is rarely made known to the client, who commonly deals with a seemingly general practitioner. A clergyman can presumably perform many of his tasks in almost any setting, but he is likely to behave differently within the church building than he does, say, when calling on a sick parishioner.

Our primary strategy for dealing with differences of this sort will be a fairly systematic analysis of professional role relationships, generalizing where possible and particularizing where necessary. In the remaining chapters of Part One we shall continue our examination of the professions in historical and comparative perspective, observe the strategies and tactics of occupations seeking to gain or improve professional status, and, finally, the processes whereby recruits are inducted into the awful mysteries and emerge as more or less qualified practitioners.

In Part Two we shall turn to a rather detailed examination of professionals in their setting, distinguishing clients, peers, those in complementary occupations, employers, administrative subordinates, and even the public as constituting common or possible alter egos in professional roles.

Finally, in the single chapter of Part Three we shall attempt a summing up, particularly with respect to the endlessly troublesome question of the social responsibility of the possessors of knowledge beyond the ken of the layman.

IN the range of human societies—historical, near-contemporary, and modern—something approximating professional services and their practitioners have appeared rather commonly. Priests and curers, rainmakers and soothsayers were to be found in most ancient civilizations, and also in most nonliterate societies before their extensive contact with the modern world. Many of these practitioners would not fully qualify as professionals by the criteria discussed in the preceding chapter. Yet some services are the functional equivalent of contemporary professional practice, although differing in quality, particular procedures, and, most conspicuously, in the institutional setting of their work.

There is a sufficient mystique surrounding the specialized service of the professional that the service may take on, for the layman, the character of a "miraculous cure." There is enough affinity between esoteric knowledge and the claim to supernatural powers that professionals may be regarded by the laity as possessing skills not generally available to the ordinary adult, not because the professional is simply more knowledgeable, but rather because he has a privileged access to occult powers. This is a distinction that will serve us well subsequently, in dealing with the medicine man. We should not leave the subject at this point without noting that all sorts of commonly acknowledged professionals tend to leave implicit the *ultimate* source of their confidence in their admonitions. And there are occupations, such as that of clergyman, which have been little affected by the onslaught of rationality and new knowledge. (It is true, of course, that some clergymen have become increasingly oriented to individual problems, to social problems, and to the challenges of a secular society. These new orientations scarcely rest on a new set of theological principles, but rather on an attempt to keep relevant in the contemporary world.) In these occupations it is still possible to declare, on completely nonrational bases, that the incumbent has some portion of the authority given by the Apostolic Succession (Roman Catholic) or has had the "call to preach" (Protestant evangelical sects). The former is only a more sophisticated and bureaucratized version of the latter, and both would have to be regarded as an attempt to bring into professional practice a peculiar claim to knowledge, namely, that it had been revealed from sources not accessible by the most advanced rational techniques available to the highly educated layman.

One must resist the temptation to identify as professionals in ancient and tribal societies all those performing valued services beyond the competence of the ordinary socialized adult. This simple criterion is in fact likely to have a fair correspondence to quasi-professional positions in societies where there is generally very little division of labor. But where specialization is extensive, any occupational role may be performed by a minority, and others be unqualified without comparable training. In contemporary economically advanced societies this would indeed mean the professionalization of everyone,[1] or at least everyone gainfully occupied save only the unskilled. No, we are safest if we insist on the unusual degree of specialized skill and training, relative of course to variable social settings. We should thus exclude the artisan who chooses (or has thrust upon him by the accident of birth) a particular handicraft specialty, but is not thereby set apart as superior to those engaged in other productive roles. The professional or quasi-professional *is* set apart, though perhaps primarily because he commands mysterious forces rather than matter-of-factly in terms of the training time required to acquire his awesome skill.

We shall examine, first, the position of the medicine man and similar positions in nonliterate societies. Theories of social evolution no longer assume that nonliterate societies are in an arrested state of evolution and can be safely equated with prehistoric human cultures. Yet the temptation is strong, particularly when similar patterns of organization appear in widely diverse cultures without detectable chances of diffu-

---

[1] Harold L. Wilensky, "The Professionalization of Everyone?," *American Journal of Sociology*, 70:137–158, September 1964.

sion among them. The similarity will become clear in our brief examination of professional functions in ancient civilizations, both those that have some historic linkage with Western societies and those that have little or none.

The emergence of the professions in something like their contemporary form can be most readily traced to the Middle Ages and Renaissance, particularly to the universities and the later formation of learned societies. Rational solutions began competing with traditional ones and with conventional acceptance of fate. A somewhat similar situation is to be found when we return to tribal and similar traditional societies, but this time with our attention turned to modern types of professional practice in settings where they compete with older forms of handling human interests and problems.

The professions in nonliterate societies

We should have to tamper with our previously enunciated scale of professionalism to a marked degree in order to include distinct (and highly valued) services in nonliterate societies. It is perhaps simplest to characterize these roles as quasi-professional, or possibly proto-professional, in view of the tentative evolutionary interpretation that we are about to advance. Not all of these performers of valued services are even full-time practitioners, and some rest their claims to special prowess more on spiritual identification than on cognitively acquired knowledge and skills. Yet some of the functions performed are ubiquitous in the human condition, and some have enough congruence with professionalism to warrant a more than casual glance at some social types that resemble modern professionals at least in their oddity.

THE SHAMAN: PROBLEMS OF MAGIC, SCIENCE, AND RELIGION

One prototype of the contemporary professional is the shaman, or medicine man. (We are inclined, for reasons presently to be adduced, to view this position, suitably loosened in specification, as *the* prototype of the professional position.) "Shamanism" comes from certain central Siberian nonliterate tribes, and in its strictest meaning refers to a type of activity relying prominently on alleged spiritual forces directed toward practical vicissitudes of a harsh human existence. Indeed, there is a strong overtone of a kind of demonic possession, to use archaic language, or personality traits that verge on the psychotic, to use a scarcely more informative modern idiom.[2] Because of the rather common occurrence of comparable specialties and functions in nonliterate societies, there is an apparently unchallenged acquiescence among anthropologists in using the terms shaman or shamanism to refer to the similar roles wherever found.

We think that the interesting theoretical question relevant to our subject is this: Under what circumstances will a specialized professional type appear, and when not? We think that it is safe to say that in the current state of comparative social analysis—and that is rather a dismal state—this question is unanswerable. Yet we shall attempt here some preliminaries to an answer, for we are convinced that the regularities are far beyond chance or mere accidental appearances.

AN EVOLUTIONARY VIEW

Most historians of the ancient world and comparative anthropologists and sociologists harbor, at least secretly, some belief in the reality of social evolution. To sustain this view it is not necessary (and it is not methodologically tenable, in view of evidence) simply to rank known societies and cultures on a single, rectilinear evolutionary scale. Neither is it necessary, or proper, to assume that there is a single invariant course of developmental change, all aspects of the system being coordinated. Cross-sectional diversity may be attributed to environmental adaptation, and not necessarily to arrested development. What is essential is to allege that more complex social structures supersede simpler ones, that certain elements such as verifiable knowledge are cumulative, and that reversals of direction are improbable without a

---

[2] See William A. Lessa and Evon Z. Vogt (eds.), *Reader in Comparative Religion*, 2nd ed. (New York: Harper & Row, Publishers, 1965), Chap. 10, "Shamans and Priests."

radical and disruptive change in relevant conditions—for example, a natural, medical, or military catastrophe.

These comments are prefatory to an examination of what appear to be proto-professionals in nonliterate and ancient societies. For whatever historical reasons, there are substantial differences among societies in the store of verifiable knowledge and rational technique relating to the nonhuman environment and man's adjustment to it or control over it. It appears fairly clear that nonliterate or barely literate societies have only very small stores of useful knowledge, the degree of sophistication of course being somewhat variable in amount and kind. Yet it appears proper to ask whether certain kinds of knowledge (or alleged knowledge and skills) are more likely than others, and indeed, whether the "knowledge" is of sufficient degree and difficulty that it cannot be commonly shared—that is, that it is likely to be associated with specialized roles in social systems.

A clear, affirmative answer can be given to this query with respect to matters of health and life. In societies of which we have any record, it is universally or almost universally true that illnesses—including wounds and broken bones— are not only the concern of specialized role assignments, but that those roles are almost invariably set apart from ordinary role assignments within familial and kinship structures. In other words, these services are rendered on some sort of community basis, and not confined to the immediate kinship unit.

Now the point of alluding to evolutionary theory is speculative but possibly interesting. Under evolutionary assumptions, it would be proper to posit a kind of limiting, primal state, in which physical suffering and death are viewed fatalistically, along with other vicissitudes of the human condition. No such society has been observed or recorded.

A next theoretical stage would be the appearance of explanatory systems, normally animistic, with the correlative idea that these forces can be propitiated and perhaps even manipulated. Yet at this early stage, the normally socialized adult has these powers and responsibilities, probably reinforced with a set of community sanctions since more than individual welfare may be involved. But the forces are likely to be regarded as so powerful, and the outcomes so uncertain and so important, that differences in skills in handling them are likely to be assumed or alleged. One should suppose that a next step is the allocation of specialized responsibility within the kinship system. (Whether the allocation is by ascription or on the basis of presumed performance is an interesting but not critical question at this point.)

By extension of the same notion, the next step in evolutionary development should be an extrafamilial role allocation: the appearance of the true medicine man, shaman, or other variety of specialist. The exact role requirements and indeed the mode of selection may vary widely, as indeed they observably do, but questions of health and life are always included.

The validation of any such evolutionary scheme may be forever impossible, since prehistoric evidence can only be recovered by hazardous inference from archaeological remains. And of course the quest for origins is not crucial to an interpretation in terms of cross-sectional similarities, say, in the ubiquitous hazards in the human condition. Yet the differentiation of a quasi-professional role in nonliterate and ancient societies invites evolutionary speculation, the more particularly when virtually all other significant roles are determined by kinship position, age, and sex.

Let us turn then to a somewhat closer look at the "medical" quasi-professional in nonliterate societies, though our interest is not in an ethnographic survey but rather in some interesting variations in type. The first observation to be made is that the ubiquity of such a specialized role is not beyond dispute (the possible exceptions giving some slight hint of support for an evolutionary interpretation). The universality of the medicine man is simply asserted by Carr-Saunders and Wilson,[3] for example. Indeed, they go further, with the sort of incautious generalizations that

---

[3] A. M. Carr-Saunders and P. A. Wilson, "Professions," in *Encyclopedia of the Social Sciences* (New York: The Macmillan Company, 1934), Vol. 12, pp. 476–480.

encyclopedias generate: These authors assert that "... every society has its priesthood; many early communities knew the lawyer and the physician while even the most primitive accorded a special position to the medicine man."[4]

We shall note that these simplicities turn out not to be exactly true, and the exceptions are not merely a problem of semantics—though those will plague us. A distinct position for a priest, properly identified, is far from universal, and it is not beyond question that every lost society, everywhere, had a specialized position for the more action-oriented medicine man. Sigerist, an historian of medicine who has done his ethnographic homework rather better than most comparative anthropologists, says, simply, "We cannot expect to find medicine men in very primitive groups ..."[5] and cites some doubtful cases to illustrate his point. But his skepticism, and implicit evolutionism, lend some credence to his position.

THE INTERTWINED TRILOGY: MAGIC, SCIENCE, AND RELIGION

After one has identified the common feature of concern for healing and for preserving life, the variations are understandably wide. It is not uncommon for the professional's activities to intermix three analytically distinct orientations: the *religious* quest for assuring immortality; the *magical* manipulation of non-empirical forces for the achievement of observable cures; and the *technical* use of bonesetting or herbal remedies. (We shall return below to a fuller examination of these distinctions.) But the relative importance of these distinguishable ingredients is highly variable from one group to another, and the distinctly "priestly" role is not uniformly combined with the others. Thomas was therefore correct, in an early essay,[6] in dis-

---

[4] *Ibid.*, p. 476.

[5] Henry E. Sigerist, *A History of Medicine*, Vol. I, *Primitive and Archaic Medicine* (New York: Oxford University Press, 1951), p. 163.

[6] William I. Thomas, "The Relation of the Medicine-Man to the Origin of the Professional Occupations," in University of Chicago, *Decennial Publications, Investigations Representing the Departments*, First Series (Chicago: University of Chicago Press, 1903), Vol. IV, pp. 239–256.

puting Herbert Spencer's contention that the priesthood is to be taken as the invariant prototype of professional occupations. Thomas observes that Spencer was misled by a rather late, and peculiar, historical circumstance : the clergy's monopoly of literacy and learning in medieval Europe, a circumstance to which we shall return. But secular professions had long preceded that clerical monopoly, and some started without pronounced elements of either religion or magic.

Let us now take on frontally the problem of dealing with the common admixture of science, magic, and religion that constantly recurs in the practice of occult arts in ancient and tribal societies, and from which the modern world is by no means exempt.

Analytically speaking, religion is concerned with the achievement of otherworldly goals, or the belief in states of being not subject to sensory observation. Science (and its now common counterpart, technology) is concerned with the explanation and control of observable outcomes by the understanding and control of observable antecedents. Magic is the difficult part of this trilogy to deal with analytically, for it is most neatly viewed as the manipulation of supernatural or at least non-empirical forces for the achievement of observable events. But this commonly puts it in close contact with what is, analytically speaking, strictly religious behavior and that association persists almost universally. It also raises a whole series of questions of serious significance in the analysis and prediction of human behavior. One may properly ask, for example, is magic simply bad technology (as viewed by an external and possibly unfair view of technical causation) ? That is, is magic simply a kind of ignorant but well-meaning misunderstanding of causal sequences ? Often yes, and that is the reason that "secular magic," that is, magic that is not deeply imbedded in religious systems, is commonly subject to successful displacement by more knowledgeable and demonstrably superior technique.

The writings on science, magic, and religion generally represent a state of rather regrettable confusion. (The distinction between science and technology is a late, and very sophisticated, distinction, and will not trouble us in these exotic domains.) Even Malinowski,[7] who put forward what we regard as the only tenable theory of magic, turned chatty rather than analytical in distinguishing between magic and religion. The distinction is indeed commonly obscured, both in the ancient and, most conspicuously, in the modern world. The supernatural forces that are to be attuned to, supplicated, or controlled, are rarely distinguished in any neat way. Thus the forces that assure immortality, an unobservable state, may be the same as those that cure the sick, produce rain, or assure good harvests. And those who claim control over these forces may or may not be specialized according to the particular results sought.

It is not, or should not be, terribly surprising that premodern medicine (or, for that matter, pre-modern engineering or law or architecture) often mixed what now appear to be procedures that Sigerist[8] properly characterizes as empirico-rational with others, seemingly equally secular in orientation, that now appear to be ignorant and superstitious.

Here one must recall that a rational, calculating orientation to the achievement of real and observable outcomes is highly relative to the state of technically efficient knowledge. Many of the recipes for producing cures of specified ailments available in the papyri of ancient Egypt include mixtures of (subsequently confirmed) pharmaceutical specifics and of substances that appear to the eye of the present, sophisticated observer as pure magic.[9] But, lacking anything approximating *experimental* controls, and, with *experiential* results as a guide, these remedies may have produced results for reasons more narrowly restrictive than the practitioners supposed. If some ingredients of recipes, now appearing to

[7] Bronislaw Malinowski, "Magic, Science and Religion," in Malinowski (ed.), *Magic, Science and Religion, and Other Essays* (New York: Free Press, 1948; paperback: Garden City, N.Y.: Anchor Books, 1954), pp. 17–92.

[8] Sigerist, work cited in note 5, pp. 297–373.

[9] *Ibid.*, pp. 335–348.

be laden with substances that were merely exotic or whimsical, produced results, how would one know, outside of genuinely short-term experiments, which were efficacious, which were negatively indicated but overbalanced by effective specifics, and which were simply irrelevant to the purpose at hand?

It is easy to read into primitive and archaic medicine a quite unjustified prescience, just as it is possible to take the curious combinations of ingredients as purely magical, in the sense that no real and technically correct acts were even contemplated.

No, the situation is more complex, and very instructive. There is no reason at all to deny to nonliterate and ancient societies a rational orientation to life's ubiquitous problems. We may share, and that enthusiastically, with Malinowski[10] the correct perception that rational technique will be used, within the available limits of knowledge and efficacious action. We shall also have to add, however, several other observations, only part of which Malinowski came to understand.

The first of these observations is that the state of useful knowledge is variable in time and space; yesterday's superstition or experientially based technique gets set aside and outmoded as mere nonsense, or gets confirmed as reliable procedure.

Second, in a world in which nonrational forces seem to prevail, but ordinary activities also work with somewhat variable efficacy, it is not surprising that: (a) techniques that have a higher probability of success win out against competitors; (b) there will be a lot of bad technology, since the forces determining events are poorly understood; (c) there will be a somewhat clear distinction between observable and efficacious instrumental acts—now identifiable as rational technology—and the eking out of this rational orientation by the use of some of that broad spectrum of acts that we have agreed to call magical acts; (d) one should not expect from relatively undifferentiated social systems—or, as we

---

[10] Malinowski, work cited in note 7.

shall see, of the most highly differentiated—an absolutely sharp and inviolate distinction among purely technical and efficacious controls, the reliance on spurious technical controls, the attempt to command unseen and mostly purely imaginary forces, and the seemingly simple, essentially religious stance of facing the inevitable.

The nuances are in fact more complex, and deserve to be made explicit. If Malinowski is correct—and we see no reason to doubt it—persons in a nonliterate society not only use the rational techniques available, but seek to improve upon them. But, the argument goes, the desired level of predictive control over events is rarely assured, and in its absence, nonrational (magical) techniques are used as supplementary and not as competitive procedures. We doubt that any modern profession is exempt from such practices. Although Ackerknecht says that the medicine man is more nearly the prototype of the priest than of the modern physician,[11] we remain unconvinced. The fundamental source of Ackerknecht's error was that he accepted uncritically the Lévy-Bruhl thesis that primitive thought is "prelogical,"[12] and therefore lacking elements common in the technical, problem-solving orientations of modern medicine (or most other professional performance). On the evidence, that view is plainly wrong.

There is a somewhat different distinction between religious and magical stances made by some authorities.[13] This distinction rests on the supposed difference between supplicating deities or spirits and attempting to manipulate both seen and unseen objects and powers. We do not find this distinction very persuasive, as the act of supplication, even

---

[11] Erwin H. Ackerknecht, "Problems of Primitive Medicine" in Lessa and Vogt, work cited in note 2, pp. 394–402.

[12] See, for example, Lucien Lévy-Bruhl, *Primitive Mentality* (New York: The Macmillan Company, 1923).

[13] See, for example, Lessa and Vogt, work cited in note 2, "Introduction" to Chap. 7 on "Magic, Witchcraft, and Divination," pp. 298–300. A similar distinction appears in the "Introduction" to Chap. 10, "Shamans and Priests," *Ibid.*, pp. 451–452, based mainly on a selection from Robert H. Lowie, "Shamans and Priests Among the Plains Indians," pp. 452–454.

if purely oral and without other ritual or symbolic action, seems designed to change what would otherwise be an unwanted outcome—that is, the "patient" remains ill or dies. A prayer that a cure be made or rain delivered is as manipulative as the rattling of knucklebones or amulets. The circumstance that the procedures for seeking help may be performed by different persons should not dissuade us from that conclusion, for role specialization in terms of differences in techniques commanded by the performer is scarcely surprising.

Livingstone, the medical missionary to Africa, recorded in his reports a dispute he had with an African rainmaker.[14] The account is both amusing and instructive, although it is a little surprising to find it recorded, as the author by no means won the argument. Both practitioners claimed to be able to alter the course of events, to produce rain, the rainmaker by control over unseen forces and the missionary by appeal to presumably different sources. Each claimed usual success, though of course neither could prove it, particularly since each had to have some explanation for admitted occasional failure. One can suppose that the good Doctor Livingstone, before being found by Mr. Stanley, may have had a somewhat better case for his services as a physician—although there too he could not guarantee success.

A further distinction between religion and magic that has been suggested is that between *ad hoc* or what might be called emergency action and more periodic or calendrical ceremonies.[15] This distinction may have some relevance to our concerns if indeed it leads to specialization of roles, but the periodic rituals may well be communal, without a specialized functionary, whereas emergency action is entrusted to a qualified professional.

---

[14] The relevant passage from David Livingstone's report, *Missionary Travels and Researches in South Africa,* is reprinted in William I. Thomas, *Primitive Behavior* (New York: McGraw-Hill, Inc., 1937), pp. 782–783.

[15] See Lessa and Vogt, work cited in note 2, "Introduction" to Chap. 10, pp. 451–452; William J. Goode, *Religion Among the Primitives* (New York: Free Press, 1951), pp. 48–55.

The universal or nearly universal incidence of a shaman or comparable functionary in nonliterate societies almost exhausts the generalizations that one can make on the subject. It is not even clear that there is an invariant assumption that the practitioner is imbued with spiritual forces rather than merely having the power or technique for controlling them. Thus in some instances the authority of the performer derives solely from the equivalent of a "divine call," revealed in a vision or other identifying event. In other instances there is a lengthy apprenticeship to an established professional, the identification of eligibility often being by direct inheritance. Yet the two principles are not mutually exclusive, as the one called may still have to be trained—which, of course, is the assumption among the trained portion of the contemporary clergy.

Nor is there any uniformity in other dimensions of professionalism. Some medicine men have no other productive tasks; others do. One supposes that this variability would be related to the size of the group and its economic capacity to support a full-time occupation. In some instances the practitioner is paid for his individual services, at least in the form of a token gift; in others, the services are public, the shaman being maintained by the equivalent of a taxation system or as a dependent of a chief or other political patron. (There is no record of complaints about "socialized medicine" in the latter instances.)

In no case can the medicine man claim a monopoly on all presumably efficacious magic and technique, but only on that beyond the knowledge or power of the laity. The curer, like the modern physician, may be called only after domestic remedies have failed. This implies that the threshold of demand may be variable rather than absolutely fixed by tradition.

The primitive professional practitioner would not rank very high along the scale of professionalism suggested in the preceding chapter. That may be as derogatory of the scale as of the medicine man or his equivalent, for he is set apart from the laity, presumably is committed to a calling, and indeed may enjoy a high degree of autonomy in his performance. Thus the intermediate points on our scale may be relevant only to more complex civilizations, and some of them only to modernized societies.

BASES OF SPECIALIZATION

The degree of professional specialization within nonliterate societies is also variable, and its bases warrant attention, at least speculatively. One common source of extensive role differentiation is of course mere size of membership. This was Durkheim's original explanation of division of labor.[16] Yet size is more likely to be an important condition for, but not a cause of, specialization, and in any event most of the societies reported in ethnographic sources are relatively small. Similarly, the amount of useful knowledge collectively possessed may lead to specialization, particularly when that store exceeds individual capacity to assimilate and use the information in its entirety. Again, however, this is scarcely a critical problem in most nonliterate societies, where cumulation of knowledge is somewhat difficult.

Most of the specialization encountered in these societies can be accounted for by the intersection of two principles: the *salience* of the knowledge or skills for individual or collective welfare, and a distinction among *functions* actually performed. We have noted the analytical distinctions among religion, magic, and rational technique. These distinctions do not precisely match forms of professional specialization found in nonliterate societies, although something like a differentiation between priests and shamans occasionally occurs. Other functional distinctions may rest on the particular magical powers commanded or particular cures attempted. The aboriginal Australians, who combine an extremely elementary productive technology with an extremely complex classificatory kinship system, add to the confusion by having three types of medicine men.

---

[16] Emile Durkheim, *De la Division du Travail Social*, 2nd ed. (Paris: Alcan, 1902). English ed., trans. by George Simpson, *The Division of Labor in Society* (New York: Free Press, 1960).

We have suggested that matters of health and life are intrinsic to the human condition; their salience is thus assured, and we have found nearly universal professional specialization with respect to these problems, the professional commanding extraordinary knowledge, technique, or powers not available to the laity.

Other problems bespeak the *social* uncertainties of the human condition: personal love and hate, conflicts between kin groups or villages. Nonliterate societies abound with diviners, sorcerers, and compounders of beneficent or destructive magical potions. Yet such specialists are rarely full-time performers, the goods and ills to be controlled are highly variable from one group to another, and in many cases they are not recorded at all—such magic, perhaps, being well within the competence of the individual or some member of the family. Lacking any clear principle that would predict the occurrence of such specialties, we shall have to fall back on the comparative analysts' last resort and attribute these phenomena simply to "cultural differences."

What of other specialized performers? Here is where the notion of salience is especially useful. In contrast to the universality of concern over health and survival, other problems are much more conditioned on the variable circumstances and settings of nonliterate societies. In societies practicing a settled agriculture in a precarious climate, attempts to control weather and prevent other dangers such as insect devastations are likely. Indeed, food supplies of many nonliterate societies are precarious, and fertility rites and other magic to assure food are nearly universal. Often, however, these appear to be within the collective power of the group and do not require exceptional performers.

Just as the geographical setting of nonliterate societies is variable, so is their relation to other groups. Some societies have not had to be concerned with alien and hostile neighbors. In others, military specialization is the norm, though the full-time military professional is rare. Rather, able-bodied males or an age-grade of males generally conduct offensive and defensive war. Frequently, the all-purpose medicine man performs magic to assure success, and may determine from auguries known only to him whether the time is propitious for an expedition.

Size appears to be one factor in determining whether governors (rulers, chiefs) are exempt from other duties and in that sense have a kind of professional position. Yet many exceptions may be found in the association of size and political differentiation, and other bases for explaining differences among societies are not at hand. Even the association of a government, properly speaking, with external conflict, though common, is not invariant. Yet we may add that when the political function is specialized, the performer is likely to be put through an apprenticeship that at least includes the law and lore of the group over which he will subsequently exercise authority.

Those specialists that we have been able to identify in nonliterate societies accordingly share several characteristics of professionalism in modern societies, often in rudimentary and incomplete degree: esoteric knowledge and skills, used in service to a community and not solely for self or kinsmen, and exercised with considerable autonomy (since the ordinary adult could scarcely instruct the expert).

The professional in ancient civilizations

The occurrence of specialization in ancient civilizations is not sharply different from the situation in nonliterate societies. The differences, however, are instructive, as they indicate that ancient empires were in some ways closer to contemporary societies than to tribal and similar orders. First, the formal organization of the state clearly set apart rulers from ruled, and was always associated with other social differentiation, if for no other reason than that the rulers could and did associate to themselves advisers, implementers, and other subordinates. Second, concentrations of wealth appeared, whether the result of greater economic and technical efficiency, or simply from the exploitation of indigenous and conquered subjects. Third, written language made possible some accumulation of knowledge (or at least doctrine) through successive generations; at the very least, teachings, recipes, and procedures could be passed along intact rather than being subject to attrition through faulty recall. Literacy of course was by no means universal. Indeed literacy alone necessarily set apart its possessors from the common run of people. In Pharaonic Egypt, both physicians and priest-magicians attended schools for scribes prior to further training, along with those who became simply scribes.[17]

PROFESSIONALS: PRIESTS AND OTHERS

It is much too facile to identify the priesthood as the primal source of professionalism, as we have noted with respect to nonliterate societies. The priesthood certainly possessed specialized knowledge in Babylonia, Egypt, ancient Israel, and even in India. In some instances the priests appeared to have a monopoly on learning in the strict and esoteric sense. Sigerist, however, is at pains to demonstrate a clear functional division between priests and physicians in Egypt.[18] The common attribution of genuinely secular medicine in the Western world to the Greeks is challenged by Sigerist, who credits this innovation to the Egyptians. Of course, any allegation of first origins is likely to invite the recital of earlier antecedents. The question in the instant case is whether at least some portion of Egyptian medicine was genuinely secular. It appears so, although such medicine was not necessarily free from elements that now appear magical, and perhaps, here and there, a ritual reference to a divinity. Lefebvre notes that Egyptian medicine did not even have a special god in Pharaonic times, that being a much later invention under the Ptolomies;[19] Sigerist disagrees,[20] so we are left with uncertainty on this point.

Sigerist, incidentally, makes the interesting observation that surgery, and most particularly the repair of visible ills such as fractures and wounds, is more likely to be approached in

---

[17] Sigerist, work cited in note 5, pp. 323–324.

[18] *Ibid.*, pp. 297–356; see also Gustave Lefebvre, *Essai sur la Médicine Egyptienne a l'Epoque Pharaonique* (Paris: Presses Universitaires de France, 1956), Chap. II.

[19] Lefebvre, work cited in note 18, p. 20.

[20] Sigerist, work cited in note 5, p. 323.

what he calls an "empirico-rational" manner than, say, the treatment of fevers or other symptoms of physiological malfunction.[21] In the latter situation, the forces causing the disorders are, after all, unseen, and it is scarcely surprising that both the interpretation and the attempted therapy should rely on unseen and—we should now say—spurious forces. But just as Malinowski's Trobriand Islanders fully understood that not even powerful rituals would build canoes or plant yams,[22] the most untutored primitive would scarcely resort to magic to set bones or close wounds.

Of course we are not concerned here solely with the history of medicine, but with all forms of professional specialization. Ancient Egypt perhaps offers the widest variety of specialties requiring considerable training and skill: the scribes, priests, and many varieties of healers, but also embalmers, and, in some degree, professional soldiers.

The question of the position of the military among specialized occupations appears to have been poorly documented by historians. We learn about military formations and a little about military technology and of course about the outcome of battles, but virtually nothing about the leadership of armies. To be a common soldier was in some instances a duty of citizenship (for example in the Greek city-states); in others, military forces were conscripts or essentially mercenaries in the sense that the reward for service was the booty that victorious forces shared; but both citizen-soldier and conscript might also take booty as all or part of their reward. What we know little about are the military leaders; not just the political conquerors—Darius or Alexander or Caesar—but the field commanders and officers in charge of troops. On inferential evidence we may assume that most of the ancient empires afforded something like an officer class, a category of "professional" military men primarily involved in warfare or in preparation for war. This inference derives from the clear fact of an hierarchical military organization, from the fairly ordinary state of attack or defense, and, most subtly and most significantly, from the circumstance that

---

[21] *Ibid.*, pp. 343–344.

[22] Malinowski, work cited in note 7.

military operations were a major source of innovation in both social and physical technology. The inference stands despite the nominal amateurism prevalent in Greek and early Roman armies, the top command rotating among civilian-soldiers, and, in the Roman case, election of officers.[23] Yet in Rome a "professional" army had emerged by the end of the second century B.C. according to one authority,[24] or by the third century A.D. according to another:[25] What are a few centuries among historians?

MEDICINE REVISITED

Greek and Roman medicine appear to have had Egyptian origins. Nevertheless, it is in Greece at the time of Hippocrates (fifth century B.C.) and thereafter that we encounter a truly secularized medical fraternity, rational in orientation, but also explicitly oriented to the norms of service and loyalty to a calling.[26] The case is relatively clear that Graeco-Roman medicine was secular, yet the formalities required that the Hippocratic oath be sworn by Apollo and Aesculapius.[27]

There is an irony here that should not escape us. Hippocrates represents not only modern ideals of correct professional conduct—including the duty to pass along the knowledge, the loyalty to one's peers, the protection of the patient by avoidance of exploitation and the observance of privileged communication—but also the *private* conduct of medical practice by a freeborn Greek citizen. Yet Greek medicine continued to develop even after the Roman conquest, and Greek physicians served their conquerors as retainers or even as nominal slaves.[28] (We say nominal slaves, for a man possessing esoteric and useful knowledge not shared by his

---

[23] See Charles B. MacDonald, "Army," in *Encyclopedia Americana,* 1959 ed. (New York: Americana Corporation), Vol. II, pp. 287–293.

[24] *Ibid.*, p. 288.

[25] See Elbridge Colby, "Army," *Encyclopaedia of the Social Sciences* (New York: The Macmillan Company, 1937), Vol. II, pp. 210–218.

[26] See Fred B. Lund, *Greek Medicine* (New York: Paul Hoeber, 1936).

[27] *Ibid.*, p. 21.

[28] See Victor Robinson, *The Story of Medicine* (New York: Tudor Publishing Company, 1931), Chap. V, "Greek Medicine in Rome."

patron or master may not be free to change his location or clients, but is unlikely to suffer most of the indignities of ordinary slavery.)

Medicine also flourished in the ancient Buddhist regime in India, approximately contemporaneous with classical Greece. Neither medicine nor any rational science fared well later under Brahmanism, with its otherworldly orientations and rigid regime of castes, the priestly Brahmans having the unchallenged ascendancy in position and function.[29] Some elements of Indian medical knowledge reached the West through a curious circumstance. Nestorian Christians, harassed for their heresy throughout Asia Minor, found refuge in Jundisapur in Persia. There the Nestorians, who had become specialists in medicine, united with remnants of the authentic Greek traditions and with Indians to provide a link with the later Islamic developments, which, in turn, became the link to the revival of medicine in late medieval Europe.[30]

The history of medical knowledge (and myth) is better recorded than is the character of medical practice. In the Roman world it is doubtful that any professionals were in "private practice," unless the priesthood may be so regarded —but the priests were more nearly public servants. The steep and rigid stratification system assured that medical services—along with other specialized functions—would be accorded to those who could afford (or own) them.

RATIONAL LEARNING

The Graeco-Roman world was able to encourage and afford a command of literacy among part of its citizenry, and among that literate minority there was some dedication to rational learning. In much of the development of science, literature, and the arts there was a great deal of cultivated amateurism—the hobbies of the wealthy (the wealth from landed estates or, less probably, from mere commerce)— and of patronage of skilled dependents. Professionalism as such was by no means widespread, though occupational

---

[29] *Ibid.*, pp. 139–145.
[30] *Ibid.*, Chap. VI, "Arabian Medicine in the Middle Ages."

specialization in arts, crafts, and entertainment was. The Roman Empire developed an elaborate legal system, which provided a code that exists in amended form to this day. Yet it is not proper to speak of the professional lawyer, since every citizen was assumed to be equally eligible to be a litigant, a lawmaker, or a judge. Specialization certainly occurred, but it was in a sense surreptitious; and since law was scarcely distinguishable from politics, the successful representative of an interest was as likely to be influential as he was to be especially knowledgeable.

Modern professional practice owes a good deal to the direct historical antecedents of the ancient "Western" world—and, by infiltration, a little to the Orient. Yet the continuities are easily exaggerated. From a strictly comparative, rather than sequential, point of view, the ancient world provides perhaps clearer conclusions. First, specialization is once more seen to derive from *salience* of perceived interests. Second, size and organizational complexity provides an opportunity for refinement of specialization; by the same token, the sense and reality of communality is lost, with the result that specialized services resting upon esoteric knowledge and skills were generally reserved to the wealthy and powerful sectors of the social order.

The near-modern world

The older "learned" professions of contemporary modernized societies owe their immediate origins to two organizations of medieval Europe: the university and the guild.[31] Although under the control of the Church, the universities taught law and physic (medicine) in addition to theology. Because of Church control, all students were required to take at least minor clerical orders—a requirement that was gradually relaxed and finally abandoned around the sixteenth century.[32]

Had the universities held and maintained a monopoly on the training of "recognized" professions, the historic path

---

[31] See Carr-Saunders and Wilson, article cited in note 3.
[32] *Ibid.*

to the present close association between professionalism and advanced formal education would be straight and clear. The circumstance, however, is rather different. Certain skills grew both in importance and in the sophistication required for their practice, but received no recognition from the universities—which persevered in a steadfast conservatism that is not unknown today. Thus, particularly in England, surgery, the art of the apothecary or pharmacist, and the practice of common law became organized in what were essentially guilds. Instruction in these fields thus tended to involve more apprenticeship than formal precept, which may have been an advantage.

The history of medicine, perhaps better (and certainly more copiously) documented than other persisting professions, offers instructive evidence of the continuing strain between orthodoxy and innovation. After the fall of Rome, secular medicine virtually disappeared in Western Europe, and was gradually reintroduced because of the Islamic preservation of classical sources. Yet "Arabism" became a kind of orthodoxy, countered by another which insisted on a return to the Greek originals. These were, in effect, two variants of the same orthodoxy. Those who would expand the array of drugs and challenge the efficacy of received remedies, who would observe anatomy, physiology, and pathology rather than reciting the classical sources, were often treated with the same savage intolerance that religious heretics received.[33] The battles indeed have persisted through ensuing centuries; one has only to recall the relatively recent struggles over the germ theory of disease or the slow acceptance of asepsis in surgery. The particular succession of issues needs not concern us. What is of enduring importance is the homely truth that new knowledge or innovations in technique and practice threaten the very basis upon which established professionals rest their claims to expert competence. Medicine, and later the sciences, engineering, and a host of specialized technologies, are especially subject to strains between tradition and innovation, for they deal with observable and calculable states and events, and rest upon a

---

[33] See Robinson, book cited in note 30, Chaps. VIII–X.

rational orientation toward understanding and control. Neither theology nor law stand in the same relation to the natural order as do medicine and other technologies. Both emerged as learned specialties in the medieval universities, but their subsequent internal disputes were more doctrinal or in that sense philosophical than questions of accuracy of observation or efficacy in practice. It is only in very recent times, and by no means uniformly, that scientific knowledge of the social order has been urged as relevant to the proper training and practice of these long-established professions.

Europe in the Middle Ages afforded numerous occupational specialties, particularly in the towns and cities, and the number has increased apace, particularly since the beginning of industrialism. Yet most of these specialties were properly speaking crafts, organized into guilds. A few "craft" occupations, such as English barristers and surgeons, subsequently emerged as established professions.

Science in its post-Renaissance development remained safely outside the universities until at least the latter part of the nineteenth century, when physics here and there gained a toehold under the guise of "natural philosophy." Indeed much of the prior scientific development was at the hands of amateurs, who organized "academies" for scientific discourse but provided no systematic instruction for themselves or others.

Even the arts of warfare, much esteemed in the emerging nation-states, rested upon essentially amateur military leadership and a sort of apprenticeship. So-called professional armies were in effect merely salaried military units; whatever specialized technical competence they possessed and passed along to new recruits more nearly represented that of the craft guild than the learned profession. The first formal school for officer training appears to have been established by Napoleon in 1802, a school that evolved into the French military academy at St. Cyr.[34] Other military academies were established in the latter part of the nine-

---

[34] See Elbridge Colby, "Military Training," in *Encyclopaedia of the Social Sciences*, Vol. X, pp. 464–471.

teenth century, with curricula that have become increasingly
academic.

Several additional points need to be noted concerning the
historic roots of modern professionals. The first is the importance of the university as the mechanism of both training
and, to some degree, of scholarly or scientific innovation. The
university's monopoly of abstruse but useful knowledge has
never been complete. Indeed, the common posture of university faculties has been not to seek to expand jurisdictions but to resist recognition of new specialties. This stance
persists in most European universities, which are highly
limited in number and generally under fairly extensive
centralized control by a Ministry of Education or its equivalent. The highly decentralized character of publicly supported
higher education in the United States, and the existence of
numerous private institutions, combine to assure diversity
and the probability that at least one or a few colleges or
universities may be induced to add a new occupational curriculum. The point of present concern is that the link between professionalism and *formal* higher education has
strong historic foundations.

The second point is closely related : The establishment of
formal and somewhat impersonal criteria for recruitment
and training reduced (though it by no means eliminated)
the probability of a kind of hereditary apprenticeship. Indeed, as long as the university-trained professional was
required to enter a *celibate* religious order, such inheritance
of position was at least nominally forbidden. Granted that
the truly "popular" university is only beginning to be established in Europe, within the privileged group with prior
educational qualifications for university study, a degree of
openness was engendered in selection and training for professional careers.

A third point about the university as the source of professional authentication is the consequent professional position
of the teaching scholar. The European universities early
established the relative autonomy of the individual professor
in determining the dimensions of his subject and how it

should be taught, and the faculty as a collectivity determined what subjects were to be taught. "Profession" and "professor" clearly derive semantically from the same root. Although it is not unknown for teachers to be in a kind of servitude to their young charges, that has not been true in the traditions of university teachers in the Western world.

The professions in modernizing societies

Among the many associated characteristics of countries that are economically underdeveloped are meager facilities and opportunities for education at all levels. Yet particularly in the modernizing sectors of such countries there is a rapidly growing demand for highly trained people, both in the various medical arts to satisfy needs that are universal, and in the engineering fields essential to an industrial economy. The attempted solutions to this problem are several, not mutually exclusive: (1) to "import" professionals, at least on a temporary basis—the Soviet Union did this in the 1920's and much of contemporary "technical assistance" is of this character; (2) to send nationals abroad for advanced training, with the considerable risk that they will not return; (3) to establish indigenous universities with a view to becoming "self-sufficient" in the production of professionals. The third solution is the most difficult, at least over the short run, as universities require faculties, libraries, and laboratories, all of which are expensive if they are of good quality.

The social position of the professional in modernizing societies is likely to be even higher than it is generally. It is, however, not without its ambiguities. The professional trained abroad, whether a national or foreigner, is likely to excite some resentment, particularly if he is the least bit patronizing. The professional, in turn, is likely to find his assistants, his facilities, and virtually everything else "off standard."

The problem, indeed, has broader ramifications. Since the world has become a singular system in many respects, including the store of technical knowledge,[35] it is clearly not necessary in newly modernizing societies to replicate the gradual and now accelerating process of professional development. Public officials and at least part of the general population will insist that they want only the best. Yet the best may be neither attainable nor necessary under local circumstances, and at times may be less satisfactory than somewhat less advanced techniques and procedures. A physician may be so specialized, for example, that he cannot treat the ordinary run of human ills, or an engineer so accustomed to sophisticated instruments that he is helpless in their absence.

The considerable discussion of the alleged oversupply and underemployment of professionals in some underdeveloped countries is mostly wide of the mark. This may be true, here and there, for any specialty in view of the effective market demand, if not in view of "needs" otherwise evident. Yet the situation in most developing countries is that professionals as a category are not numerous,[36] but some of the more traditional occupations such as law are oversupplied. Training in law is easier and less expensive than training in the natural sciences, engineering, or medicine. Moreover, legal training has often been the principal route into relatively secure employment in the civil service. In Latin America there is certainly some redundancy in the supply of lawyers, particularly in capital cities, but the usual shortages in less traditional fields.

A further occupational problem in modernizing societies is the relation between the professional with modern training and his traditional counterpart, if any. This is most common in the case of "medicine," for we have observed that specialists in healing are virtually universal. It cannot be assumed that traditional healers will be immediately displaced once modern medicine is introduced. Cost and accessibility are important considerations, but so is the question of confi-

---

[35] See Wilbert E. Moore, "Global Sociology: The World as a Singular System," *American Journal of Sociology*, 71:475–482, March 1966.
[36] See Wilbert E. Moore, *Order and Change: Essays in Comparative Sociology* (New York: John Wiley & Sons, Inc., 1967), pp. 110–111.

dence. Particularly in villages and among the ubiquitous urban poor one may expect continued primary recourse to the traditional sources of solace, with some of the more knowledgeable (and possibly more affluent) of the inhabitants seeking out the new magicians if matters become desperate.

The modernizing societies thus display an array of professional talent that is even wider than that intrinsic to the contrast between the older and the newer skills in the most highly developed (and also very rapidly developing) societies.

A comparative perspective

For the material comforts and amenities of life, there is a somewhat elastic demand, even where affluence prevails and grows. But that demand is bound to have finite limits, since both time and storage space place restraints on mere physical accumulation. It is doubtful that there is any limit on the demand for services, given a highly productive economic system. And there would seem to be no effective limit on the expansion of knowledge, for omniscience or infinite wisdom —even if collectivized and not resident within any individual—seems an unattainable goal.

The professions, though not uniquely in the contemporary world, combine the quest for greater knowledge and the use of that knowledge in providing rather sophisticated "services" for the laity, some of whom are professionals in their own domains.

The proportions of the labor force that, by fairly loose but conventional distinctions, are professional range from 1 per cent to 12 per cent, where any data are available at all.[37] Here is an instance where quantity and quality are likely to be highly correlated. The highly developed, post-industrial societies provide not only more professionals per capita, over a broader range of specialties, but also at a higher level of average or upper-level skill than poor countries can afford.

---

[37] *Ibid.*

If there is any sure trend prediction anywhere—and there are several—it is that the proportion of professionals will increase everywhere. The rates will undoubtedly differ, and it is not at all sure that those countries farthest in arrears will grow fastest. The converse may well be true. For in civilizations with very refined techniques of physical production, and more and more elaborate bodies of specialized knowledge having some potential utility for human concerns, it is quite possible that the process of "universal professionalization"[38] will proceed faster over the next few decades than will the desperate measures taken in poor countries trying to catch up.

---

[38] Wilensky, article cited in note 1.

*Chapter three: The professionalization of occupations**

THE quest for fully professional status among the practitioners of various technical occupations is real and earnest. The quest implicitly recognizes a scale of professionalism such as put forward in Chapter 1. Particular tactics adopted by one or another occupational group, organized by an association, recognize *criteria* of professionalism, if not a scale or sequence. The result may well be a kind of checklist approach, once the criteria are enumerated with some degree of common assent. Since symbols may hide the absence of reality, and the manipulation of symbols is often easier than the changing of actual organizations and behavior patterns, it is scarcely surprising that a considerable part of the observed behavior of organized technical occupations consists in the conscientious manipulation of symbols.

One can almost envision the process of self-authentication by an occupational group: Service orientation? Provided in our adopted code. High admission standards? We have achieved a university curriculum. Autonomy? Well, in our salaried position we do the best we can. None of these polemical tactics—and who is the antagonist?—can get around the essential criteria of professionalism that have considerable commonality as between highly trained practitioners and the laity.

The criteria of professionalism differ in details that are relatively minor. The process of professionalization consists, at the crudest level, of the filling out of those criteria. Yet two recent discussions of this problem are most apt, those by Wilensky and Goode.[1] Both authors, for somewhat dif-

---

* Chapter by Gerald Rosenblum, supplemented in modest degree by Moore.

[1] Harold L. Wilensky, "The Professionalization of Everyone?" *American Journal of Sociology*, 70:137–158, September 1964; William J. Goode, "The Theoretical Limits of Professionalization," in Amitai Etzioni (ed.), *The Semi-Professions and Their Organization* (New York: Free Press, 1969), pp. 266–313.

ferent reasons, doubt that the process of professionalization is to be extrapolated endlessly, and adduce arguments to the general effect that there are early limits to the expansion of professional occupations in any time-honored sense of the term. Wilensky argues, in brief, that bureaucratization threatens the service ideal even more seriously than the threat to autonomy in practice. The process whereby clearly professional elements, such as high performance standards, enter into the normative expectations for a growing number of occupations does not insure that the occupations have become truly professional. Goode, accepting this argument, notes that of the rapidly multiplying technical specialties, few require both trust (particularly in the necessary reception of privileged communication or what Goode calls "classified knowledge") and autonomy in practice.

We present here a theoretical interpretation of the process of professionalization that we believe to be consistent with the extensive literature on the subject (but not repeating it) and consistent with the historical and contemporary evidence concerning occupational specialization.

Occupational and professional specialization

The inception of a new occupation implies that certain specific work activities are valued enough such that those activities become distinctly differentiated from others and publicly recognizable. When the activities become sufficiently regularized they come to be bounded by rules. That is to say, repetitive action (structure) gives rise to normatively governed subsequent action. Behavior has normative consequences; and norms, sociologists have long maintained, have behavioral consequences.[2] Why else would they persist? When differential behavioral activities and normative patterns arise in the sphere of work activities, we confront a new occupational role.

Briefly put, an occupational role denotes market-related work that has come to be sufficiently standardized so as to be

---

[2] Wilbert E. Moore, *Order and Change: Essays in Comparative Sociology* (New York: John Wiley & Sons, Inc., 1967). See Chap. 11, "Social Structure and Behavior," pp. 171–219.

recognizable by relevant lay members of a society. Though such members may be *technically* ignorant, they are aware of the functions performed by occupational role incumbents and thereby attach expectations to them. Of the universe of occupational roles we take the inception of professional activities as problematic. We ask how these come into being.

Professions are a subset of a larger occupational class known as the services.

Service may be defined most generally as any act of an individual so far as it contributes to the realization of the ends of other individuals. The universal existence of differentiation of social functions of individuals makes mutual service an inexorable necessity of all life in society. Starting with the elementary biological differences of sex and age it becomes more important with increasing complexities of social differentiation.[3]

Colin Clark has argued that, with economic development, the labor force moves from primary to secondary and finally to tertiary, or service, areas of activity.[4] Though latecomers to the process of modernization may not entirely replicate this sequence,[5] it does appear that the wealthier a country is, taking product per capita as the standard, the more decisively service-oriented is its labor force.[6] And so it is that the "service industries" have assumed an ever larger share of the labor force as societies become increasingly occupationally differentiated during the course of modernization. Indeed, the United States has already been referred to as a "service economy" and the professions appear to be perhaps the most rapidly expanding group in the service structure of this country.

We define a profession, for present purposes, as an occupa-

---

[3] Talcott Parsons, "Service," in Edwin R. A. Seligman (ed.), *Encyclopedia of the Social Sciences* (New York: The Macmillan Company, 1934), Vol. 13, p. 672.

[4] Colin Clark, *The Conditions of Economic Progress*, 3rd ed. (New York: St. Martins Press, 1957), p. 492.

[5] Wilbert E. Moore, *The Impact of Industry* (Englewood Cliffs, N.J.: Prentice-Hall, 1965), p. 64.

[6] Simon Kuznets, "Quantitative Aspects of the Economic Growth of Nations: II, Industrial Distribution of National Product and Labor Force," *Economic Development and Cultural Change*, Supplement to Vol. 5, July 1957.

tion whose incumbents create and explicitly utilize systematically accumulated general knowledge in the solution of problems posed by a clientele (either individuals or collectivities). Professional activities are the most closely contingent on new knowledge of any of the occupational spheres. Additional increments of knowledge not only are immediately relevant for professions that already exist but also provide the foundations upon which new ones are built.

The notion that occupational specialization and market extensity bear a relation to one another goes back at least as far as Adam Smith.[7] The relationship implies that a sufficient demand will exist for certain work effort such that a body of individuals may devote themselves full time to satisfying it. It was on this basis that, Weber suggested, factory production comes into being. "An economic prerequisite for the appearance and existence of a factory . . . is mass demand, and also steady demand—that is, a certain organization of the market."[8] Thus the factory production of standardized goods was contingent on a large and fairly permanent body of ready consumers.

We may argue, similarly, that mass demand makes for the standardization of services as well as goods and "from a broad point of view all social institutions may be regarded as examples of standardization."[9] The greater the demand for a skilled service, we suggest, the more rigorously institutionalized the occupational role assigned to provide it becomes.

One cannot speak of professionals as dispensing a series of unique services in treating a series of unique problems unless one is prepared to move to the lowest level of generalization in which no two events are alike and scientific the-

---

[7] Adam Smith, *An Inquiry into the Nature and Causes of the Wealth of Nations* (New York: Modern Library, 1937), especially Chap. III, "That the Division of Labour Is Limited by the Extent of the Market," pp. 17–21.

[8] Max Weber, *General Economic History*, trans. by Frank H. Knight (New York: Collier Books, 1961), p. 129.

[9] George Soule, "Standardization," in Edwin R. A. Seligman (ed.), *Encyclopedia of the Social Sciences* (New York: The Macmillan Company, 1934), Vol. 14, p. 319.

orizing is an impossibility. To use the term *professional role* is to imply certain regularities encompassed finally by institutions, and hence standardization. Marshall[10] asserts that professional service is "unique and personal." That is a very interesting and conspicuously false notion. If every professional problem were in all respects unique, solutions would be at best accidental, and therefore have nothing to do with expert knowledge. What we are suggesting, on the contrary, is that there are sufficient uniformities in problems and in devices for solving them to qualify the solvers of problems as professionals. The handling of the unique qualities of the individual case is likely to distinguish the competent from the unusually successful professional. That is an insight that has little relevance to the essential point, which is that professionals apply very general principles, *standardized* knowledge, to concrete problems requiring solution or palliative measures. Yet it remains true that the client's problems and the professional's knowledge may have a rather small overlap. Wilensky notes the problem of the expert "as a man who knows so much [that] he can communicate only a small part of it."[11] This "tacit knowledge," which is not readily available for critical appraisal, will tend to enhance professional prestige through the solution of highly individual problems. This in no way taints our general comments on the importance of standardization in the course of professionalization.

This standardization is determined, first and foremost, by a knowledge base which, however fragile it might be as regards new inputs, has fairly well-defined boundaries. "The antithesis to a profession is an avocation based upon customary activities and modified by the trial and error of individual practice."[12] The profession, on the other hand, involves the application of general principles to specific problems, and it is a feature of modern societies that such

---

[10] T. H. Marshall, *Class, Citizenship, and Social Development* (Garden City, N.Y.: Doubleday & Company, Inc., 1964), p. 148.

[11] Wilensky, article cited in note 1, p. 149.

[12] Alfred North Whitehead, *Adventures of Ideas* (New York: The Macmillan Company, 1933), p. 73.

general principles are abundant and growing. This gives rise to a growing sense of shortage of experts, which sense may be poorly informed.

As we have argued in the first chapter, there are six steps that must be ascended in the institutionalization of an occupational role whose incumbents create and explicitly utilize systematically accumulated general knowledge in the solution of problems posed by a clientele. If the proposition relating demand and the inception of a professional role is valid, we may expect these steps in our scale to be traversed in close relation to the degree in which people claim to require the relevant services. Some occupations may not traverse the entire scale, precisely because the essential knowledge on which the rest is built is shaky.[13] Though they may become institutionalized, their incumbents must settle for something other than the configuration we have put forward. And since it is autonomy which ultimately will elude their grasp, this "something other" may also be read as "something less."

Again, we may look to the growth of new knowledge as being the likely source of new occupational roles. The advent, then, of major scientific strides provided the initial impetus for many occupations now classified, some with grave reservations, as professional. Initially, it appears that these esoteric and as yet novel services are the outcome of talented innovators perceiving practical benefits embedded in basic discovery.[14] These innovators are not yet practicing a profession, since no occupational role has, at this point, been institutionalized. For this to occur the market must widen.

If, as the information at hand suggests, demand for services is a function of affluence, we might reasonably infer that early provision of services was enjoyed by a relatively small elite in a society characterized by rather pronounced inequalities in income and knowledge. Further, we may suggest that the *historical* experience has been for profes-

---

[13] William J. Goode, "The Librarian: From Occupation to Profession?" *The Library Quarterly*, 31:306–320, October 1961.

[14] A. M. Carr-Saunders and P. A. Wilson, *The Professions* (Oxford: Clarendon Press, 1933), pp. 296–297.

sionalism to emerge as the demand for rather exceptional and expert services makes itself known in the lower, and more heavily populated, reaches of the stratification hierarchy. The demand becomes more extensive, if somewhat more diffuse. With increasing modernization the growing demand for services appears to be related to the expanding middle levels of this hierarchy and to rising minimum standards of well-being in the strata below.[15] Luxuries, it has often been observed, frequently become necessities as societies modernize, and goods and services that were formerly a household responsibility increasingly move through the market.

An increase in demand, then, mediated by the mechanism of social mobility, may be taken as the source of growth in any given occupation.[16] In fact, Caplow argues, paradoxically, that there is a tendency for the supply of professional practitioners to *decrease* together with increasing demand as a result of an invigoration of professional controls on entry.[17]

From the point of view of the labor market, one may view professional institutions as providing barriers that place limits on who may enter the market in providing demanded services. Thus a true market situation connotes not only demand, but also supply in relation to it. An occupation's economic and prestige position may be enhanced by inducing demand; it may also be enhanced by reducing or at least limiting supply.

Goode notes that "characteristic of each of the established professions, and a goal of each aspiring profession, is the

---

[15] Eliot Freidson, "Medical Personnel. II. Paramedical Personnel," in David L. Sills (ed.), *International Encyclopedia of the Social Sciences* (New York: Free Press, 1968), Vol. 10, pp. 115–116. Corinne Lathrop Gilb, *Hidden Hierarchies: The Professions and Government* (New York: Harper & Row, 1966), p. 89.

[16] Moore, work cited in note 2, Chap. 7, "Changes in Occupational Structure," pp. 98–117. Also Peter M. Blau, "The Flow of Occupational Supply and Recruitment," *American Sociological Review*, 30:485–486, August 1965.

[17] Theodore Caplow, *The Sociology of Work* (Minneapolis: University of Minnesota Press, 1954), p. 170.

'community of the profession.' " And one of the features of this "community" that is specified by Goode is that:

> Though it does not produce the next generation biologically, it does so socially through its control over the selection of professional trainees, and through its training it sends these recruits through an adult socialization process.[18]

The professional community then serves as the labor allocator through which a would-be professional must pass on his way to market his services. Such barriers would be an absurdity without an abundant demand for the services in question and one function these barriers perform is the standardization of the relevant services, that is, the institutionalization of an occupational role.

It is by these mechanisms that we are witnessing an example of "balkanization" of labor markets. Barriers to entry narrowly circumscribe the kinds of personnel who may operate within them. Clark Kerr uses the term "institutional markets" which operate,

> . . . not by the whims of workers and employers but by rules, both formal and informal. These rules state which workers are preferred or even which ones may operate in it at all and which employers may or must buy in this market if they are to buy at all. Institutional rules take the place of individual preferences in setting the boundaries.[19]

For the professions these rules include much of what we have put forward as the ascending steps of professionalism. One of their functions, we are now arguing, is to standardize the service within rather well-defined limits.

In effect, then, professionalization involves the creation of an institutional market. Early in the process (and in our scale) professional associations, at their inception, operate somewhat as an avant-garde for establishing performance

---

[18] William J. Goode, "Community Within a Community: The Professions," *American Sociological Review*, 22:194–200, April 1957; quotation from p. 194.

[19] Clark Kerr, "The Balkanization of Labor Markets," in E. Wight Bakke and others (eds.), *Labor Mobility and Economic Opportunity* (Cambridge and New York: Technology Press of the Massachusetts Institute of Technology and John Wiley & Sons, Inc., 1954), p. 93.

criteria concerning specific services. The early ideals thus established may be quite wide of actualities. Frequently, Gilb notes,[20] early professional associations were populated by a small body of elite practitioners who attempted to standardize performance by good example, not exactly the most reliable way to insure compliance.

But these early associational formations were to provide the lever with which the gap between the ideal and the actual could be narrowed; this lever was government cooperation through licensing statutes which would insure standardized performance.

Thus licensing is viewed by government as a regulatory device. From the standpoint of private groups it may be seen as a means of employing government to standardize admission requirements and minimize competition while at the same time protecting the public from injury to its health and welfare.[21]

As Gilb points out, part of the impetus in seeking government help was the notion that "to be a profession means to present a reliable, uniform face to the public; collectively, to have the public's confidence and respect."[22] Accordingly, associations of professionals sought and, after the turn-of-the-century, increasingly obtained state licensing laws which were drafted in part by their own membership.[23]

Licensing, of course, is not a distinguishing feature of professions but it is important to note that whereas autonomy may be reduced by licensing in other areas, among professionals judgment tends to remain within the fraternity. Thus, not only do professionals help to draft the laws,

Legislation including salient features of professional codes is common for those professions which have developed formal codes, generally accepted by their practitioners and the public. In such cases violation of the code often constitutes grounds for suspension of a license.[24]

---

[20] Gilb, work cited in note 15, pp. 31–34.

[21] The Council of State Governments, *Occupational Licensing Legislation in the States* (Chicago: Council of State Governments, 1952), p. 5.

[22] Gilb, work cited in note 15, p. 41.

[23] Council of State Governments, work cited in note 21, pp. 21–22.

[24] *Ibid.*, p. 42.

Further, training requirements, approval of schools, preparation and administration of licensing examinations and, finally, initial determination of code violations—all these activities are frequently carried out by members of the professional body itself. Thus it is the professionals themselves who often set the standards while it is left to government, when necessary, to mete out sanctions.

Thus far we have argued that the movement along the scale that we have put forward is likely to occur in relation to increasing demand for the services in question. We suggest that such has occurred historically as societies underwent modernization and demand for skilled services appeared in the less privileged but increasingly knowledgeable and financially potent levels of the stratification hierarchy. With increased demand new recruits are drawn into the service and it is at this point that difficult questions of relative training, competence, and background enter the picture. Our suggestion has been that institutional controls became operative here and functioned to standardize performance similar to the standardization of goods for a mass market. Thus the public comes to be assured of certain uniformities, within limits, of various services wherever they may happen to seek them out.

But it is at this point that the analogy between goods and services begins to diverge and it is instructive to explore this divergence. The leveling of uneven quality of goods destined for a mass market is accomplished by means of large-scale manufacturing techniques. Thus mass demand is satisfied with products meeting minimum quality specifications, turned out in increasing *quantity*.

With skilled services it appears that just the opposite may occur. That is, an upgrading of quality, driving out (or not permitting in) the incompetent performer achieves standardization at the *expense* of quantity. The legitimate professional practitioner is one who has met increasingly stringent criteria and his numbers may as a result have been reduced.

In the United States, accreditation partly accounts for the fact that only 20 per cent of the medical schools that have ever been established in this country still exist.[25] Thus, according to one source,

In 1900 there were 157 physicians per 100,000 population, but by 1929 this ratio had dropped to 125 per 100,000. Thereafter it rose until 1940, when it leveled off. Since then the ratio has hovered around 133 per 100,000.[26]

Further, entry may be denied long before the individual presents his credentials. The lengthy and expensive training with income foregone for several years may deter otherwise able recruits. Thus, the Webbs pointed out a half-century ago that,

. . . the most potent, as it is the most universal, means of rendering difficult the access to a brain-working profession is the requirement of a particular kind of professional training, extending over a specified number of years.[27]

Similarly, Friedman and Kuznets indicate that the substantial investment in professional training is at least a partial deterrent for many would-be practitioners.[28] There seems to be little doubt that along with enhanced quality enjoyed by consumers of a service, a favorable economic position is enjoyed by its purveyor as a result of such restrictive practices.

---

[25] Gilb, work cited in note 15, p. 59.

[26] Monroe Lerner and Odin W. Anderson, *Health Progress in the United States: 1900–1960* (Chicago: University of Chicago Press, 1963), p. 222. More recent figures based on somewhat different data show some late increase in the physician-population ratio. "The total number of M.D.'s and D.O.'s per 100,000 total population remained at 149 from 1950 to 1963 and increased to 158 by 1967." U.S. Department of Health, Education, and Welfare, *Health Resources Statistics,* Public Health Service Publication No. 1509, 1968 (Washington, D.C.: Government Printing Office, 1968), p. 121. See also Table 77, p. 123.

[27] See *The New Statesman*, "Special Supplement on Professional Associations: Part II," p. 39, April 28, 1917.

[28] Milton Friedman and Simon Kuznets, *Income from Independent Professional Practice* (New York: National Bureau of Economic Research, 1945), p. 94.

Professionals and aspirants

In the light of these remarks we confront the paradox that the professions as a class of occupations appear to be increasing more rapidly than others. Here we refer once again to the nature of institutional markets. Those who operate within these various markets stand as noncompeting groups relative to one another. Thus, the doctor does not compete with the lawyer and neither competes with the engineer. It would appear that the growth in the over-all class of occupations known as professions comes less from larger numbers entering old fields than from the rise of new fields themselves, or new specialties within old fields, and hence new institutional markets being carved out of the American occupational structure.

Among these latecomers to the professions the scale sequence we have suggested may not precisely replicate the experience of earlier arrivals. One major difference would be the rapidity with which the institutional market is created. We expect that the later the appearance of a new occupational group the less protracted will be its journey to professional status if that status is in fact attainable.

But perhaps the most important difference that may be noted is that many of the older groups began as "free professionals," operating as part of the "old middle class" of self-employed practitioners. Only recently has this group begun to experience the confines of bureaucratic membership and salaried income.

Many of the newer groups are likely to have emerged or have grown substantially as a direct consequence of large-scale employing organizations. Often they may never have enjoyed a "free" state.

Freidson makes the important point that professional authority is at its highest "when the numbers of its members is small in relation to demand, and when the clientele is unorganized."[29] Under such circumstances the professional re-

---

[29] Eliot Freidson, "The Impurity of Professional Authority," in Howard S. Becker and others (eds.), *Institutions and the Person: Papers Presented to Everett C. Hughes* (Chicago: Aldine Publishing Company, 1968), p. 29.

serves for himself the final word regarding appropriate services while the individual consumer of these services has little power to exert in countermanding professional advice. As suggested by Freidson,[30] and of interest here, where the consumers of services are in fact highly organized, professional authority may be curtailed or possibly eclipsed entirely. Such indeed may be the case where the "client" is a corporate enterprise and the professional its salaried employee.

It is perhaps a commonplace to note that the large majority of workers today are employed in large-scale organizations. Many of the older, and formerly "free" professions, have not escaped this trend. But there are important differences in this over-all shift. Whereas the older groups may become salaried employees in large organizations, the consumers of their services are not their employers and remain unorganized individuals, as in the case of medicine.

Where the client and the employer are one and the same, and where the latter is an organizational entity, the professional is in a radically different position. In this case he may well represent but one of an array of specialties which, in concert, *contribute*, within a complex division of labor, to a unified product or service, the "ultimate" consumer of which the professional may never see or consult with. The situation of the engineer as it emerged in the 1940's may serve as an appropriate example of what is intended here.

A growth in the number of engineers was accompanied by a considerable change, which had begun earlier, in the character of engineering employment. In contrast to earlier times, when most engineers were either self-employed or worked with few other engineers on a consulting basis, the typical engineer became one of many, in some cases one of several thousand, engineers working for a large firm. Work was increasingly subjected to much closer controls than normally prevail in other professions. In many firms, strict working hours and use of the time clock were required of engineers, as well as production workers. Engineering services apparently began to be considered by management as a variable, rather than a fixed, cost of production, and engineering employ-

---

[30] *Ibid.*

ment tended to fluctuate with fluctuations in product demand, in much the same manner as employment of production workers. During the Great Depression, unemployment among engineers was considerably more widespread than in most other professions.[31]

Thus, professionalization, though contingent upon mass demand, appears to have become differentiated as regards the nature of the consumer. Many aspiring professions, such as computer programming, have arisen as a result of mass demand for standardized *goods,* which has called into being more efficient automated production facilities served by this specialty within the context of large organizations. Thus mass demand comes to be *indirectly* related to the rise of a professional service which results from the exigencies of large-scale productive technology.

Much of the model of the free professional serving an unorganized clientele may be preserved in the context of organized services where the professional serves the client directly. This, of course, is true of medicine, but it is also true of such fields as social work and teaching. In these cases standards imposed by the professional body itself are more likely to be preeminent in the determination of how services are to be rendered.

Where the employer is also the consumer of services and is, further, an organized entity supplying other consumers, it is highly probable that the determination of appropriate services will shift to this "intermediate" consumer. Thus, management may know nothing about a profession, but it may well know what it wants.[32]

Under such circumstances, professional organization may have less power in determining the quality and quantity of services than the employing unit. Thus, the presumed benefits of professional certification to assure the client of competent services may be less strategic where the client can

---

[31] Eldon J. Dvorak, "Will Engineers Unionize?" *Industrial Relations,* 2:46–47, May 1963.

[32] Melville Dalton, "Conflicts Between Line and Staff Managerial Officers," *American Sociological Review,* 15:342–351, June 1950.

assure himself of such competence and also dictate the manner in which it is utilized.

We suggest, then, that professional services may be divided into three major types. The first is the familiar free professional catering to an unorganized clientele. The employer and the client are here one and the same and professional authority is at its maximum. The second concerns the professional working within an organization but serving unorganized clients. The employer and the client are different but the professional maintains a good deal of his authority. Finally, there is emerging the case in which one may speculate that most new, and some older, professions will find themselves. Here the employer and client are the same and highly organized. In such cases the organization stands intermediate between the professional and the ultimate consumer and professional authority is at a minimum.

As regards this last case our scale of professionalism is likely to be altered considerably. To start at the top and work down, autonomy is obviously considerably reduced as a distinctive attribute. A service orientation is very likely to shift toward an emphasis on an employment *contract* and while training standards may be upheld, the professional organization component may well come to resemble that of a labor union. The element of a calling may become variable as opportunities to move into administration will be high.

In this era of organized "consumer sovereignty," as it concerns skilled services, the growth of the census category of professional and technical workers might well emphasize the term technical as many heretofore distinguishing professional attributes have to be taken as not really fulfilled. The true professionals—those that qualify on all points of our scale—continue to represent a relatively small segment of the technically distinguished portions of the labor force.

*Chapter four: The formation
of a professional*

TWO criteria of professionalism—a high educational level
and commitment to a calling—point to the importance of
recruitment, training, and the internalization of professional norms. The process by which a child or youth chooses
an occupational career (or drifts into it) and prepares for
it represents a rather intricate mixture of personality characteristics, selective procedures used by teachers and admis-
sions officers, and the actual acquisition of occupational skills
and normative orientations. The process is by no means fully
understood, but we are permitted to move from the known
and to speculate about the unknown.

Recruitment and selection

Those who enter occupations in contemporary society that
qualify in varying degree as professional are the survivors
of complex selective and sorting mechanisms. Given the
relatively high prestige of professional positions, a naive
first assumption might be that occupants of those positions
are the successful contestants in a universal competition.
Not only would this exaggerate the rectilinear and unambiguous quality of an occupational prestige scale (thus implying that all those in less-than-professional positions are
relative failures), but also would exaggerate the openness
of occupational choice to all persons participating in such
crucial sorting mechanisms as the schools. To become a professional requires a combination of accident, ability, and
choice, and the relative importance of these is difficult to
decipher.

SOCIAL ORIGINS

If we, for the moment, simply accept the United States Census designation of professional occupations, it is clear that
they are among the most hereditary of occupational cate-

gories. A very disproportionate number of professionals
come from families with professional fathers. Blau and
Duncan have analyzed extensive American data on occupational mobility and find that sons of self-employed professionals occupy the same occupational category at nearly
twelve times the frequency that would be expected if fathers'
and sons' occupational standing were independent. Sons of
salaried professionals enter either self-employed or salaried professional positions with three times the expected
frequency. Occupational categories "neighboring" the professions in relative status—managers, proprietors, and
nonretail salesmen—also supply a disproportionate share
of professionals in the following generation. One has to go
to the opposite end of the occupational prestige spectrum to
find a comparable degree of occupational inheritance: the
sons of farm laborers are over five times as likely to follow
their fathers' status as would be expected if the children of
the rich had the same opportunity to be poor as do the children of the poor.[1]

Now some of this selectivity by social origins may bespeak
genetic inheritance of talent. Since such genetic factors are
still impossible to disentangle from differential opportunities
for educational achievement and attitudinal factors in occupational choice, it is well to focus on the latter.

The child growing up in a professional family has at least one
parent (and usually both) with a relatively high educational
attainment. Similar or higher attainments for their children
are a uniform parental ambition.[2] Parental ambitions become
expectations for performance by children, commonly supported by preschool preparation and in-school assistance and
encouragement. The well-documented cultural deprivation of
Negro children shows up in the substantial underrepresenta-
tion of Negro professionals, though a whole succession of

---

[1] Peter M. Blau and Otis Dudley Duncan, *The American Occupational
Structure* (New York: John Wiley & Sons, Inc., 1967), pp. 26–48; see
esp. Table 2.5, p. 32.
[2] Henry Borow, "Development of Occupational Motives and Roles," in
Lois W. Hoffman and Martin L. Hoffman (eds.), *Review of Child Development Research* (New York: Russell Sage Foundation, 1966), Vol.
II, pp. 373–422.

later obstacles must also be accorded some "credit" for the result. Professional and technical workers comprised 8 per cent of the white population in 1950, over 13 per cent in 1966. The corresponding percentages for nonwhites were 3 in 1950 and 7 in 1966.[3] Although the rate of increase for nonwhites is larger, the gap remains great. On the other hand, female professionals represent a higher proportion of the female labor force than do professional males among the male labor force. (The respective proportion in the United States in 1960 were 13.8 per cent and 10.8 per cent.) Women were heavily concentrated in medical and health services (4 per cent of the female labor force) and teachers other than college (6 per cent of the female labor force).[4]

The strongly "hereditary" character of the older professions again represents a mixture of explanatory factors. The older professions are also those most likely to require formal education beyond the collegiate level. Thus it might be thought that what we are observing is an application of a simple "means test," assuming that more advanced education has meant higher parental income and thus the ability to pay for advanced education by children. The situation is not exactly that simple, as clergymen are relatively poorly paid, as were college professors until fairly recently. However, it should also be noted that the professional training of the clergyman or professor is more likely to be financed by scholarships or other impersonal assistance than is training in law and medicine.

One obvious element in the degree of generational succession is simply the historic age of the occupation. Very new occupations—say, computer programmer or electronics engineer—cannot be hereditary; law, medicine, and the military may be.

The degree of openness of professional occupations regardless of social origins is thus a function of the entire selective

---

[3] U.S. Bureau of the Census, *Statistical Abstract of the United States, 1967* (Washington, D.C.: Government Printing Office, 1967), Table 328, p. 231.

[4] U.S. Bureau of the Census, *U.S. Census of Population, 1960; Special Reports: Characteristics of Professional Workers*, Final Report PC(2)–7E (Washington, D.C.: Government Printing Office, 1964), Table B, p. x.

and sorting process, beginning practically with infancy and proceeding through various stages of formal education and personality development. Dentists are more likely to be drawn from ethnic minorities than are physicians, through a mixture of differential means and, probably, differential prejudice. Teachers, at all levels, are more likely to be upwardly mobile in the generational sense than are, say, attorneys.

ROLE MODELS AND EARLY COMMITMENT

What we have been saying about social origins underscores the strong parental influence in occupational choice. This is of course clearest where the child selects and prepares himself for the same occupation as that of his father. Here he is provided throughout his childhood and youth with a "role model," and probably with several, since common occupation is a strong basis for selecting the family's circle of friends. In situations where the child is destined for a different, but still professional, occupation, the common features of professional orientations—which we shall be documenting in subsequent chapters—still provide a somewhat more generalized set of expectations. Even for the upwardly mobile potential recruit, it is probable (though by no means uniformly true) that parents will have exposed the child not only to achievement expectations but also to a partially vicarious sense of occupational attainment.

Although we know of no systematic evidence on the influence of teachers, we have observed that individuals in successful careers—especially in the professions—are able to name several influential teachers, ranging back to elementary school, and to recall the grade and the subject matter. With the possible exception of negative nostalgia for a tyrant, other teachers are blurred. If this observation should prove to be correct, it would force amendment to the usual supposition that teachers have little or no effect on attitudes and choices. The occasional teacher may be included as one of the individual's "significant others."

The nature of occupational choice is still rather poorly understood. Despite the statistical significance of social origins for professional recruitment, the process is by no means automatic. For many children, even those from professional family backgrounds, moving toward an adult occupation consists of a complex mixture of narrowing the range of choices (or having them narrowed by poor educational performance) ; exploration of alternatives by use of information, misinformation, and sheer fantasy ; and considerable components of chance. It remains true that children and youths from "good" backgrounds generally perform better in school, and if they do not, are more likely to be given assistance and guidance in career perspectives. By the same token, the child from a background of deprivation who still performs well in school may still be discouraged from "unrealistic" aspirations and shunted into a less demanding (and eventually less rewarding) "vocational" curriculum.

THE SEARCH FOR TALENT

The uncertainties of competitive placement for adult occupational positions are real enough for the youthful aspirant. If he seeks to prepare himself for a position of considerable prestige and, often, relatively high income, the way to his goal may appear strewn with a succession of formidable barriers. This perception is in varying degrees correct, but it does not follow that each is manned by a "gatekeeper" intent solely on keeping people out. Although the various professions lay claim with some sincerity to a desire not to lower standards but to raise them, and some groups may seek to reduce competition under the guise of maintaining standards, there is at the same time a competition for identifiable talent. The academic disciplines represented on university faculties attempt to get students exposed to their subject matter at earlier and earlier school grades ; they are joined in this contest by at least some of the "helping" professions. The competition gets keener in secondary schools, and indeed up to the point when fairly irreversible decisions are made. Note that this quest for talent may initially affect only those students with the highest academic achievement, but their short supply will also lead the talent scouts to discover compensating qualities in students with more modest records. And since school performance records (particularly grades, if not failing) predict other school performance but have a poor correlation with adult occupational achievement,[5] the second and later scouting expeditions may be as successful as the first.

Professional socialization

The transformation of a generalist into a specialist in some professional field varies not only with the field of specialization, but also to a certain extent with individual and idiosyncratic characteristics. Professional socialization involves acquiring the requisite knowledge and skills and also the sense of occupational identity and internalization of occupational norms typical of the fully qualified practitioner. The various occupations relatively high on the scale of professionalism differ in their demands for formal education, as well as, obviously, the specific content of both knowledge and norms. Our concern here is to deal, as necessary, with particularities, but also to attend to some features that may differ somewhat in magnitudes or scale but not in kind.

EDUCATIONAL LEVELS AND REQUIREMENTS

The point in childhood or adolescence when career choices are made (or drifted into) is also somewhat individual; yet this decision can be postponed longer in some fields than in others. An inviting hypothesis would be that those specialties that require only a baccalaureate degree, or a little longer, should require rather early decision. The corollary of this would be that the longer the required formal education, the later the final decision can be delayed. Indeed, it is part of the genteel traditions of the "learned professions" that the professional is broadly educated before he turns, at last, to his specialty. With the increasing complexity of technical fields, that is a standard difficult to maintain. The contempo-

---

[5] See Donald P. Hoyt, "The Relationship Between College Grades and Adult Achievement: A Review of the Literature," *ACT Research Reports*, No. 7, September 1965 (American College Testing Program, Iowa City) ; John L. Holland and James M. Richards, Jr., "Academic and Non-Academic Accomplishment in a Representative Sample Taken from a Population of 612,000," *ibid.*, No. 12, May 1966.

rary professional may be a gentleman, by conventional social definition, but he is not an amateur.

No, there seems to be scant relation between brevity or length of formal training and the requirement of early decision. Youngsters intent on a medical career will normally need an early choice in order to acquire some natural sciences and mathematics in secondary school; the same is true for those headed for engineering, where baccalaureate terminal degrees are still common, and also for those going into physical science disciplines, where a doctorate is virtually mandatory. Teaching in elementary or secondary schools commonly requires only collegiate training or a Master of Arts (or equivalent). Yet that decision can be postponed a couple of college years. The professor or researcher in physical sciences will normally have made early decisions; his counterpart in the life sciences may have discovered his interests later, and in the social sciences and humanities later still. Yet here we are dealing with training times at least rivaling those of the physician.

Now one explanation for *both* the length of total education and the necessity of early specialization would be that the amount of knowledge to be acquired differs radically by field of knowledge and its application. Undoubtedly there are differences of considerable importance in the substantive content and requisite skills among professions, and we have attempted to represent that, at least crudely, in our scale item representing educational requirements. Yet the twofold exceptions give us pause: the normal three-year post-baccalaureate training of lawyers, and much longer for humanistic professors, on the one hand, and the technical complexity and early decision required of engineers. Clearly, one important element in accounting for the differences is not the amount or complexity of what is to be learned, but rather the conventionality of a graded curriculum through long years of gradual preparation as against a demonstration of broad-ranging competence followed by rather intensive specialization over a relatively short period.

Educational requirements may be conventional as well as real, and it is not surprising that older members of any established profession have generally spent fewer years in school than their younger counterparts. (The various academic disciplines are a bit ambiguous on this point, in view of the conscientious effort to make the Ph.D. degree a less leisurely affair than it has been.) Specialization within medicine has lengthened the training period, beyond the standard curriculum required of all physicians. The lawyers, we shall see, have kept their specialization surreptitious and thus do not recognize it by postgraduate work, residencies, and internships. Aspiring semi-professional occupations such as social workers or public school teachers have more or less successfully sought legislative assistance in specifying length of training for state certification. The school teachers have turned out to be one of the more effective occupational lobbies in American legislatures, for they have succeeded not only in securing legislation specifying total strength of formal training, but also proportion of time successfully completing pedagogical courses, and even the semester credits to be fulfilled in named (and mostly intellectually vacuous) courses.

The interplay among educational levels that senior and otherwise responsible practitioners of a profession think appropriate for admission to their ranks, the levels that have been given governmental approval owing to efforts of professionals in getting legislation on licensing, the levels demanded by (often aspiring) occupational associations, and those "necessary" will not detain us here, for that problem is treated, gingerly, later. We are at this moment concerned with how the individual qualifies, whatever the merits of the qualifications.

The educational requirements for professional authentication are certainly variable through time, and also across political frontiers where private or public certifying bodies follow jurisdictional boundaries. The strong trend toward professional communication across such boundaries reduces the idiosyncracies, but does not eliminate them; authenticated professionals are scarcely more prone to rational and sensible compromises and reasonable innovations than are others who occupy a privileged position.

For the individual professional aspirant, qualification generally represents a set of formal requirements, presumably
graded by difficulty in order to build on his previously acquired knowledge and skills. It is common for the curriculum
to be set by his mentors (who are also, often, his judges).
Where and when individual discretion sets in is almost as
variable as questions of broad occupational choice in the first
place. Here, however, we do have a reliable predictive principle: the longer the required training time, the later the subspecialization sets in. And it is commonly true that those
who drop out of the most advanced training become more or
less proficient general practitioners: the troop commander
in the army, the arts college teacher, the small-town attorney,
the suburban pastor, the general practitioner in medicine,
the town engineer, the social worker, the hospital nurse.

Sorting never ceases, and the neophyte professional is faced
with some small prospect of outright failure and thus of
secondary or tertiary selection or drifting. Some "skid"
badly, and others find their possibly appropriate place in
the multidimensional professional world.

THE RELATION OF EDUCATION TO PRACTICE

The curricula of professional schools, whether at collegiate
or postgraduate level, always entail an irrational mixture of
several components:

1. What the professors learned, which is necessarily a collegiate generation earlier and usually a full biological generation gone into antiquity.

2. What the qualifying (and certifying) authorities think
should be known; for a variety of not very subtle reasons,
the persons serving on review or certifying committees are
likely to represent a full biological generation—or more—in
ascendancy over the new aspirants.

3. What the "new revolutionaries" on the professional school
faculty think is appropriate for the training of future professionals.

It should surprise no one that conservatism is the norm and
innovation the exception in professional education. The sal-

vation of the system is almost certainly external to it: the organization and institutionalization of social change has finally, and ironically, come to permeate those intellectual centers that might have been thought to be its instigators. Medical, legal, engineering, clerical, and even academic faculties are uneasy. All might well be. Each specialty has been shaken by intellectual and secular changes for which the ordinary teacher of professionals was unprepared.

Our immediate concern here is with professional socialization; we shall return to other aspects of the current intellectual ferment. If the teaching and learning of a set of professional skills gets badly out of phase with what is happening in the experiential world of research and application, however, the negative feedback will not be long in making its impact felt.

Of the older, established, professions, it is probably only medicine that has set its training schedule to accommodate specialties (mostly, after the M.D. degree, the requirements for which are mostly conventional and sometimes silly). Virtually from the beginning of professional training, the student physician presumably learns what it is like to be a professional physician.[6] Becker and his colleagues dispute this view, on grounds that the medical student primarily learns to be a student, and only much later learns to be a physician.[7] Part of the difficulty certainly arises from the interplay of generalities and specialties. The student first learns generalities, or at least "backgrounds." However, if he is aimed toward a career in research endocrinology or public health parasitology or psychotherapy, he also learns more than he needs to know. He is qualifying, but somewhat irrelevantly.

Irrelevant knowledge abounds in every established professional field. It is scarcely surprising that "abstract" and

---

[6] Mary Jean Huntington, "The Development of a Professional Self-Image," in Robert K. Merton, George G. Reader, and Patricia L. Kendall (eds.), *The Student Physician* (Cambridge, Mass.: Harvard University Press, 1957), pp. 179–187.

[7] Howard S. Becker and others, *Boys in White: Student Culture in Medical School* (Chicago: University of Chicago Press, 1961), esp. Chap. 21, "The Development of the Medical Student."

"irrelevant" should get confused, and that those who claim professional standing command, and demand of neophytes, irrelevant knowledge that has no abstract, and therefore inferential, value.

The more or less formal educational systems designed to prepare young adults for the world of work convey with varying degrees of accuracy the formal requirements and formal rules of conduct appropriate to particular occupations. Verbal prescriptions and admonitions are rarely adequate; some form of apprenticeship or on-the-job training is a normal part of occupational socialization. Both in the context of formal training and in the situation of the newly recruited worker, formal precept is supplemented (and at times supplanted) by more knowledgeable associates. Thus in professional schools the less advanced students derive both cognitive and affective cues from those farther along in training. The extensive attention to peer groups in the literature often misses the point that their members may not be truly equal. One of the ways in which nominal peers are influential in socialization as *significant others* is that those who are more advanced know and exemplify the norms, and thus are accorded respect as well as liking or affection. This means that peers are less different from adult role models than might at first appear. In both cases it is the expectations of significant others that induces normative compliance and, normally, an actual sharing of attitudes and beliefs. This sharing, whether or not fully articulated, then constitutes an occupational identity, which is collective as well as individual. The individual *belongs*.

The frequency with which initiates to an occupation are put through some form of hazing may be interpreted either as a rather irrational survival of savagery, or possibly as having a definite function in socialization. We suggest the latter is the case. If, instead of hazing, we take the broader notion of suffering, it appears to be a prominent component in the training for all occupations that exhibit strong attention to standards of competence and performance and to identification with the occupation as a collectivity. (Tomkins has

argued a similar point, his illustrations being the experiences of abolitionists.[8] We owe our particular perception of professional socialization to some comments by Goode.[9])
Some professional schools virtually sequester their trainees, setting them apart from normal social activity in what amount to "total institutions"—military academies and some theological schools provide examples.[10] Other professional schools approximate such social isolation by the sheer burden of work demanded of students—classes, laboratories, studies, and practice. Despite the possible commitment of the student to his chosen career, at least part of the demands made upon him will be unpleasant and even hazardous to his remaining in good standing.

We thus have some of the ingredients of our proposed theory : a *punishment-centered theory of socialization*. The initiate is put through a set of tasks and duties that are difficult, and some are unpleasant. Success is accorded to most of the entrants, but not all; failure is a realistic possibility. These challenging and painful experiences are shared with others, who thus have a sort of fellowship of suffering.

Now if we add the probability that peers and adult role models constitute significant others, and thus that relations with them are marked by some degree of affectivity, we are well on the way to comprehending how an occupational identity gets formed. In short, the theory is that occupational identity and commitment will be proportional to the degree that these conditions are approximated—whether for the individual or for an occupational collectivity.

Although not essential to the theory, some additional and associated features of "punishing socialization" may be noted. Some of the difficult tasks are commonly ritualized and in that sense arbitrary. The medical student bound for

[8] Sylvan S. Tomkins, "The Constructive Role of Violence and Suffering for the Individual and for His Society," in Sylvan S. Tomkins and Carrol E. Izard (eds.), *Affect, Cognition and Personality: Empirical Studies* (New York: Springer Publishing Co., Inc., 1965), pp. 148–171.

[9] William J. Goode, "Community Within a Community; The Professions," *American Sociological Review*, 22:194–200, April 1957.

[10] Sanford M. Dornbusch, "The Military Academy as an Assimilating Institution," *Social Forces*, 33:316–321, May 1955.

a career in psychiatry must memorize the bones of the human body; the law student looking forward to a practice in establishing trusts for wealthy clients must learn endless cases in torts; the doctoral candidate intending to become a statistician in a university must show that he can read French and German; and military training abounds with apparently meaningless tasks. Marks of success, too, are commonly ritualized: awards, election to honorary fraternities, certificates, and diplomas. Yet the punishment does not stop so quickly, at least for occupations high on the scale of professionalism. The medical intern does the medical dirty work around a hospital; the young lawyer does the dirty work around a law firm, or, for that matter, if he attempts to establish an individual practice; the newly minted Ph.D. who enters college teaching does not exactly have to carry senior professors' books, but he does have to teach the courses they do not want. And although greater freedom follows successful survival of trials, the *persistent* possibility of failure is characteristic of most professional and technical occupations. We are suggesting that this is an important ingredient of continuing occupational commitment. Another allegation then follows: Persons who get into positions of absolute security, with no need to expose themselves to risk and uncertainty, in fact become occupationally unproductive. (We have rediscovered Calvinism by a devious route, but there it is.)

Still another feature of occupational socialization—and again we are attending primarily to fairly technical occupations—is the learning of technical language. Note that part of an occupational patois will consist of synonyms for words in general usage, and part will refer to objects, ideas, and processes beyond the layman's ken. Aside from facilitating precise technical communication, esoteric language serves to identify and exclude and thus to confirm occupational identity. It appears also to serve a psychological function, a kind of emotional set: now I am thinking technically.

The person who successfully learns the language and skills of a trade, and survives the ordeals that punished him and his fellows will emerge, we are arguing, not only with an internalized occupational commitment but also with an identification with the collectivity, the brotherhood. Yet note that for professional and similar occupations subject to continuing internal specialization and to substantial differences in the style and setting of occupational activities, identification with the occupational collectivity must be increasingly nostalgic: shared suffering and success in the past. Note also that the shared experience need not be entirely simultaneous, as long as the socializing system endures. This circumstance undoubtedly accounts for resistance to major changes in occupational training, for such changes would destroy a bridge across age groups—a bridge increasingly difficult to maintain in technical occupations, where the young, distressingly, know more than their elders. And even if the young are punished no less, and perhaps more, suffering comes in new forms that the older worker did not experience.

The professional career

Rapid growth of new knowledge and new techniques for doing the world's work threatens some occupations with extinction and others with technical obsolescence unless the workers can somehow manage to keep current. Some professional specialties may be subject to mechanization—computerized diagnosis in medicine, computerized case-finding in law, programmed instruction in education. For the most part, however, the professional is faced with keeping up, often by finer and finer specialization.

CAREER BUILDING

For most professionals, completion of formal training, passing qualifying examinations, and, perhaps, being licensed to practice constitute in combination a ticket of admission to a career. They do not guarantee success. For success one needs the good opinion of clients, even if that opinion is not very well informed, and the good opinion of professional peers.

The *particular* tactics appropriate to career building are

likely to be peculiar to each occupation or closely related group of them, and thus to defy quick generalization. The college professor demonstrates growth by his technical publications and, less reliably, by his reputation as a teacher. The engineer, whether salaried or a consultant, establishes his merits by delivering workable plans on schedule. The Army officer builds his career on the basis of merit ratings by his superiors, leading to orderly or even rapid promotion. The clergyman with a parish or congregation succeeds by increasing membership and attendance at services, by community participation, and perhaps by able performance of pastoral duties. For the physician or lawyer in strictly private practice, which is increasingly rare, building a clientele is a question of making suitable contacts. Above all, the new practitioner must appear busy; if a chance client can reach him too readily, he may quickly lose confidence in his competence.

What is general to these fields, and others, is the expectation of *growth:* in proficiency, wisdom, and recognition. Plateaus and declines do occur, but they do not correspond to ideal norms. The professional calling is ideally not a fixed position of competent service, but a career that shows progress.

ACCUMULATION VERSUS OBSOLESCENCE

A professional characteristic, which may be made either definitional or as a generalization about professionals otherwise identified, is commitment to a calling. This means, among other things, loyalty to a collectivity[11] as well as to occupational norms. The professional is expected to meet criteria of competence and performance, and to seek and recognize excellence. And, as earlier noted, it is precisely because professionals enjoy a large measure of autonomy in their exercise of what amounts to a form of power over their clients' welfare that their responsible behavior is, ideally, self-imposed. It is true that other restraints are available: the judgment of peers, disciplinary action by formal associations, lawsuits by dissatisfied clients. Particularly for the "helping" professions in private practice, however,

---

[11] Goode, reference cited in note 6.

external controls are likely to be called on only in extreme cases; self-restraint marks the socialized practitioner.

A problem faced by most professionals in the contemporary situation is compliance with the norms of competence, as the knowledge base changes and expands. Valiant resistance to specialization can only result in growing incompetence relative to changing standards set by superior performers. The duty of keeping current is owed not only to clients but also to peers, since poor performance may reflect discredit on the occupation as a whole. The incompetent professional's peers may defend poor performance to the laity and "cover up" for him, but they are likely to admonish him privately not to repeat errors.

We have been suggesting that for at least the professional part of the labor force occupational socialization does not end with entry into the labor market. This is especially the case for those in occupations with changing standards. Whether because of changes in the market for skills or because of changes more or less internal to occupations, we may expect in the future an even greater need for adult adaptability, and in not a few instances outright retraining of a formal kind.[12]

UNSTABLE CAREERS

In view of the expectation of occupational commitment among professionals, it is not surprising that we encounter some feeling of desertion (if not treason) when a scientist becomes a laboratory administrator, a physician a hospital administrator, or a professor an academic dean. Legal training is apparently more commonly used as a bridge to other occupations, such as politics or business management, and this branching in career lines may be more acceptable to former peers; one suspects, however, at least some ambivalence toward such behavior.

At the very least, unstable careers underscore once more the

---

[12] Seymour L. Wolfbein, "The Future World of Work," in William E. Hopke (ed.), *The Encyclopedia of Careers and Vocational Guidance*, Vol. 1, *Planning Your Career* (Garden City, N.Y.: Doubleday & Company, Inc., 1967), pp. 37–44.

importance of *adult socialization,* since a career shift clearly requires the acquisition of new skills. That the skills may have been acquired gradually as a sort of a by-product of prior practice, rather than by concentrated "retreading," does not argue against their importance.

DÉFORMATION PROFESSIONNELLE

The charming French phrase *déformation professionnelle* refers to the possible distortions in character that derive from participation in the world of work—in any occupation. One mild example is the incapacity to divest oneself of occupational concerns in other social contexts: the inveterate shoptalk of professionals, the businessman who thinks only of business. Yet Wilensky's data confirm a bit of folk wisdom: "If you want a job done, give it to a busy man." It is precisely the hardworking and successful portions of the labor force that also become involved in community service and "constructive" recreation. And, conversely, it is those whose jobs are essentially meaningless who find leisure as constituting time on their hands.[13]

The subtler forms of character distortion also merit attention. Rampant and increasing specialization may result in an excessively narrow view not only of the world of work, but also of the world generally. Narrow problem-solving may inhibit thinking about whether the problem is important. The worker may become overcommitted to occupational norms and practices, resisting even those innovations that would improve his position or make his task easier. In social situations outside the workplace, popular occupational stereotypes may have some merit: the fussy accountant, argumentative lawyer, didactic teacher, crude and materialistic businessman, inarticulate mechanic or engineer, television-addicted factory worker, and tense and brittle advertising man. It would be surprising if work did not leave its mark, for roles are one thing, but they are played by more or less whole persons.

---

[13] Harold L. Wilensky, "Orderly Careers and Social Participation: The Impact of Work History on Social Integration in the Middle Mass," *American Sociological Review,* 26:521–539, August 1961.

The plight of the professional is that extreme specialization radically narrows those significant others with whom he can carry on job-centered social discourse. And the attention required by his specialty may reduce his other social involvements. Here, once more, the importance of identification with a broader calling is apparent, even if the common interests of the fraternity are in some measure nostalgic rather than strictly contemporary.

Modes of reinforcement

Just as we have argued that socialization is a continuing and not simply early and terminal process, so we should note that the conscientious performer is rarely isolated from reinforcements. In a sense, internalization of occupational norms is itself a kind of reinforcement, for self-respect may be a powerful restraint on slovenly performance or violation of standards. Additionally, even the relatively autonomous professional is not entirely out of sight of his peers. We have repeatedly used the phrase "expectations of significant others," and that about sums it up. Indifference to the opinions of peers is exceptional and plainly pathological; it is the essence of alienation.

More formal reinforcements also exist. The extremely poor performer finds no market for his services. Occupational associations—particularly among the professions and those seeking professional status—set standards of training and performance, and many provide machinery for formal charges and discipline. Even the government may be used as a disciplinary agent: the damage suit instituted by an aggrieved employer or client; the removal of a license, perhaps even a charge of criminal misconduct. The rarity of extreme sanctions means either that rules are poorly enforced or that occupational socialization and informal reinforcements serve in most cases. With some possible exceptions—abortion may be one, for the law is more severe than many members of the community would support—the probability is high that socialization works.

Part two: Professional roles

THE professional renders his expert services for clients.
Those clients may be individual or collective; they may
actively seek professional advice and help, or have the service provided as a sort of by-product of their position in some
social organization. The physician in private practice treats
patients, who seek him out. The "house counsel" or law firm
in corporate practice is primarily engaged in advice relating
to the collective welfare of the client organization. The professional soldier serves his government and thus, presumably and indirectly, the entire citizenry. The research scientist or scholar is a limiting case. It would perhaps be more
accurate to argue that scientists and scholars, except as
teachers or advisory consultants, are much like professionals
in nearly all of the scalar or definitional criteria, but must
be considered as "professional-like" if they genuinely lack
clients "needing" their services for the solving of problems
of moment. Wilensky[1] would not consider them professionals,
for want of clients. It might be argued, somewhat tenuously,
that even where the research is "basic," without apparent
practical applications to human goals or problems, the researcher's clients are in effect his fellow specialists.

The client as employer

For the professional in private practice, and for many
salaried professionals also, the client—the recipient of help,
information, and advice—is the employer. Particularly for
the private practitioner, who will be our primary concern
here, this circumstance provides some interesting strains in
role relationships.

---

[1] Harold Wilensky, "The Professionalization of Everyone?" *American
Journal of Sociology*, 70:137–158, September 1964, esp. p. 141.

Professionals in strictly independent practice—who account for a declining proportion of all professional services—respond only to initiatives taken by clients, at least by the conventions of the established occupational groups. Physicians and attorneys do not advertise their services, though they may circumspectly announce them, and certainly do not announce their fees. Dentists who advertise are an embarrassment to the more "professionally" oriented practitioners. It is also interesting to note that consulting engineers and public relations or management consultants advertise in specialized journals that reach a prospective clientele. For the physician or lawyer, however, the initiative is supposed to rest with the client, except for rare emergency situations. Even for those groups, however, listings available to professionals exist.

We come then to a paradox, masterfully explored by Eliot Freidson.[2] The reputation, the professional success or failure of the independent practitioner, rests precisely with potential clients, who are precisely those not technically competent to judge. Freidson contrasts this "client control," which operates through a "lay referral system," with the colleague control that operates through professional referral. Thus the independence of the lone practitioner is somewhat illusory, for he is somewhat insulated from the competent judgment of peers and dependent on the good opinion of the laity.

The lay referral system, Freidson notes,[3] operates so as to impose client's standards—for example, in types of medication or other therapy—that may not agree with professional standards. Thus mothers may "shop" for a pediatrician that most closely agrees with their own childrearing theories, often without the necessity of successive professional appointments but rather by the simple process of taking testimony from knowledgeable (or at least opinionated) friends and neighbors.

---

[2] Eliot Freidson, "Client Control and Medical Practice," *American Journal of Sociology*, 65:374–382, January 1960.

[3] *Ibid.*, p. 378.

We should add that client control will determine not only the success or failure of the independent practitioner, but also is likely to have a major effect on the *threshold* of professional service. Undoubtedly the degree of hypochondria or litigiousness or religious anxiety experienced by individuals is somewhat idiosyncratic, reflecting personality differences. Still, groups within a community will be found to have differing levels of demand for professional services, somewhat independent of ability to pay for them.

Occupations relatively high on the scale of professionalism differ in their degree of what we may call "public exposure." Illness and the hazards of death are ubiquitous problems in human existence; to a growing degree in economically modern societies it is expected that these problems will be treated professionally. True, part of this extension of medical service has come about through publicly financed hospitals and clinics, through welfare payments for medical services to indigent clients, through medical insurance as a fringe benefit of employment, and even, as in England, through national medical insurance. It is also true that home remedies, self-medication, and drugstore diagnosis keep the threshold of strictly professional medicine well above absolute zero. (Over the short run perhaps that is just as well, as the number of physicians in the United States has increased nowhere near as fast as the demand for their services, and their geographic distribution is highly uneven relative to population.)

The law, too, is ubiquitous in modern societies, but a great portion of the population goes through life without once seeing an attorney. Many citizens encounter the legal order, if at all, as a defendant in some charge for a misdemeanor for an illegally parked car or some traffic violation. Even if a man's guilt is in doubt and he wants a court hearing, he will rarely be represented by counsel. One reason for that is that an attorney's fee would ordinarily exceed the amount of the prospective fine. The threshold may well be lowered if a jail term is threatened. In such cases the defendant's income is likely to be the best predictor of his seeking professional help, though in law, too, notions of providing equal justice through a public defender are gradually being implemented in the United States.

Aside from possible brushes with the criminal law, the citizen's perceived need for legal counsel may be slight to nonexistent. If he is affluent enough to have accumulated some property, he may (or may not) have a lawyer draw his will or establish a trust. Again persons of some affluence may be involved in property transfers—the commonest being purchasing a house—but real estate brokers or the mortgage loan officers of a bank may make all arrangements, including title search and insurance, without the purchaser (or perhaps anyone) having recourse to an attorney.

Additionally, there is a fair chance that an American adult will be involved in an automobile accident. Aside from possible traffic violations, the settlement of liability claims may involve negotiation by attorneys and perhaps actual litigation. Yet the participant in an accident is more likely to see an insurance company claims adjuster than an attorney, the lawyers—if they get involved at all—representing insurance companies.

Even a divorce may not require the services of a lawyer (most divorces being uncontested), though the complainant at least is usually represented by counsel.

In effect, what we have been saying about law is that most individuals do not get charged with serious legal offenses, and that the bulk of legal practice relates to property, contracts, and torts (negligence and civil liability), which, again, engage most individuals seldom or never. The popular association of lawyers with "propertied interests" is not strictly accurate, but is correct often enough to confirm the stereotype.

Client control over the lawyer thus operates within narrower circles than for the physician. Yet the potential client will still seek an attorney who will *successfully* represent his interests. This may range from simply keeping the client out of trouble, say in his business transactions, to the attempted use of the attorney instrumentally, to find a feasible way of doing what the client wants to do: to get a variance on a zoning ordinance, to acquire control of another company, to negotiate a more favorable contract with a governmental agency.

For the infrequent consumer of legal services a "lay referral system" no doubt operates, though it may be difficult to find a friend or acquaintance who knows a lawyer. For the frequent client, or the man who has a regular attorney, the choice of an adviser is likely to be highly "particularistic." If the independent medical practitioner builds his practice on the basis of a reputation among a clientele, the lawyer—whether independent or in a law firm—depends upon contacts. Some of these may be of some duration—the school or college classmate, for example. Others may arise from country-club memberships, participation in other voluntary associations, or a chance exchange at a neighborhood cocktail party.

It is, of course, not true that all members of the bar are equally competent, on strictly professional criteria. (We shall explore professional judgments of peers in Chapter 8.) But the relative success of a lawyer has a low—it would be inaccurate and therefore too cynical to say a negative—correlation with technical competence. What happens in the practice of law is that "connections" make a difference. Reasonable competence, however, is essential to keeping the client satisfied, for, however painfully, the client may decide that his old buddy is not really protecting or prosecuting his interests properly; and, since money is likely to be involved, the client may hardheartedly dismiss his attorney and seek a sharper adviser and protagonist.

We are a few paragraphs away from the initial introduction of the concept of thresholds, but we now return to that focus. New specialties in the professions have difficulty in establishing clienteles, except by professional referral. Specialization may take place through the dynamics of professional practice, without primary reference to perceived demand. Even a new and independent service, the practitioners following carefully the scalar steps outlined in Chapter 1, may still have trouble locating a market, enthusiasts having exaggerated the potential demand. Architects, for example, have yet to achieve a taken-for-granted status even for the minority of custom-built residences. And marital counselors have a rather narrowly restricted clientele, despite the widespread occurrence of marital conflict and a high divorce rate. Architects have mainly wealthy or corporate clients, and marital counselors attract "sophisticated" urbanites who lack the more traditional ties to church or kinsmen, and are not quite prepared for psychiatrists or lawyers.

The potential client, seeking professional help, presents a complaint, problem, or challenge. When he is free to select his adviser he may also have the presumed freedom to determine the limit of his involvement. He may want help on a particular problem, not all his problems, a temporary arrangement rather than a continuing one. Under these same circumstances of choice, however, the professional need not accept the client on these terms. Although the professional has no real authority to impose sanctions other than the merit of his advice or refusal to continue a relationship, he may seek to convince the client that his particular problem cannot be solved in isolation from his life situation, be that medical, legal, economic, or whatever. Thus the professional adviser commonly seeks to develop what amounts to a dossier on the client, on the grounds that help in meeting the client's problem is properly contextual and not isolated. In this way the professional begins to establish his control, to counter the control of the employing client. Yet the degree to which the practitioner is client-oriented as distinct from problem-oriented is variable within and between professional groups.

THE ECONOMIC NEXUS

The private professional practitioner, whether operating as an independent or as a member of a group or firm, depends for his livelihood on the fees paid for particular services. A physician or attorney may accept an annual retainer from a collective or corporate client for more or less routine services, reserving the right of charging an additional fee for an unusual set of duties. Otherwise, the client is expected to pay for each particular service. The salaried professional is essentially on a "full retainer," and practice varies as to whether such a professional may, additionally, have private clients as long as their interests are not adverse to those of the primary employer.

There are a number of normative issues involved in setting (and collecting) professional fees. One set of principles operates according to an emulation of the open market, and indeed a true market may operate to some degree. This set of principles sets the level of fees according to the quantity or quality of services. Thus in medical practice it is common for a physician to have a standard fee for a routine office visit, a higher fee for a home call (if he ever makes one), for a check-up examination, and for inoculations and vaccinations (commonly performed by a nurse in a successful independent practice or in group practice). Even "normal" obstetrical cases may be billed at a flat fee, uniform for all such patients, and amended upward only if complications develop.

Yet there is another fee-setting principle in medicine, which, ironically—since organized medicine especially in the United States is strong on ideological individualism and on the economic welfare of physicians—is a form of private socialism. This principle is to grade fees according to ability to pay, thus giving a special sense to the classic socialist slogan, "To each according to his need, from each according to his ability." This principle has been used to encourage service to the indigent patient—whose bill is now often paid by others, as earlier noted—and to afford compensation for such cases by expecting high fees from wealthy clients.

Specialists commonly demand higher fees than general practitioners for comparable services, the rationale being the presumed greater capacity of specialists to deal with unusual situations. Of course, in contemporary medical practice, there are certain skills such as organ transplants that are commanded only by specialists. It is also true that specialists, by the norms, are supposed to take on exceptional cases regardless of fee, for the dual reason that the patient needs the treatment and that the specialist may further develop his skills.

Nevertheless, it remains true that if one has an unusual ailment it is better to be rich than poor, and in general that the quality of medical care is correlated with ability to pay. Thus, despite the greater incidence of emotional disturbance and mental disorder among the poor than among the well-to-do,[4] it is the latter who can afford private psychotherapy.

Problems also arise within what Freidson[5] calls the professional referral system. Since the client referral system may not accurately lead the patient to the proper specialist, the point of entry into the medical system is likely to be the (almost) general practitioner or, in group practice, the internist. In earlier practice, the specialist, being dependent upon a generalist for his clientele, recognized this dependence by splitting his fee with his "patron." This practice may still exist here and there but is strongly condemned by professional groups.

The quality of service also affects the legal client, and is also likely to be graded by the scale of fees. This is most conspicuous in criminal cases. (Thus, a well-to-do client is almost never convicted on a first-degree murder charge; in the rare cases of convictions, the death penalty, where applicable, is almost always avoided.) In other legal practice, there is a strong tendency for the attorney to set his fee in some proportion to the amount of money involved in the transaction, not on the amount of time spent or the technical difficulty of the case. It is not automatically true that large-sum negotiations are also complex. Again, the conspicuous case of the graded fee is the liability suit, undertaken by the attorney for the plaintiff on a contingent-fee basis—nothing if the case is lost, and a share of the award if won. The professional image of attorneys is sufficiently damaged by this practice to expect that it may not survive long, at least openly. But it does get this kind of legal service for persons too poor to afford an attorney.

Consulting engineers and other individual consultants or firms generally operate on the basis of a daily fee. If a group is involved, the fee does not all stay in the hands of the actual consultant; like the physician in group practice or the partner in a law firm, a portion of the fee is paid as a kind of internal tax for payment of secretarial staff, perhaps re-

---

[4] August B. Hollingshead and Frederick C. Redlich, *Social Class and Mental Illness* (New York: John Wiley & Sons, Inc., 1958).

[5] Freidson, article cited in note 2, p. 379.

search assistants and rent, receptionists, writers, and flowers in the reception room.

There are certain fee-setting practices, which, like the lawyer's pro rata fee, are simply contrary to clients' interests. Private architects, for example, commonly bill clients for a percentage of the total construction costs of a building. Needless to say, this scarcely encourages the architect to recommend the lowest-cost contractor, or to seek economical substitutes for high-cost materials.

Veterinarians (who would rank surprisingly high on our scale of professionalism, which does not include a prestige item) generally operate with a uniform schedule of fees. So do optometrists. Dentists, though rather variable among themselves in fee-setting, tend to have standard charges for "standard" dental problems, but have a great deal of discretion for major jobs of facial reconstruction. It is not unusual for facial repair fees of an accident victim to be affected by the financial circumstance of the patient, including his insurance coverage for medical expenses.

Understandably, members of a professional group dislike blatant competition in the price for their services. The rationale for price maintenance is dual: protection of the income level of all practitioners and protection of the prestigious position of the professional in the community. The two are closely related, but analytically and sometimes concretely distinct. Where there is a general shortage of professional services, or some members of the occupation are amply secure in their earning capacity, there will still be resentment at any "degrading" practice of rate-cutting. Aside from diplomas and bar association memberships, the most frequent framed document on a lawyer's office wall is a quotation from Abraham Lincoln: "A lawyer's time and advice are his stock in trade." Professionals, we have noted, have a strong sense of collective identity, however much they may compete with one another in practical effect.

It is rather common for local bar associations to set standard (or minimum) fees for certain legal instruments, and a minimum hourly rate for working on a case. Other professional groups also set fees. Whether such rate-setting constitutes a "combination in restraint of trade" or a legitimate bit of self-regulation by an occupational association has yet to be tested in American courts.

There is a further irony in professional attitudes and practices. Perhaps the most extreme, insistent, and blatantly biased spokesmen for the right of the individual to choose his professional adviser has been the American Medical Association.[6] Yet physicians, and indeed other professionals in private practice, do not encourage "shopping," either for price or quality; on the contrary. Any transfer, by professional views, should come from a professional referral, not from a client's dissatisfaction or eagerness for a bargain.

The whole handling of fees offers some further insights. The private practitioner is by no means averse to an immediate cash payment, particularly from a relatively poor client who may be a credit risk. Even so, direct payment is rare and commonly gauche. Rather, the client is encouraged to settle his account with a secretary, receptionist, or business office in a larger establishment. For the regular (and more affluent) client, the whole transaction is handled at arm's length: the service is rendered, and the client learns what value the professional placed on the help given when he receives a mailed statement.

Actual collection of professional fees is variable in time and circumstance. The conspicuous contemporary affluence of American physicians certainly owes something to the level of fees charged, but also no doubt owes something to a reduction in the incidence of nonpayment. The indigent client is more likely to have payments made on his behalf. Moreover, the older complaint of physicians that fees graded by ability to pay tended to yield a considerable portion of "paper income," owing to the casual attitudes and practices of the very well-to-do concerning payment of debts, seems no longer to be voiced. Have even the rich become "middle class" in their morality?

---

[6] See "The American Medical Association: Power, Purpose, and Politics in Organized Medicine," *Yale Law Journal,* 63:976–996, May 1954.

In return for the trust that a client places in a professional whose help he seeks, the professional owes various duties to the client: current competence and performance, at least by prevailing standards; preservation of the confidentiality of the relationship, and in particular of the information that the client gives to the professional; and, in varying degrees, attending to the client's welfare in the particular personal and social setting in which he finds himself.

The expectation of competence is one of the major concerns for training and admission standards, which a professional association (and occupational groups attempting to improve their acceptance as professionals) will attempt to regulate with or without licensing. But competence may not be current, and the currently competent practitioner may become lazy, careless, or cynical. The client may, of course, take his problems elsewhere, perhaps with some difficulty, if he has not meanwhile died, gone to prison, or lost a great deal of money because he followed advice given. Performance is more difficult to control than is initial competence, and the most effective control is from peers and not clients. We shall see that peer control is also not easy, partly because of the loyalty that a professional owes his colleagues.

The question of *privileged communication* is in a somewhat cloudy state. Professionals may, in the course of consulting with a client or handling a specific problem, come into possession of "guilty information," or at least of information that, if made public, might damage the reputation, the friendships, or the livelihood of clients. Physicians and lawyers have long been accorded the legal right (and moral obligation) not to divulge such information; clergymen also sometimes share this special position. Confidentiality of professional relations is of course especially important in the Anglo-American system of law, as a person accused of an infraction is not required to testify against himself, and he has the right to counsel in his defense even if he is, in fact, guilty. Other occupational groups seek to assert the right of protecting privileged communication, with very uneven success. Public officials, and particularly the military, may do so, under regulations permitting the "classification" of information deemed in the national interest, but this is scarcely on behalf of clients, except in a very indirect sense. Journalists may seek to protect confidential news sources, but the right has not been clearly established by the courts. A great many social scientists assure respondents to interviews and questionnaires that their information will be treated anonymously, but the scholars would have no legal recourse if required to produce their records in court.

There is another duty to clients that is especially germane to law, but has broader ramifications. The lawyer's duty of *loyalty* to the client applies not only to confidential information, but also to the avoidance of adverse interests. Under an adversary system of legal settlements, an attorney—or a law firm—may not represent both sides in a possible dispute. For example, it is improper for an attorney to represent the plaintiff in a civil liability claim and also the insurance company that would be a co-defendant with an insured driver in the negotiation or litigation of the claim. Yet it is noteworthy that licensed real estate brokers—who are required to prepare for and pass an examination in many jurisdictions, but do not otherwise rank exceptionally high on the scale of professionalism—do seem to represent both parties in transactions. As the broker's fee is a percentage of the sale price, the purchaser is perhaps best advised to assume that the broker does indeed want to complete the transaction, but at as high a price as possible. The New York State laws and regulations regarding licensed real estate brokers are fairly unambiguous on the point that the broker is representing the prospective seller (who will, normally, pay the appropriate commission for the service of a broker in finding a buyer).[7] A broker may also act in a fiduciary capacity for a buyer, however, as in accepting a deposit on an incomplete transaction. In any event, it is not at all clear that prospective purchasers or renters of real estate understand that the broker must be assumed to be acting in the interests of the

---

[7] (New York), Department of State, Division of Licensing Services, *Real Estate Brokers: License Laws for Brokers and Salesmen* (Albany, n.d.—app. 1966).

seller or landlord should there be a difference of interest between seller and buyer—as there always is when the trans-
actional price is at stake.

Adverse interests may even appear in medical practice.
The individual applicant for a life-insurance policy is
normally required to offer proof of insurability by submitting to a medical examination (and by waiver of the confidentiality of his prior medical records). The applicant is
supposed to make "full disclosure," for failure to do so on an
important matter would constitute an attempted fraud and
might result in cancellation of his policy. (Indeed, since
American life insurance companies pool their medical information on policyholders, the individual runs the risk of
becoming uninsurable, or insurable only at very high pre-
miums.) But what are the physician's responsibilities?
Technically, the applicant is *not* the examining physician's
client. The physician is acting in an advisory capacity to the
prospective insurer, which, incidentally, will normally pay
for the examination. Now suppose the physician finds a
serious impairment, which would not only affect the applicant's insurability, but which also should be given remedial
or palliative therapy. He must either report this to the insurance company, or advise the applicant to withdraw his application. And despite the circumstance that the applicant, who
may also be confused on this point, is not his client, the
general ethical responsibility of the physician is to urge the
applicant to go to his own physician for advice and treatment.

Whether a professional should assume some responsibility
for the general welfare of his client is a question that raises
some further troublesome issues. The idealized picture of
the general practitioner in medicine made of him a friend,
confidant, and wise adviser on matters far removed from
scalpels and pills. No doubt such relationships have existed,
with dubious propriety. Yet this role model has been supplemented rather than superseded by certain developments in
contemporary medical practice. The psychiatric emphasis
in medical training, and the consequent tendency to look for
psychosomatic sources of physical disorders and complaints,

have been further reinforced by the firm admonition to the physician to perceive the patient in his familial, neighborhood, and employment settings. In view of the extensive specialization in contemporary medicine, one would expect a growth of referrals between medical specialties. Although we have no secure evidence on this, it appears that private physicians—normally the internist in group practice—also attempt to deal with "the whole patient" by advising the patient to get help from other professionals and service agencies.

In addition to physicians, attorneys with individual clients, the pastoral type of clergyman, and even some teachers attempt to see the client in a somewhat broader perspective than narrow problem-solving would seem to indicate. The social worker also receives this kind of orientation in training, but actual practice must be highly variable. The dentist, on the other hand, is commonly reputed to limit his perspective to the patient's mouth (and possibly his wallet), but not to suggest clearly indicated medical, psychiatric, legal, or welfare services.

Since specialization is virtually forced on the contemporary professional, dealing with the "whole client" may lead to awkward questions of jurisdiction among professionals, not to mention more traditional structural sources of social support. In relatively small communities, or relatively stable suburban ones, the interprofessional referrals may be relatively knowledgeable, and the professional of primary contact may be able to know which other services are available, and which are not. In a relatively impersonal metropolitan setting the professional is both less likely to extend himself for his client and less able to enlist the named and specified services of others, if he were so minded.

NUANCES OF ROLE RELATIONSHIPS

One difficulty that privately practicing professionals have with clients is that the latter often fail to behave like the textbook case. Another way of putting this is that professionals, trained to deal with clients, have an established set of role models for clients; on the average, the practicing professional is more prepared to deal with (stereotypical) clients than are the latter to deal with professionals. The professional's view, out of reading case histories and perhaps watching some portion of the performing and consulting practice, expects to deal with a supplicant client, who brings a routine or possibly challenging problem for solution, and the practitioner solves it routinely (out of the book) or at greater challenge to his ingenuity. A major difficulty is that many clients fail to behave properly.

Here we encounter another paradox, or at least an ambivalence on the part of the professional. If the client comes with his problem poorly specified, his report of need vague, the reason for his seeking help seemingly more psychotherapeutic than technical, the consultant must somehow bring the client into his proper field of vision. He, the professional, seeks to get the *technical* meaning of the problem, and, if he is to be of service, must get the client in the appropriate role of recipient of exceptional services. Parsons and Fox[8] have explored the problem of "taking the sick role" in medical practice, and comparable problems arise in other professional contexts : the candid and needful client for legal services, the penitent sinner for the clergyman, the eager but confused student, the man who has ideas but no plan for his home consulting an architect, the official with a goal but not the technical means for its accomplishment relying on an engineer.

The unsocialized client presents one kind of problem, for, in his way, he must be turned into a suitably oriented client. The oversocialized client presents his own difficulties. Self-diagnosed, allegedly knowledgeable about his problem and its solution, he seeks for public or other authenticating reasons only the routine connivance of the professional. This situation is perhaps the more annoying in professional practice, because more threatening to the distinctively authoritative role of the expert. The professional tactic in such instances may be some variant of the honored aphorism in

8 Talcott Parsons and Renée Fox, "Illness, Therapy and the Modern Urban American Family," *Journal of Social Issues*, 8(4) :31–44, 1952.

psychotherapy: First make the patient sick. The client must be shown that his problem is much greater and more complex than he had thought, that circumstances he had not dreamed of might be involved, and that he was well advised to seek professional counsel, if a little naive in thinking that all he needed was a kind of official blessing.

The problems of role relationships also get a bit complex if the client happens to be a more or less fully qualified professional in another field. By canon, though not in fact, the physician is not supposed to treat himself or his immediate family; he is supposed not to heed the admonition, "Physician, heal thyself!" Since specialization is widely recognized in medicine, however, the physician may in fact refer his own case, or one in his family, to another. Lawyers, pretending not to specialize, rarely seek legal counsel overtly. College professors, being dedicated specialists, commonly refer and defer to colleagues, except, perhaps, for teaching practices, where everyone is assumed—incorrectly—to be equally competent.

The more interesting situation is the professional client from another occupational group. Here the professional consultant must tread cautiously, for he must forbear his possibly customary practice of mystery and meaningless charade. His professional counterpart will be able to translate into his own impressive display of esoteric and possibly irrelevant knowledge, and grow impatient.

Questions of relative rank and title may even get involved in interprofessional relations. Physicians lost their American battle for the exclusive right to the term "doctor," a right never enjoyed in Europe. (It will be noted that in this book we use "physicians" as the generic term for medical professionals; that is correct usage, "doctor" is not.) Yet for a long time physicians failed to accord a doctoral title to any but an M.D. (to whom it was always accorded), and to this day a physician will sign a letter or a technical publication with the decreasingly prestigious M.D., as though it were a peculiar distinction. A number of years ago the misplaced arrogance of physicians came to the attention of the—often misguided—public relations counselors of the American Medical Association, and physicians were advised to give appropriate titles to patients. The reform has not been universal, partly because physicians, like other high-ranking professionals, are trained to think that they represent possibly the most honorable of noble callings, and mainly because dealing with putative equals puts a strain on the professional-client role relationship.

In a civilization in which a steadily rising proportion of the labor force has one sort or another of technical training—and thus each commands a mystery narrowly shared—the position of the relatively narrow corps of highly educated and putatively cultivated true professionals is being steadily eroded. The specialist is an extremely likely client of another specialist; he will rarely welcome being patronized or talked down to. Teachers, clergymen, and engineers have had to learn this lesson; lawyers are beginning to get the message, and physicians are bound to learn, perhaps last.

The client as beneficiary

With the growing bureaucratization of professional occupations, in the minimum definitional sense of salaried employment, there is a correlative development of the rendering of professional services for a stated class of clients rather than for those who seek out such services on an individual basis.

We should distinguish a few types of such "built-in" situations, with primary reference still to relations between professionals and individual clients. The relations of the salaried professional to his employer will engage our attention in Chapter 11, where we shall more fully explore the situation of the professional whose employer is not his client. Yet it is difficult to keep the analytical distinction concretely distinct. Two types of situations will represent typological cases not unknown in nature. The one is the situation of the aeronautical engineer in a Research and Development division in an aircraft company, that company being under federal-agency contract, and the engineer working on the design of a supersonic fighter plane. Here, clearly, the demand for this kind of professional service on the part of the ordinary laity is exactly none. The other situation is that of the private or public social work or welfare organization in which the client is unable to pay for professional services, but is accorded them because some decision-makers have seen fit to think that the client needs them and has some basis of legitimate claim upon them.

Having set the extremes—the provision of professional services in the interests of everyone and therefore possibly of no one, and the provision of professional services for those who could not conceivably afford them—let us turn to a middle range of more ambiguous situations.

What we are concerned with here is the range of contexts in which the client does not seek, or cannot afford to seek, professional services, and nevertheless receives them as a by-product of his situation in the social system.

One set of situations is exemplified by the bureaucratic employee who gets certain professional, and certain other merely specialized, services as a consequence of employment. Thus many corporate employees have an annual, routine medical examination, at the employer's expense, and without report to the employer. (Where there is a report to the employer, matters get more complicated, as we shall see.)

Other professional services in corporate and similar administrative organizations may be less forthright. The knowledge that the employer has a salaried legal counselor and his assistants, experts on tax accountancy, and other experts ranging from engineers to marketing analysts, may entice the managerial (never the hourly rated) employee into seeking internal consultation on his own problems.

This kind of request may very well place the salaried professional in an awkward position. He may understand the sophisticated distinction between the collective client and the individual as a member of the collectivity. His petitioner may not. It naturally follows that the higher the rank of the person in an administrative organization, the more likely is the professional employee to waive the difference, since, politically, he will accept the reality of the commonly, and erroneously, assumed identity of interests of officers of corporations and those of the entity as such. Many a senior corporate officer has had free income-tax (not to mention stock-market) advice from a salaried professional, advice that a junior administrator could scarcely claim.

The role-strains do not end with this particular ambiguity. The salaried professional, as we shall explore more extensively in Chapter 11, has obligations to his employer, to his peers, and often to his proper clients that are included in neither of those categories. Thus if the salaried professional renders services beyond those for which he is nominally hired, he may be in improper competition with a colleague in private practice. The situation of university medical staffs is interesting in this regard—not professors of medicine but salaried physicians in "health service" units. Now these professionals are overtly employed to deal with students, who may be charged an explicitly earmarked health fee as a kind of contributory insurance premium. What about members of university faculties? It appears that the situation is rather uniformly left ambiguous. Medical care is either not mentioned as one of the standard benefits of employment, or some specific benefit such as an optional annual examination is mentioned, but not others. The normal assumption appears to be that the faculty member, and certainly members of his family, will consult private physicians; yet some faculty members may exploit the ambiguity by getting personal medical service from staff physicians.

Some professional services are normally rendered by salaried practitioners. This is true of the clergy, whose spiritual counsel is presumably not differentiated by the amount, or even the act, of voluntary contributions to church support by parishioners. Yet it is customary to award special services—notably those passage rituals marking christening, marriage, and death—with a nominally voluntary honorarium; the clergyman does not submit a bill for his services. For the salaried social worker in a private welfare agency, it is extremely unlikely that the beneficiaries of his or her activities will also be donors to the agency's support. Since it is difficult for any adult, however poor, to avoid paying some taxes, it might be argued that clients of publicly supported welfare agencies may be partial, and indirect, contributors to the cost of services received; yet certainly this is not a fee-for-service transaction. Similarly, whether an educational institution is supported by endowments, gifts, tuition, or taxes, the professional is not paid directly by the client. Here, however, some slight measure of client control may still exist, as in the case of the exceptionally popular or exceptionally unpopular college teacher. Yet the general run of professors resist giving the impression of yielding too much to students' opinions or demands, and are likely to regard the very popular teacher as "playing to the galleries" at the sacrifice of pedagogical standards.

It is clear that the salaried professional or the one in some form of group practice is less subject to control by aggregates of individual clients than is the man in independent practice. Even if the clients are beneficiaries rather than employers, however, their opinions are likely to have some effect on professional careers, at least at the extremes of popularity and unpopularity.

Professional authority and its restraints

A qualified professional is supposed to be an *authority* on his subject as a body of knowledge and an *expert* on its application to the solution of particular problems presented by clients. This places the professional in a superordinate position in the role relationship with the client, even if the latter is the employer. The role relationship gets complicated, however, in certain fairly standard situations, and these are worth exploring.

TECHNICAL AND ADMINISTRATIVE AUTHORITY

Professional authority in its pure form is in the nature of *advice*. Since the client has sought it, there is some supposition that he will follow through. If, however, he fails to do so, the only penalty is that the consequences may be contrary to the client's best interests. Professional authority does not normally carry administrative or legal sanctions.

In certain situations technical and administrative authority may be mixed. Thus teachers, aside from maintenance of classroom discipline, also have the sanction of grades. In the case of infraction of rules, sanctions may be imposed directly by the teacher or by higher administrative authority. If imposed by the teacher, he or she is exercising administrative, not professional, authority. Even study assignments are more nearly orders than advice, since penalties are imposed for nonperformance.

Roman Catholic clergymen, too, may mete out required penance for the confessed misconduct of a parishioner; the parishioner runs the risk of expulsion if he fails to comply.

Another standard situation is that of the salaried professional with administrative backing, which, of course, is also true of the teacher. Thus, professional advice may become genuine "orders" if compliance is a condition for continued employment. A company-sponsored medical examination may result in specific instructions for changes in diet and regimen; if these instructions are made known to the employee's administrative superiors—thus raising again the question, who is the client?—the employee is essentially constrained in his conduct. A similar constraint applies if the employer's rules require that speeches or publications be cleared by the office of the corporation counsel. In this last situation there is small likelihood of confusion. The professional is not giving primacy to the interests of the individual but to those of the corporate entity.

CLIENT FREEDOM AND ITS PENALTIES

When the client is free to reject or simply ignore professional advice, he does so at his own peril. The professional can scarcely be held accountable for failure not of his doing. Incidentally, this may be a latent function of the records kept by methodical physicians—invariably known in American medical practice as the patient's "chart." Of course, since the records remain in the physician's custody, they could always be "doctored" should a dispute arise. It is also noteworthy that the hospitalized patient sacrifices most of his discretionary options, so that, once more, "orders" become just that.

In strictly private practice the client's freedom is balanced by the freedom of the professional to refuse to continue in an advisory capacity if the advice is ordinarily ignored or ignored in serious instances. The professional has enough risks of failure without the added threat of being known as the adviser of an irresponsible client. There is one situation, however, in which the professional is supposed to protect the client from his own folly, and that is the refusal of medical, legal, or other services when, in the opinion of the professional, they are not needed. The difficulty with this is that the potential client, having convinced himself that he has problems beyond his capacity, may be hard to convince of the contrary; if the professional remains adamant, the client may simply take his case to a more compliant practitioner. Some clients, we have observed, simply do not behave "reasonably," thus violating the normative expectation for *their* conduct in the arena of professionalism.

*Chapter six: The professional and his peers:
identification and self-regulation*

IF the professional has various duties to clients in return for
the trust accorded the adviser, he also has responsibilities to
his professional peers. His relations with colleagues are by
no means untroubled, as we shall see in this and several suc-
ceeding chapters. They start with common interests, and
may proceed to diverse and even divisive interests.

Identification: the brotherhood

Both among the high-ranking professional occupations, and,
perhaps even more noticeably, among those attempting to
gain full professional acceptance, there is a strong and normatively supported tendency to emphasize the collegiality of
the occupation. Terms such as "colleague," "fellow," and
even "brother" abound as references to peers, particularly
before the laity. We noted in Chapter 4 that occupational
identification is a prominent part of professional socialization, and suggested that a principal element in its effective
internalization is a shared nostalgia for serious trials successfully sustained. We should add that there are elements
of pride in being associated with a "high" calling, and
identification with historic heroes in the development of
theory or practice. The use of technical language for discourse among peers serves not only to communicate but also
to identify who belongs and to reinforce the common interests. When specialization makes communication difficult, it
is also likely to impair the sense of professional "community."[1]

Despite the inveterate practice of judging and ranking of
nominal peers, which goes on in every technical field, there

---

[1] William J. Goode, "Community Within a Community: The Professions," *American Sociological Review*, 22:194–200, April 1957.

is a general reluctance to share this information with out-siders.[2]

Where professional specialization and referral occurs, the choice of a specialist may imply a judgment of differential merit, but even that may not be overtly articulated. An extreme manifestation of collegiality is the reluctance to criticize the judgment or skill of a fellow professional. This is most marked among physicians in American professional practice. A patient dissatisfied with the results attained by one physician who seeks out another may elicit from the latter a cautious statement to the effect that he probably would not have followed his predecessor's course, but then adding that it was a "reasonable" one that simply reflected a difference in judgment. This restraint was by no means always the situation in the stormy history of medical theory and practice.[3] The contemporary situation perhaps reflects in part a confidence in the technical levels of competence that in turn rests upon considerable standardization in medical training.

Even attorneys, although caught up in an adversary system of negotiation and trial, are more or less restrained in *public* criticism of a colleague's competence. Criticism is built into the professional performance of scientists and other scholars, but the norms discourage *ad hominem* arguments and favor attention to substantive issues. As teachers (that is, with clients) the scholars may still criticize colleagues, but with even greater restraint. It is, however, a little difficult to characterize a colleague's procedures or conclusions as, say, idiotic, without implying something about the competence of the perpetrator.

A major exception to the norm of collegiality is afforded by dentists in general practice. A client who has had prior dental work and goes to a new dentist encounters a substantial risk of being told that all previous work has been shoddy and incompetent and must now be competently re-

---

[2] *Ibid.*, pp. 198–199. See also Everett Hughes, *Men and Their Work* (New York: Free Press, 1958), p. 94.

[3] Richard Harrison Shryock, *Medical Licensing in America, 1650–1965* (Baltimore: Johns Hopkins Press, 1967), pp. 36–37.

paired. What brick mason did that? the new dentist gently inquires.

In no case, however, is criticism of professional standards or practice by the laity encouraged, again with the possible exception of students, who may be regarded as developing professional skills. How is the layman to judge? Well, partly by results. And conspicuously bad results or other conspicuous misconduct causes suffering throughout the fraternity, for the reputation of the calling as a whole has been in some degree impaired.

The rationale of regulation

The legitimate purposes of regulating admission to professional practice and subsequent performance can be stated simply: to protect the potentially gullible client from incompetent and unscrupulous "experts," and to protect the qualified practitioner against unfair competition. Less laudable purposes may also be served, under these guises.

The client is in no position to judge competence, except, possibly, at the extremes, and even there his view may differ from that of the expert; what appears to be extreme competence may appear to colleagues as mere showmanship, and what appears as extreme incompetence may appear to colleagues as reasonable conduct in a situation fraught with difficulties and possibly bad luck. Even on ethical matters, it should surprise no one that complexity is more nearly the rule than the exception, and thus that judgment rather than merely routine compliance with unambiguous rules governs even the most scrupulous practitioner.

The claims of professional bodies to regulate admission to their occupations and the performance of those in it are neither untainted nor unchallenged. Self-regulation may serve to preserve and even enhance standards, but may also be used merely to enhance occupational prestige, to control the number of authenticated practitioners in order to reduce competition and increase income, and, not uncommonly, to protect a particular orthodoxy against reasonable and even superior alternatives.

No one of the older "established" professions has been able to command a complete monopoly of its claimed field of competence, a circumstance that will engage our attention in the following chapter. Nineteenth-century American medicine abounded with hydropaths, naturopaths, osteopaths (who still exist) and chiropractors (licensed now in some American states), not to mention faith healers and purveyors of patented cure-alls. Until the twentieth century the professional lawyer had little competition except for such people as the untrained justice of the peace, and, importantly, self-help. Now tax accountants, trust officers in banks, insurance adjusters, marital counselors, labor arbitrators, and a host of others are engaged in matters that are in part legal. The trained clergyman of the past competed with the evangelical preacher who simply had a "call," and now competes also with social workers, marital counselors, clinical psychologists, psychiatrists, and sports directors of the Young Men's Christian Association.

The rationale of regulation is precisely the opposite of an open market for services, on the grounds that an open market will cause harm to the ill-advised and ill-informed. Again we encounter an anomaly. The salaried spokesmen for organized American medicine enunciate economic doctrines more archaic than those of virtually any conservative economist, but they are in fact unalterably opposed to an open market for services in diagnosing and treating human physical or emotional disorders.[4] They seem to be seeking an *unrestrained* monopoly, with no public review of fees or rules of allocation of services, but only the rules and criteria set by the organized profession itself. There is no precedent for an unregulated monopoly of a legitimate service in any modern society, and the physicians' long, bitter, and totally unprincipled struggle is now on its way to an overdue defeat.

The notion of regulation of various occupations is in fact solidly established, as we shall observe presently in our discussion of licensing. The idea that the regulation should come from the occupation itself in the first instance, and al-

[4] "The American Medical Association: Power, Purposes, and Politics in Organized Medicine," *Yale Law Review*, 63:938–1022, May 1954.

ways include occupational representation, is made sensible by the importance of competence. Difficulties arise with respect to two problems: (1) the self-regulating specialists are likely to claim a large and preclusive jurisdiction, and to have a small tolerance for novelty in training or technique; (2) where there is extensive specialization *within* the occupation, neither the older generalist nor the specialist in another field is in fact able to judge either competence or performance. This latter consideration is the reason that American medicine, having recognized specialization, turns over the regulation of specialists to their own kind. It is also the reason that the bar examination in American legal practice is archaic and anachronistic, having very little to do with the practice of law, and why the genuinely public oral defense of the thesis by the candidate for the Doctor of Philosophy degree—still practiced in many European universities—is downright silly.

The forms and agencies of regulation

Once the need for regulation of admission to professional practice and continued competence in performance is recognized by some interested parties, there exist various forms and degrees of implementation. They are not mutually exclusive, and all in combination will not prevent practice by unprincipled scoundrels or prevent willfully irrational people from supporting them.

ASSOCIATIONS

It is sometimes supposed, at least since the comments of De Tocqueville early in the nineteenth century,[5] that there is something special about American character or social structure that leads to a proclivity to form associations. This is at most a matter of degree, however, for we find this set of phenomena closely associated with urbanizing and industrializing societies everywhere.[6] What we do note is that

[5] Alexis De Tocqueville, *Democracy in America*, ed. by Philips Bradley (New York: Alfred A. Knopf, Inc., 1945), Vol. 1, pp. 191–192.
[6] Wilbert E. Moore, *Man, Time and Society* (New York: John Wiley & Sons, Inc., 1963), pp. 104–105.

urbanization and consequent contiguity and ease of communication lead to the identification of common occupational interests; occupations, strictly speaking, are likely to emerge only in such settings.

The guilds of medieval towns and cities[7] were among the progenitors of contemporary professional associations, as we observed in Chapter 2. The guilds set rules and practices of apprenticeship, provided for a graded career as proficiency increased, *and set standards of technical and personal conduct for their members.*[8] It may be argued that the guilds were especially attentive to standards and competence, as they were commonly of different social origins from the then-recognized and university-based "true" professions: clergymen, lawyers, physicians, and professors. For the man of gentle, or genteel, origins, explicit codes of conduct would be thought unnecessary, as being taken for granted. (One may still find university professors who regard codes of professional conduct as degrading, since "everyone" knows, accepts, and practices proper behavior; that is, of course, a simple refusal to face modern complexities, and turns out to be nonsense.)

For those occupational associations not having an ancient lineage, it has been typical that practitioners (or enthusiasts for an intellectual specialty, which may be treated as a hobby) have got together in local groups, discussed their common occupational and intellectual interests, and encouraged one another in the pursuit of common purposes. In due course, if several such local groups are formed, it occurs to some good organizational types to try to bring them together in a national association, complete with officers, annual meetings, and some kind of stated purpose and program.

The evolutionary development of professional and disciplinary associations is remarkably uniform. Initial criteria for

---

[7] Max Weber, *General Economic History,* trans. by Frank H. Knight (New York: Collier Books, 1961), pp. 110–115. Henri Pirenne, *The Medieval City* (Princeton: Princeton University Press, 1925).

[8] Wilbert E. Moore, *Industrial Relations and the Social Order,* rev. ed. (New York: The Macmillan Company, 1951), pp. 17–21.

membership are primarily those of self-identified interest or practice in the subject, and initial adherents seek out others of like mind. Technical qualifications for inclusion are generally of small moment in early phases of associational organization. By the same token, however, nontechnical criteria may be used freely, the associational membership viewing the organization as a club, and congeniality may well be put above competence in admitting new members.

If the group achieves some standing as representing an occupational specialty or intellectual discipline, the standard tendency is for technical criteria of membership to be given increasing prominence, at the expense of well-disposed amateurs. Technical criteria, however, are likely to permit the membership of qualified persons not notable for their pleasant relations with colleagues.

What a professional association, adopting technical qualifications for fully-authentic membership, loses by way of friendly discourse among a group of common believers it is likely to gain by the recognition of membership as an authenticating agency for its constituency.

This, then, is the prime form of professional self-discipline: the setting of admission standards for persons who think it advantageous, or wise, to be accepted as members of a less-than-open professional association.

Such a control system clearly affords ample opportunities for abuse. For example, some elements of the "club" may persist, so that qualified persons are excluded on grounds of race, ethnicity, and, commonly, sex.[9] On the other hand, the quest for expansion of membership may lead to lenient interpretations of stated qualifications, and possibly to off-grade classes of membership that can be confusing to the layman. Additionally, the founders may have an exaggerated influence, doubly devastating when they would be disqualified by current criteria for membership. Moreover, the claims to competence and to sole jurisdiction over a problem may be overstated or plainly specious. Yet it remains true

---

[9] Corinne Lathrop Gilb, *Hidden Hierarchies: The Professions and Government* (New York: Harper & Row, 1966), pp. 46–49.

that peers are the most competent judges of technical qualifications and performance, and that the existence of a professional association virtually guarantees that some portion
of adherents to or practitioners of a specialty will be attentive to the good reputation of the collectivity. If a conspicuous miscreant is not a member of the appropriate association,
its spokesmen can disavow him with ample and unctuous
piety. If he is affiliated with the proper and relevant association, his conduct may be brought under review by his colleagues; the reputation of the collectivity may require the
imposition of sanctions, ranging from reprimand to dis-
missal.

Since membership in professional associations is rarely
compulsory—a point to which we return in Chapter 9—the
officers may not be able to speak for or exercise discipline
over all qualified constituents. And without further forms
of control, the association operates effectively only as an
authenticating agency, and that effectiveness depends upon
the degree to which, in fact, qualified practitioners as judged
by other criteria are represented by the association, and the
degree to which relevant clienteles accept the authentication
as valid.

DEVELOPMENT OF CODES

One prominent way in which professional associations
operate as agencies of self-regulation is in the development
of codes of conduct. What these amount to are private systems of law which are characteristic of all formally constituted organizations, with two notable features that are not
prominent in the administrative regulations of public or
private bureaucracies: (1) The codes highlight proper relations with clients or others outside the organization, rather
than procedural rules for organizational behavior. (2) Codes
are also commonly understood as not self-enforcing. In the
bureaucratic setting, regulations are supposed to be moni-
tored, and discipline imposed, by hierarchical superiors. The
professional association, being nominally a society of equals,
must adopt other procedures; normally, these will rest primarily on an internal, quasi-judicial body commonly known

as a "committee on ethics," which will review complaints and, if necessary, recommend disciplinary action.

Although codes are an almost universal feature of professional and quasi-professional associations—the principal exceptions being a number of "purely academic" disciplinary associations mainly inhabited by university professors—their origins and excuses differ substantially.

One provocation to the promulgation of a code of professional conduct may be an external scandal or complaint. If we may speak, illustratively, of our own discipline of sociology, two types of problems in very recent years are responsible for halting steps toward a professional code for sociologists. One problem was a bit of research, sponsored by a private and by no means disinterested source of funds, which reached conclusions delightful to the sponsors on the basis of an opinion survey; the "population sample" was so distorted that it virtually excluded any member of the genuinely relevant population that would have held contrary views. The other problem, which at this writing is still receiving consideration by leaders throughout the social science disciplines, relates to the conduct of research, particularly in foreign areas, under auspices of United States mission-oriented agencies. These agencies (for example, Department of Defense, Central Intelligence Agency) also engage in clandestine quests for tactical and strategic "intelligence." The whole issue of the conduct of social science research outside the United States has provoked at least one disciplinary association into a statement of policies,[10] to the appointment of committees with a possibly comparable set of outcomes in other associations, and to an extensive report and set of policy recommendations by a committee of the National Academy of Sciences–National Research Council.[11]

---

[10] American Anthropological Association, "Statement on Problems of Anthropological Research & Ethics, by the Fellows of the American Anthropological Association" (printed leaflet, 1967).

[11] National Research Council, Advisory Committee on Government Programs in the Behavioral Sciences, *The Behavioral Sciences and the Federal Government* (Washington, D.C.: National Academy of Sciences, 1968).

Although it remains true, as noted in passing a bit earlier, that many members of disciplinary associations still insist that codes are unnecessary because the concerns of members are strictly intellectual or academic, the fact is that growing numbers of fully authenticated members are in fact serving clients in the strict sense, or are financially sponsored by dubious sources.

It would be a mistake to infer from our illustration that impropriety in professional conduct is exclusively, or even mainly, a problem in new and therefore immature fields of practice. Medicine, law, engineering, and religion offer periodic examples of the human capacity for grievous misbehavior. As these examples come to public notice, or occasionally to the more circumspect notice of legitimate and therefore outraged practitioners, two solutions are commonly sought—usually not by the same people. The one solution is to tighten the admission standards for acceptance by the qualified group, including, if necessary, personality tests or appraisals that will permit weeding out those who have not internalized the norms or may violate them too easily in the presence of attractive alternatives. The other solution is to adopt new rules, or clarify existing ones, and increase both the inspection of current compliance and the efficacy of enforcement. The two solutions, of course, are not mutually exclusive, but the second may be made to appear more responsive to immediate complaints.

Codes, then, may be responsive to threats or complaints that might do collective damage to the peer-group of professionals. It requires no brilliant insight to predict that changes in codes will come from sources of dissatisfaction, as long as we include professional peers among the potentially disgruntled.

Symbol and substance may get confused in social relationships, however. When established professions are observed to have certain common characteristics, those attributes may become definitional to all parties : to the accepted practitioners, to the laity, and to those occupational groups seeking to enhance their relative position (not to mention scholars analyzing the professions). Since a code of ethics is commonly taken as one criterion of professionalism, it is not surprising to observe aspiring groups ticking off the defining criteria, and formulating professional codes instrumentally. Thus the practitioners of a vulnerable and venal occupation, that of funeral directors, responded to Jessica Mitford's scathing attack[12] by protesting that the "professional" associations have a firm code of ethics for proper dealing with clients.[13] The replies were not convincing, but they were instructive.

The formalization of a set of normative principles offers scope for both moralists and legislative draftsmen. The task is by no means an easy one, however. Modern legal systems offer two leading alternative approaches. The "Roman law" system (often and improperly called the civil law system), typical of most of Western Europe, represents an attempt at a logical *and complete* set of rules, with all contingencies foreseen and taken into account. The Anglo-American common law tradition rests, in principle though decreasingly in fact, on fewer and more general normative principles, which are made cumulatively more precise and more complex by decisions in particular cases ajudicated in courts.

The congruence is by no means perfect, but it appears that in their construction of private legal systems professional bodies tend to emulate the public law within which they operate. The Anglo-American style is to accumulate precedents out of cases; not surprisingly, this is most conspicuous among bar associations, for that is precisely the tradition in which lawyers are trained.

Without review and enforcement mechanisms, professional codes may be little more than window dressing, perhaps more designed to give false comfort to the laity than to guide the practitioner. Yet it is also important to stress the efficacy of informal controls. The physician in group practice or in the hospital setting, the attorney in a law firm, the Army officer, the university professor work in situations

---

[12] Jessica Mitford, *The American Way of Death* (New York: Simon & Schuster, Inc., 1963).

[13] See, for example, *The New York Times*, November 20, 1963, pp. 1, 44.

in which other experts are watching, or may do so at virtually any time.

Recognition of an occupational specialty as a distinct curriculum leading to distinctive degree in a university is an important, though not absolutely essential, step in the process of professionalization. In view of the tremendous range in higher educational institutions in the modern world, and in the degree to which whatever standards are set in some fields apply to others, university recognition of an occupation is no guarantee of quality. One or a few universities with rather pliable standards may simply be used as a spurious authenticating mechanism for an occupation. Nonetheless, if practitioners include those who genuinely seek an upgrading of standards, successful results may ensue from an interaction between the professional association and the professional schools. In some fields and at some stages of professional development, the leading practitioners in a field may be well in advance of both the faculties in the training centers for the field, and in advance of what youngsters are being taught. In more mature fields, the university-based professionals take the lead in upgrading standards.

Occasionally, changes in professional education result from essentially external sources. In the United States, the famous report on medical education by Abraham Flexner[14] revealed such variable and generally low standards that the profession was goaded into remedial action. Accreditation committees were formed; giving medical education a university base, pioneered at Johns Hopkins, became the norm rather than the exception; night-school medical education virtually disappeared, to the possible disadvantage of some able students from poor families.

If substantial improvements are made in the standards of training for teachers, the reforms are also likely to come in

---

[14] Abraham Flexner, *Medical Education in the United States and Canada: A Report to the Carnegie Foundation for the Advancement of Teaching,* Bulletin No. 4 (New York, 1910).

part from the outside,[15] since professional educators have tended to be somewhat isolated from other university faculties.

Law schools in the United States still display wide variability, and many of them lack university affiliations. The state bar examinations were long thought to be an adequate safeguard of quality. Once dissatisfaction with that procedure began to grow, there began a ferment—now in process—for curriculum reform. The American Association of Law Schools, an organization to which most of the proprietary night schools do not belong, may be the effective agent of change.

The American clergy is scarcely organized, except along denominational lines, and the standards of professional training are extremely varied. Even the qualifications of college and university professors are varied. For denominations, higher education has substituted disciplines, and at times we encounter both, as in "Catholic sociology." The disciplines generally have national associations, some elements in which are concerned with training standards. Yet colleges and universities are sufficiently independent in the United States that attempts to set and improve training standards in any field involve slow and delicate measures. When the demand for college teachers is high, as at present, unqualified universities may turn out substandard Doctors of Philosophy, and other unqualified institutions accept them as authentic. Since professors, unlike physicians and attorneys, do not deal with serious matters but only with knowledge and its imparting to students, perhaps the damage is not too severe.

Our concern here is with professional self-regulation, and control of training is as important as technical and ethical control of performance. For the "mature" professions, the faculties of professional schools may serve in part as the collective conscience as well as the innovators in knowledge and technique. Such faculties, being in a sense at the center

[15] See, for example, among his many works on the subject, James B. Conant, *The Education of American Teachers* (New York: McGraw-Hill, Inc., 1963).

of professional concerns, and being by trade and training articulate, are in an influential position to influence the course of professional development. This will happen, however, only if a considerable portion of such teachers are, in fact, respected for their outstanding merits. If professors are poorly paid relative to practitioners, and if the positions tend to attract "rejects" from the profession, no leadership can be expected and even meritorious reforms are likely to be treated with derision.

In most established fields the professional schools act as the first formal gatekeepers: in setting admission standards, standards for performance in the course of training, and requirements for the appropriate degree. In some cases this may be final authentication, depending on licensing requirements, and whether the license involves a further screening of applicants or is simply a formal recognition of successful completion of training at a recognized institution. No less a sociological observer than Max Weber, several decades ago, noted the successful attempts of various occupational groups to use diplomas and certificates as their claim to position and remuneration quite apart from useful work done. And, with quiet but acidulous perception, Weber doubted the relative influence of a thirst for education as compared with a "desire for restricting the supply for these positions and their monopolization by the owners of educational certificates."[16]

Other "professional" schools have a more ambiguous relationship to practice, and therefore to self-regulation of the occupation. Training for careers in business administration, and to a lesser degree in public administration, is firmly based in American universities, and not infrequently at the post-baccalaureate level. Weber had already in 1925, or earlier, one suspects with a trace of condescension, noted diplomas from business and engineering colleges as harbingers of many other off-grade certificates of competence.[17]

---

[16] Max Weber, *From Max Weber*, ed. by H. H. Gerth and C. Wright Mills (New York: Oxford University Press, 1946), p. 241. The original of *Wirtschaft und Gesellschaft* was published in Tübingen by G. C. B. Mohr in 1925.

[17] *Ibid.*

Yet these schools have yet to establish their exclusive command over careers, or even to demonstrate that formal training is clearly superior to mere experience in business or public life.[18] The same is true of graduate schools of journalism. Other schools lack university bases. One type, exemplified by courses for real estate brokers offered by proprietary schools, has a curriculum designed to prepare candidates to pass state licensing examinations. (Courses in university schools of business administration may also serve similar functions, or may be taken by candidates as partial substitution of the "experience" requirements for licensing.) Some law schools are strictly trade schools in this sense, and indeed some are still profit-oriented organizations. Another type is the school set up, usually by a trade association, in order to "professionalize" an occupation with a view to enhancing its prestige with prospective clients. Thus life-insurance salesmen may become Certified Life Underwriters and add CLU after their names. Stock salesmen now have a similar opportunity. Now in effect "certified" means successful completion of courses and passing examinations, all administered by the school itself. Such training may indeed increase the technical competence of the participants, but for the present the most that can be claimed is that the successful candidate for certification has a mark of differential prestige, not that only such persons may practice the trade. In order to achieve a higher position on the scale of professionalism, these occupations would need to be exclusively open to bearers of the appropriate educational credentials, preferably authenticated by universities, or at the very least, those not so qualified should be subordinate to those who do. The latter would then be the "full professionals," in a fair position to organize for maintenance of standards and proper conduct. It seems fairly clear that the life insurance and securities salesmen are attempting to emulate the Certi-

---

[18] Bernard Barber, "Is American Business Becoming Professionalized? Analysis of a Social Ideology," in Edward A. Tiryakian (ed.), *Sociological Theory, Values and Sociocultural Change: Essays in Honor of Pitirim A. Sorokin* (New York: Free Press, 1963), pp. 121–145; Wilbert E. Moore, *The Conduct of the Corporation* (New York: Random House, Inc., 1962).

fied Public Accountants, who have achieved both recognition and control.

The professions, we have noted, do not seek an open market for services, but rather a protected monopoly. Despite the conspicuous political conservatism of many professional practitioners, they share with other conservatives a readiness to seek the interference of government when it serves their interests. Licensing represents a conspicuous example.

The legal status of occupational licensing is wondrously varied and complex in the United States. This arises in part from the existence of fifty state jurisdictions. Indeed, some licensing regulations are local ordinances, thus greatly multiplying the potential variation in the rules.

One outcome of this jurisdictional diversity is a mind-boggling assembly of occupations that some legislature at some time has been persuaded to believe was sufficiently mixed with the public interest to require its practitioners to be licensed.[19] The most frequent categories are the established professions, other technical occupations such as electricians and plumbers where the purchaser or patron is unlikely to be able to judge shoddy and possibly dangerous performance, and a host of "personal services" such as barbering and beauty parlor operating, where the rationale is presumably some consideration of the patrons' health.

The rules and procedures of licensing are almost as various as the occupations licensed. Yet here we can again detect a fairly clear scale of variation. At the one extreme is the uncommon situation in which a state board of examiners is authorized, to be appointed normally by state officials. These examiners then set the kinds of knowledge or demonstrated competence that they consider important for admission to an occupation. The examination is then open to anyone pre-

---

[19] See Walter Gellhorn, *Individual Freedom and Governmental Restraint* (Baton Rouge: Louisiana State University Press, 1958), Chap. 3, "The Right to Make a Living." See also U.S. Public Health Service, National Center for Health Statistics, *The Licensing of Health Occupations* (Washington, D.C.: U.S. Government Printing Office, 1968).

senting himself, after payment of the requisite fee. There are still jurisdictions in the United States where the bar examination is of this type, so that self-education and apprenticeship remain at least theoretically available avenues to professional careers.

At the other extreme is the situation in which the license is *pro forma,* being granted upon presentation of "credentials," the most important of which is evidence of successful completion of the training approved by an accredited school. Accreditation, in turn, may be a state function, but more commonly is a state recognition of a regional accrediting association, an association of professional schools, or the professional association as such.

Particularly for the established professions, but not uncommonly for other occupations, references attesting to the good moral character of the candidate are required. It appears probable that these are checked off rather than evaluated.

Like the adoption of canons or codes by professional associations in order to quieten a scandal, licensing may come about from essentially external sources. This is relatively rare. Rather, particular occupational groups seek recognition, seek protection from competition by the relatively untrained, and seek to establish a preemptive jurisdiction over services that may in fact be in considerable and justified jurisdictional dispute.

A recent, and in some jurisdictions still current, dispute over licensing proposals may illustrate several points. American psychologists, usually through state associations, successfully sought recognition of psychology as a licensed profession in a considerable number of states. Psychology over the last several decades has undergone a considerable shift of emphasis, to the degree that university-based proponents of the discipline are in a minority. Applied psychologists of various types, and particularly clinical psychologists serving private clients, have come to numerical dominance. Now the trained and professionally oriented clinical psychologists faced two kinds of threats, which provide classic examples, often repeated. The one threat was from charlatans. Prior to licensing, *anyone* could announce himself as a psychologist, offering to "cure" emotional disorders. The other threat was from medically-trained psychiatrists, who were trying to establish exclusive jurisdiction over man's mind and emotions. Licensing authenticated the clinical psychologists' claim to share that jurisdiction.

The actual license laws initially proposed, and here and there passed, illustrated another recurrent problem: the attempt to define jurisdiction in the broadest possible terms. The psychologists attempted to license by "whole title"— that is, anyone identifying himself as a psychologist. This caused considerable consternation among numerous sociologists who identify themselves as social psychologists, and had no enthusiasm at all for submitting themselves to review by a board of clinical (or any other) psychologists. Matters were made no better by the legislative definitions of psychologists in terms broad enough to include virtually all social scientists. Tender negotiations between the American Psychological Association and the American Sociological Association generally resulted in waivers and more restricted definitions. The psychologists, in these negotiations, were reputedly dismayed to be in difficulties with an interest group not initially identified as a target or adversary.

At first glance it may appear that licensing, state-appointed examining and review boards, and similar measures of professional authentication mean that the occupation itself has abandoned self-control, or has had it taken away by agencies not controlled. Such appearances are deceiving.

At times the legislation providing for licensing commissions is vague on criteria of membership on the commissions, seemingly leaving selection to the appropriate official's discretion. In other instances, the qualifications for members of licensing boards are made explicit in terms of "qualified" members of the appropriate occupation. In either case, the examiners are almost uniformly comprised of members of the occupation examined. To suppose that they are the most forward-looking or most meritorious as judged by their colleagues would be naive. An occupational group loses a measure of its independence when it successfully secures licensing. It trades off that potential loss against the gains of the right of a legal monopoly—to be court-tested when jurisdictions in fact overlap—and the right of recourse to the courts to bar both unauthorized practice of its specialty and to require compliance with professional codes by authorized but miscreant practitioners if private, associational sanctions prove inadequate. The latter situation is rare, in part because of the wise and sensible adoption of the admonition not "to wash dirty linen in public." Yet it is not unknown for an unpopular colleague, against whom many non-actionable complaints may exist, to encounter legal action for disqualification (unfrocking, disbarment, drumming out of the corps, loss of license) if he provides a technical opportunity to his adversaries.

The limits of self-regulation

Self-regulation, we have seen, is not a simple matter. Aside from the circumstance that standards must be established and codes adopted, a professional body is not a universal mutual-policing organization. Individual self-policing and informal policing by colleagues are likely in fact to be the most effective agencies of control. When an organized association becomes involved, not all members will be equally concerned about standards of competence and performance; some will benefit by being off-grade.[20] Codes of conduct may be promulgated by a minority, and accepted with less than total enthusiasm by the relevant electorate; by some, the acceptance may be tactical or cynical, designed to assuage the anxieties of dubious clients or professed for the benefit of prestigious brethren with the full intention of pursuing a "practical," less-than-ideal course of action.

One function of the university-based professional school faculty is that of setting high standards, both in competence and in ethical performance. In most established professions the formal educational unit is the original sorting and authenticating agency. Yet, in the view of professional practitioners, the faculty and curricula of professional schools

---

[20] Jerome E. Carlin, *Lawyers' Ethics: A Survey of the New York City Bar* (New York: Russell Sage Foundation, 1966).

could probably be graded on an awe-contempt scale.
At the awe end of the scale would be professors in leading
medical schools and in the older academic disciplines in major graduate schools. At the contempt end would be the
hacks in lesser faculties and in less-well-established specialties, who teach because they cannot successfully practice.
Medical school faculties, for example, have proved to be a
major counterbalance to the ridiculous stances taken by the
American Medical Association. On the other hand, relatively
few law faculties command awe from practitioners, for the
scholarly orientation of teachers of law is still relatively
rare. Many faculty members and administrators of military
academies are assigned to their posts as a limited tour of
duty, and receive thereby little extra respect.

For a professional school faculty to serve as more than
mere givers of the magical word, which will assure formal
qualification in examinations and admission to the fraternity, that faculty must be exemplary and a constant
source of current or nostalgic comparison for the practitioner. That situation is conspicuously true, now, of the
"academic" disciplines (not always including engineering)
of medical school faculties, and perhaps one or two others. It
is conspicuously not true of schools of law, journalism, or
education.

What we are suggesting is that the identification with professional peers and the adoption of one or another means of
self-regulation are less than consensual phenomena. When
the question at hand is one of strict maintenance of professional standards, or especially of their improvement, the
proponents are likely to be a minority; they may or may not
be able to mobilize an essentially apathetic or hostile majority. Professional self-regulation becomes in effect a delegated responsibility: organizational activists, professional
school faculties, persons willing and anxious to serve on review and examining bodies.

The whole matter gets further complicated by rapid change
in professional affairs (Chapter 7), by the ambiguous ways
of gaining professional prestige (Chapter 8), and by the
circumstances of professional organization (Chapter 9).

For example, persons asked to serve on committees of bar examiners, and willing to do so, may be prestigeful in terms of professional success (though the most eminent attorneys are too busy to serve), and represent exactly the most reactionary traditions in the profession. Physicians who become presidents of the American Medical Association and the salaried staffs hired by the association may indeed represent a majority or major and cohesive minority of practicing physicians in their outmoded and illogical positions. It is a sobering thought. The consistency with which the association advocates anachronistic policies indicates majority support, substantial minority support with an apathetic majority, or "rigged" and explicitly oligarchic control. None of the alternatives is attractive in terms of the professional in modern society. The self-regulation of the medical fraternity is often above reproach, including that performed by various national associations of specialists, local committees, and so on. The behavior of the American Medical Association as an organized entity on issues of public policy is unworthy of a professional body.

Who is to judge competence, performance, jurisdiction? The age-and-prestige structure of long-established professions puts power where it may be least meritorious: among those who have been successful, and recognized, according to criteria that may or not be currently relevant in view of latest information and techniques. It may be a matter of common sensibility to human problems that has built "grandfather clauses" into all new, more stringent requirements of competence for admission to professional status. Also, viewed cynically, those currently accredited are unlikely to accept new and more exacting criteria for admission unless the present members of the club are exempt from new admission standards. The Anglo-American legal system is hostile to retroactive legislation, and that, once more, demonstrates the congruence of private and public law.

In any event, it is always easier to select, govern, and control admission to an occupation than it is to keep current competence under surveillance. Yet we have observed that formal and informal professional inspection does produce a kind of self-regulation. Similarly, informal competition from conspicuously more knowledgeable juniors has led to both formal and informal systems of continuing learning in order to keep current. No profession has yet made such activities mandatory. That day will come.

Licensing, which will without doubt be pursued by new and assertive occupational specialties, will almost certainly turn out to be either *pro forma,* which means that it is significant only in rare instances, or it will become a victory that would have made defeat preferable. Licensing may encase rather than release a rapidly developing occupation. Lobbying being what it is, it is much easier to get a new—and possibly silly—law enacted than it is to get an existing silly law rescinded or sensibly amended.

An occupation's claim to self-regulation, which is a kind of collective assertion of autonomy, has a doubtful relation to the individual autonomy of the professional. If the occupational association seeks autonomy in order to establish its authenticity as an acceptable and responsible service, the consequences for the individual practitioner are ambiguous, but probably favorable. If the autonomy of the group is made the basis of a kind of private police state—which happens in some local medical societies—then we have to reconsider the meaning of autonomy. Organization and licensing may be made the basis of a genteel terror. We have ample evidence for doubting that collectivities are uniformly superior to conscientious individuals. Old truths haunt us: Collective autonomy and individual autonomy may turn out to be inconsistent goals. Identification with peers may become subservience to peers, and that ends the effective sense of personal responsibility.

Chapter seven: The professional and his peers: specialization and jurisdiction

THE modern expert who professes to deal with some limited set of human problems, or at least problems that his fellow humans think are worthy of attention and support, is an heir to all of the age-long vicissitudes of the human condition and also of a host of new circumstances that his antecedents could not have anticipated.

Professions multiply and subdivide. We shall be concerned in this chapter with both of these verities, for beneath the general expansion of occupations appearing to have some professional qualifications in modern and modernizing societies, there remain fundamental questions of how to specialize, how to allocate responsibilities, and, occasionally, how to put the specialized counsel into a unified program of practical action.

The information explosion

Occupational specialization is commonly the joint product of several forces: growth in population size and in the size of work-doing organizations; increasing technical and economic complexity and social interdependence, resulting in a demand for both new goods and new services; and expansion in the collective supply of useful knowledge, making the competence of any individual or occupation increasingly fractional. There is a high probability that any one of these developments (which, however, are not totally independent) would result in increased occupational specialization. In combination, they are certain to do so.

Since the occupational groups of primary concern here are especially involved with higher learning and its application, it is in the rapid expansion of information that we should find the most important source of specialization, although the professions are also affected by increasing size and complexity.

Some modern professions, we have seen, have ancient origins, and others date at least from medieval Europe and the Renaissance. Yet more proximate influences are conspicuously important in both old and new professional specialties. We believe the modern expansion of information has its principal source in the "Scientific Revolution" of the sixteenth century, which chiefly affected the physical sciences, and to a lesser degree, the life sciences.[1] With the appearance of philosophical rationalism in the eighteenth century, human institutions began to be viewed critically and dispassionately. It is particularly this latter development which justifies the somewhat romantic phrase, "rise of the rational spirit."

Its hypothetical essentials are the use of fact and logic for the solution of problems, a questioning of traditional solutions or even of traditional identification of problems, and a deliberate attempt to master "nature" as well as understand it.[2]

Partly as a consequence of scientific advance and mainly as a consequence of the growth of manufacturing marking the Industrial Revolution, technical innovation became increasingly deliberate. Although Kuhn maintains that the explicit marriage of science and technology took place in the nineteenth century—previous scientists being little interested in practical applications[3]—a case can be made for earlier relationships. The American Philosophical Society, founded by Benjamin Franklin in 1743, emphasized from its inception both observational and experimental sciences, on the one hand, and "useful arts" on the other.[4] But then so

---

[1] Thomas S. Kuhn, *The Structure of Scientific Revolutions* (Chicago: University of Chicago Press, 1962).

[2] Wilbert E. Moore, *Order and Change: Essays in Comparative Sociology* (New York: John Wiley & Sons, Inc., 1967), p. 62.

[3] Thomas S. Kuhn, "Comment," on paper by Irving H. Siegal in National Bureau of Economic Research, *The Rate and Directions of Innovative Activity: Economic and Social Factors* (Princeton: Princeton University Press, 1962), pp. 450–457.

[4] Any current *Year Book* of the American Philosophical Society (Philadelphia) contains "A Brief History of the American Philosophical Society."

had the Royal Society in England, dating from 1662. After
merger with another learned society (the American Society)
in 1769, the full title of the organization became, and remains, The American Philosophical Society, Held at Philadelphia, for Promoting Useful Knowledge. At that time six
committees or sections were established:

1. Geography, Mathematics, Natural Philosophy, and
   Astronomy
2. Medicine and Anatomy
3. Natural History and Chemistry
4. Trade and Commerce
5. Mechanics and Architecture
6. Husbandry and American Improvements[5]

The term "philosophical" clearly was used in its etymological
sense of "love of knowledge," and that, we think, typifies
the rational spirit. It is to be noted, moreover, that some of
the specialties enumerated referred to regular occupations
(for example, medicine, trade and commerce, and, perhaps,
architecture), but the American social structure scarcely
afforded a livelihood for other fields of competence. Rather,
these were interests of amateurs, who earned their living at
other pursuits.

It was out of developments such as these, and their counterparts in Europe, that came a considerable part of the commitment of time and resources to developing both science
and practice. The American experience is additionally noteworthy because of a widespread enthusiasm for education
at all levels. Particularly after the Morrill Act of 1862,
establishing land-grant agricultural and mechanical colleges,
the devotion of resources to the pursuit of the practical arts
began an acceleration that has been interrupted only rarely
and briefly to this day.

For the older established professions, new developments
were often seen as threatening, and bitter conflicts kept
occurring between the conservatives, who commonly had the
positions of power and prestige, and the innovators. Conservative physicians fought a rear-guard action against

---

[5] *Ibid.*

new discoveries in anatomy and physiology, in drug therapy, and against such theoretical developments as the germ theory of disease. Some surgeons long rejected the practice of aseptic surgery, and even opposed anesthetics.

Clearly, the rational spirit was not all-pervasive. Law was little affected by scientific and technical developments until relatively recent decades. In the Roman law system, codes could be tidied but not radically revised. In the common law system, precedent—under the doctrine of *stare decisis*—was more important than the novel elements in the case at hand.

The older universities resisted valiantly the recognition of new sciences or new technologies, but, particularly in the United States, competing institutions were established that were provoked by, or at least open to, a desire for innovation. Even the clergy felt some impact, not only from the jarring effect of the Darwinian theory of evolution, but from such developments as the "higher criticism" that attempted reexamination of texts, traditions, and interpretations.

THE BENIGN CIRCLE

Social change is a ubiquitous characteristic of human societies, but only in the modern world is it proper to state that most change is either deliberate or the by-product of such intentional intervention.

To a remarkable degree, in the modern world every economy or society gets about the technology it deserves, or at least what it is willing and able to support.[6]

Especially in the United States, but also in high degree in other economically advanced societies, large and growing resources are devoted to research and application. The "knowledge industry" is the fastest-growing sector of the American economy; even without expenditures for defense technology, the Research and Development budgets would be very large.

The production of new knowledge and the development of new applications have not been automated. A major part of the investment in the knowledge industry, therefore, has

---

[6] Moore, book cited in note 2, p. 88.

gone into collegiate and higher levels of training for both old and new specialties. As more people with advanced training set about their adult careers, a growing number and proportion of them will be devoting some or all of their working time to the production of new knowledge, leading to new applications. At the same time, these people exercise influence to get even larger budgetary allocations to training and research. Assuming that knowledge is a desirable goal, we have then a benign circle or even a spiral. For it appears that Ogburn's thesis that growth in technology is exponential, as a steadily richer technical base offers ever-more-numerous combinations,[7] may be applicable not only to patentable inventions but to knowledge generally. (Certainly Ogburn did not argue that the short-term curve was smooth, or lacking in plateaus and reversals. The allegation is a long-term and high-level generalization, and, with those stipulations, valid.)

There is no evidence that modern man is more intelligent than previous generations, but we devote more time, energy, and resources to the cultivation of intelligence and to innovations of almost infinite variety.

Deliberate change, one aspect of which we have been discussing, has become organized and institutionalized.[8] Thus the complex social interdependence that we noted as a major source of occupational specialization is reflected in the relations among the change-producing agents themselves, and these are almost entirely technically trained individuals with fairly high ratings on the scale of professionalism.

Professional specialization, then, is both a cause and a consequence of the explosive growth in reliable knowledge. This is still a circle, but not all of its features are benign.

THE UBIQUITOUS THREAT: OBSOLESCENCE

The human mind as a data storage and retrieval system is a wondrous evolutionary development. Even when aided by

---

[7] William F. Ogburn and Meyer F. Nimkoff, *Sociology*, 3rd ed. (Boston: Houghton Mifflin Company, 1958), esp. pp. 644–648.

[8] Wilbert E. Moore, *Social Change* (Englewood Cliffs, N.J.: Prentice-Hall, Inc., 1963), p. 110.

libraries, filing systems, and computers, however, any individual's central nervous system has severely finite limits.

With extremely rapid social change, the pace of collective experience becomes too rapid for the individual to keep current. . . . If we take the example of the person technically trained, his rate of accumulated experience is far less rapid than the rate of innovation produced by the aggregate of experts. He may be able to protect himself by specialization—to know more and more about less and less. He may be able to restrict access to his specialty, enforce employment security through seniority or tenure positions, or become an administrator because he is no longer technically competent. He may, however, become plainly obsolete, and require a period of retraining if he is going to continue a productive career.[9]

Even the specialist may become obsolete, for the specialty may still change too fast for the individual to keep current, or it may be superseded by advances in knowledge that make the knowledge or skill unnecessary or inadequate. To an increasing degree a professional career (and some others as well) will have to be regarded as a continuous learning experience, not the application of verities acquired in youthful training.

Specialization within professions

The older tradition of the learned professions was that of the cultivated gentleman, a man normally coming from a proper social background and usually trained in classics and history at secondary school level or the university before acquiring his technical training. Something of this tradition is kept alive in the modern professions, and particularly in those requiring training beyond the baccalaureate degree. But in fields such as medicine or engineering, a fairly substantial degree of "anticipatory specialization" begins in the secondary school, and that tendency accelerates at more advanced levels.

---

[9] Moore, book cited in note 2, p. 248.

Far from being a man of "universal" learning, an amateur
of science, literature, and the arts who also, and almost incidentally, has an occupation of high prestige, the contemporary professional is likely to be able to master only the
rudiments of his calling but not to encompass its full range.

General practitioners may still be found in medicine, though
their number grows steadily smaller and older. And even the
so-called general practitioner, unless he is located in a really
isolated area, is likely to refer patients to specialists—not
to the same degree as the internist, who is his closest successor, but the difference is not radical. For the young person trained in medicine, a number of career options may be
available: medical research as compared to practice, salaried
practice in a teaching hospital, a salaried advisory position
in an insurance company, joining a group of medical specialists, independent specialization, or, improbably, general
practice. And if he decides to specialize, he will require additional training, and he has a great many additional options
more or less open.

American lawyers have resisted overt specialization, not
even preserving the English distinction between advice
(solicitors) and litigation (barristers). Despite this reluctance to confess specialization, the complexity of law and
its rapid change makes a "general practice" in effect impossible. There are two principal informal ways of accomplish-
ing specialization without quite seeming to do so. One is the
increasingly common establishment of law firms. If the size
of the firm's clientele and practice justifies a considerable
number of partners, they may in effect become covert specialists, conferring with each other rather than referring the
client. If the firm also can afford salaried lawyers, the "attorney of record" may assign the actual legal research or
preparation of a contract or brief or will to a subordinate
who is a specialist not seen by the client. The other form of
informal specialization is reputational. Among the prospective clientele for legal services, some attorneys get to be
known as trial lawyers, others as effective negotiators with

federal agencies, others as specializing in divorce cases, and so on.

Although the avoidance of specialization bars formal referrals—except for a few more or less recognized specialties such as patent law—a lawyer may be "too busy" to take a case which is actually remote from his surreptitious specialty and suggest an "appropriate" attorney or firm. Despite all this pretention to generality,

> ... the legal guild grudgingly admits that there are judges; public prosecutors; criminal lawyers for defendants; tax, patent, and maritime lawyers; divorce lawyers; and ambulance-chasing liability lawyers. And then there are labor lawyers and house counsel for corporations, not to mention the derogated members of the fraternity who sit in legislatures and draft laws.[10]

None of the older professions has been immune to specialization.

> Even within the clergy, which has had to contend with no great burst of new information, the size of congregations and denominational organizations permits the demarcation of theologian, administrator, preacher, and pastor.[11]

Military officers have been supposed to be able to assume responsibility for any position in the service appropriate to their rank, on a tour-of-duty basis. Specialization in tactics and the technology of weaponry, to say nothing of such essential services as accounting, contract negotiation with civilian suppliers, inventory control, communications, medical care, intelligence—to name a few—make the all-purpose officer a myth. Indeed specialization, often requiring highly esoteric skills, is so extreme that many of the positions must be filled by "civilians in uniform," for the military academies and advanced military schools cannot begin to supply the appropriately trained specialists.

Engineering obviously is at the forefront of technical specialization, the engineers being the chief perpetrators (or

---

[10] Wilbert E. Moore, "Economic and Professional Institutions," in Neil J. Smelser (ed.), *Sociology: An Introduction* (New York: John Wiley & Sons, Inc., 1967), pp. 273–328; quotation from p. 324.

[11] *Ibid.*, pp. 323–324.

effective implementers) of changes that affect others as well as themselves. Problems of specialization are so great, including the hazard of hasty obsolescence, that engineering education is on the verge of requiring training beyond the collegiate level, and some specialties do already.

If we look at the major source of professional training, the university, it is apparent that specialization is rampant. First, there are at least three alternative career lines —at least in terms of major emphasis; they need not be exclusive: teaching, research and writing, and administration. Additionally, the university as a major source of the "information explosion" divides that information into sets and subsets, by fields or disciplines and then by specialties within them. The university has perhaps become more nearly an aggregate of scholars rather than a community of scholars. On intellectual interests, "nominal colleagues in the same department or discipline find nothing interesting to say to one another, even though each can identify real peers on other campuses."[12]

What members of college and university faculties do discuss are matters of common *professional* interests, in a narrow sense of the term, not intellectual ones: admission and graduation standards, curriculum, selection of new colleagues, and judgment of younger colleagues for promotion. Beyond departmental boundaries, there are common interests in relations with students and administrators, and perhaps problems of salary levels and academic freedom.

Because of the well-known emphasis on publication in university careers, the correct strategy of the young faculty member is generally to specialize quickly so that he may come to the attention of an identifiable segment of the discipline. The generalist (who is probably the better teacher, at least for undergraduates) runs the risk of receiving scant attention from his peers: "But what's his field?" The college or university professor, however, may have an alternative to successive narrowing of his specialty. Once he has

---

[12] *Ibid.*, p. 324.

firmly established his reputation, he may be afforded the luxury of viewing the field in broader perspective, to become, in effect, something of a generalist.

Partly because of the survival of the idea of the professional as a broadly learned man, and partly because the boundaries and jurisdictions of professions are poorly understood by the laity (or perhaps anyone), the professional may be asked for judgments on matters quite outside his technical competence. Accustomed to the role of expert in dealing with clients, the professional may show no reluctance to air his opinions. Since the occasions for spurious expertise are likely to be social or in other contexts outside the strictly professional role, there is generally another expert around who holds different, and perhaps equally unfounded, views.

Universal competence is impossible, we have argued, even if that universe is defined somewhat narrowly as an academic discipline or a fairly well-bounded profession. Yet the initial statement is wrong if we permit the universe to be very narrowly defined. We shall note in the following principal section of this chapter that new "unaffiliated" specialties may grow up in substantive or technical areas not yet claimed or settled by well-established fields. Actuaries, for example, must be well grounded in mathematical statistics, and particularly in probability theory, but the compass of the field is sufficiently small and well-bounded to permit mastery. Computer programmers are also scarcely a branch of another field, and although internal specialization is already under way, it is probably still possible for an experienced programmer to command or quickly learn the various languages whereby one "communicates" with a computer.

The lesson to learn from this important amendment is a principle of social change: the complexity of an identifiable field of human knowledge and its application is likely to be related to its age as a distinct occupation or discipline. (Some occupations may become simplified, it is true, such as through the substitution of mechanical for manual acts, but the process as a whole thus becomes more complex. This more nearly represents specialization than simplification.)

Time was that a physician could know "all" of medicine, a lawyer "all" of law, a chemist "all" of chemistry. For these relatively long-lived fields, that is no longer true.

PRINCIPLES OF SPECIALIZATION

The two primary bases for specialization with a profession are (1) the substantive field of knowledge that the specialist professes to command, and (2) the technique of production or application of knowledge over which the specialist claims mastery. The two principles are of course by no means mutually exclusive, since substantive knowledge and methodology are likely to have some relation to each other. In biology, for example, there is currently a fairly clear division between those who have gone beyond the cell as the organic unit in order to study differentiated cell structure—the molecular biologists—and those who continue to observe the structure and behavior of organic units—the organismic biologists. This division of substantive interest, however, arose because of the introduction of the electron microscope, which permitted very high degrees of magnification and thus permitted very precise intracellular observation.

Virtually every one of the academic disciplines and of the older, established professions offers examples of both principles of specialization. Thus the covert specialization in law affords opportunities to be a substantive expert on labor law, tax law, or oil and mineral law. The skills of the lawyer may be in the conduct of court trials, in legal research—the establishment of the legislation and court cases relevant to a legal issue—as adviser, or as negotiator. Indeed, in contemporary practice the senior attorney's principal "skill" may be the ability to attract clients to the law firm, and not in the practice of law, strictly speaking.

The complexity of specialization, and the way in which several criteria of specialization may intersect and overlap, is perhaps best illustrated by contemporary medical practice. The basic division between physicians and surgeons— somewhat minimized in American medicine in view of common training, but institutionalized in England by separate professional bodies—is essentially that between substance and technique. That does not end the matter, however, for the surgeon may still specialize in parts of the body and thus acquire exceptional knowledge of the appropriate anatomy and physiology along with the particular techniques for excision or repair.

Other physicians are also specialized by the techniques commanded: anesthetists, radiologists, pathologists, and, in a sense, psychiatrists. The most elaborate specialization appears to the part of the body treated: ophthalmology, urology, dermatology, gynecology, cardiology. Others specialize by the patient's age: obstetrics, pediatrics, geriatrics. And some may specialize in types of diseases or disease entities, such as cancer or virus infections, although technical names seem to be lacking for such specialists.

Few fields have even approximated medical specialization, for in American practice specialization is both recognized *and controlled*. Most medical specialization is no longer simply a process of self-determined preference for the types of problems and patients the physician cares to deal with. That was the situation a few decades ago. A man with his M.D. degree and state license could practice any or all branches of medicine and surgery. If he proved to be a conspicuous failure, he could simply take up some less risky specialty, perhaps in a new community. Now the American Medical Association not only passes on the merits of proposed new specialties, but insists on special training, internships, and examining boards to determine the fitness of those who propose to practice in a given subfield.

At least some other professions are likely to follow similar lines of development, whether in response to scandalous incompetence of a professed specialist or simply through the quest for authentication (and exclusive jurisdiction) by the specialists themselves. If this takes place, and the profession still claims to deal with "whole clients," something like the internist in medical practice may need to be reinvented, to act as a coordinator and referral agent for specialists.

The old trades and the new

The rapid multiplication of new occupational specialties derives, we have noted, from the increased size and complex interdependence of social units and increased knowledge of possible utility for human concerns.

Some new occupations appear, as it were, around the borders of established professions, representing ancillary and complementary services. At times these specialties represent skills not commanded by the professional, and at the same time not requiring full-scale professional training. In other instances, new specialties simply occupy territory claimed but not occupied by the established professions. Specialties that arise from "centrifugal" tendencies of professional practice, and their relation to those holding central positions, will engage our attention in Chapter 10. Here we shall attend to the appearance of new specialties, of some degree of professionalization, that are not closely linked with the older professional spheres. Needless to say, because of the large areas of competence claimed by many professions, old and new, this seeming independence does not prevent disputed jurisdictions.

NEW KNOWLEDGE

If the major consequence of the burgeoning output of the knowledge industry is to place a "system overload" on the generalist in conventional and established fields, a secondary consequence may be the development of new and very technical fields of professional practice. The development of high-speed computers rested upon a combination of some specialized mathematical theory and a subset of electronic engineers.

Their potential and actual use in widely disparate business and research settings created a demand for computer programmers. Now this is a specialty that does not yet have a firm university foundation, yet requires a distinct and not trivial set of knowledge and skills. Although a technical field, conventional engineering training is inappropriate. The programmer requires a combination of "information theory," "communication theory," and some specialized mathematics. What the future standards *and affiliations* of programmers may be is now difficult to forecast; for the moment they appear as a new profession relatively high on the scale of professionalism.

Similarly, some theoretical developments in applied mathematics—and this does not constitute a contradiction in terms—has led to some other new specialties. These include "rational decision theorists," who attempt to advise managers systematically to analyze and evaluate factors in complex decisions, rather than relying on precedent or intuition. Somewhat related is the development of a group of specialists who may be given the generic term of "systems analysts." Their techniques and approaches include such specialties as linear programming for economic planning, operations research for improving productive efficiency, queuing theory for the efficient and serial allocation of goods or services, and cost-benefit analysis for evaluating both primary and secondary effects of programs. Again, this may or may not remain a distinct specialty, but that appears to be its present status. Its practitioners have been mainly recruited from mathematics and engineers, though some are trained as economists. The specialty may end up being adopted as one approach to problems by more conventional fields.

NEW NEEDS

It appears that more new professional-type occupations may arise from the demand side, the identification of new needs on the part of a potential clientele, rather than from the simple availability of new knowledge. Of course, there is no reliable way of measuring such influences, so the appearance may be wrong. In any event, it is not difficult to identify a considerable number of occupational specialties, of varying degrees of professional status and pretensions, that have been responsive to the growing complexities of personal, economic, and social problems.

One example of a relatively new specialty clearly owes its origin to the growing size and complexity of work-doing organizations. This is the group of organizational analysts. They supplement, and indeed may encompass, such specialists within established fields as industrial engineers (including "efficiency experts"), personnel psychologists, and so-called "human engineers," who study man-machine relationships and human adaptation to varying environments. The organizational analysts may emerge out of sociology or even engineering, but to a growing degree have a university base in graduate schools of administration that emphasize administrative theory and something like systems analysis rather than the study of cases.

Other new specialties represent complex relations between social systems (for example, industrial relations and public relations) or problems in interpersonal relations (for example marital counselors and the several professions dealing with man's psychic and emotional state).

Problems of social adjustment and control of the environment also invite new attempts at expert solutions: the vocational counselor to aid in planning career choice and preparation; the gerontologist to aid adjustment to old age and retirement; "corner workers" to attempt to prevent juvenile gang violence and, perhaps, hasten maturity.

Many of these occupations exemplify the process of professionalization and the quest for professional identity and self-regulation discussed in Chapters 3 and 4. In some instances the practitioners may be chiefly self-identified, and with little by way of a distinct discipline to warrant their claims to expertise: public relations advisers come to mind. In other instances the need became conspicuous and persons were assigned to deal with the problem as best they could, only to be superseded by persons specially trained: industrial relations advisers and administrators come to mind. In still other instances, and particularly when universities have not responded to the demand, business or industrial trade associations have perceived a need, identified the few existing experts on a subject or skill, and arranged for specialized training courses in order to multiply their number: computer programmers come to mind.

Jurisdictional problems were not unknown among the limited number of old-line professions, but they were relatively rare until the process of subspecialization and the formation of new professional-type occupations began in earnest. True, medicine earlier had its problem of competing orthodoxies, but many were defeated or simply encompassed as specialties that did not supersede general medical training. Jurisdictional disputes that arise within organized professions—whose patient is he? whose case is it? whose client is he?—can generally be resolved by informal or formal negotiation with the peer group, without public knowledge or participation. More awkward problems occur when claims to expertise are disputed, and the claimants do not share a common professional background and a common current association.

PROBLEMS OF UNAUTHORIZED PRACTICE

Medicine and law continue to provide the most numerous instances of jurisdictions disputed with other specialists, for several reasons: they are established, they are uniformly licensed, and each makes very general jurisdictional claims.

The jurisdictional claims of physicians have not narrowed through time, but broadened—the process being hastened by the doctrine that the physician is dealing with the whole man, and this despite the internal specialization that we have noted. Pharmacists and the pharmaceutical chemists that develop new drugs provide little threat, as these occupations have found it convenient to cooperate with physicians. It is the ownership of man's psyche and emotional problems that is most disputed. The psychosomatic approach of the general practitioner or internist is supplemented by the medically trained psychiatrist. For relatively untrained counseling the general practitioner might compete with the clergyman. The latter has not given up his claim, often now on the basis of some training. Meanwhile, clinical psychologists and psychiatric social workers have made their appearance, and teachers are not averse to trying a bit of psychotherapy also. It appears that the jurisdictional disputes would have been more widespread and more acrimonious if the extent of the demand for services were not well beyond the capacity of any single competitor to supply them.

Law has found itself in jurisdictional contests on many fronts:

... with labor arbitrators, management consultants, social workers, fiscal policy economists, investment advisors, real estate brokers, private investigators, and, seemingly, anyone in sight. Well, the lawyer is trained to be combative, or at least litigious, but he can scarcely claim to be in charge of social relations generally.[13]

Representatives of these, and other, established, and licensed, professions may seek to prevent intrusions on their domain by court action. In some instances, however, the competitor is also licensed, and legislative definitions of jurisdictions are no more likely to be clear and exclusive than are professional practices themselves. The reluctance of professionals to advertise as individuals does not apply to organized collectivities. Contesting professional groups may run public relations campaigns to convince potential clients of their exceptional (and exclusive) merits. In a sense, the principles of the market once more appear in areas of human concern from which they had been mainly excluded.

COMPETENCE, CONTROL, AND COORDINATION

The anxieties expressed by established professionals (and sometimes by their salaried spokesmen) may have some merit, even if the motives of the sounders of warnings are not entirely disinterested. The urgency of a need is likely to produce proposed solutions, even though the informational and technical basis for rational solutions does not exist. This is why quackery and charlatanism plagued medicine for so long, and we should be naive indeed if we thought that it has entirely disappeared: witness bogus cancer cures and nearly lethal diets. Yet certainly the dangers of practicing magic rather than rational technique are likely to be greater in a new, untried, and perhaps relatively undisciplined specialty than in one subject to greater peer-group control.

---

[13] Moore, reference cited in note 10, pp. 324–325.

The rapid multiplication of specialists, some of whom offer competing alternatives for solving the client's problems, poses for the client problems of rational choice. This is one major function of such authenticating mechanisms as licensing and a university base for training. These do not constitute total remedies, however, particularly when the client may require the coordination of several specialists. The internist in modern group medical practice serves this function, particularly for the ambulatory patient. For the hospitalized patient, many more services may be provided. Over these the patient has little control: they are determined by administrative decision.

The high school, college, and professional school similarly offer a range of specialized services, only partly subject to the student's discretion, and at times with dubious coordination. The provision of possibly unsought services is a conspicuous feature of the Army. Except for certain special judicial proceedings such as juvenile courts and some domestic courts, law offers little by way of coordinated specialization except through such overt or covert referral as the private attorney may supply.

The problem of determining the merits of new professional specialties is exacerbated by the problem of getting them coordinated for the particular needs of the client. For the corporate community, and increasingly for governmental agencies, this "packaging" of specialists is performed by firms of management consultants or by the latest variant, the firms of systems analysts. "Bring us your problems," they say, "and we will determine the expert specialists needed for portions of its solutions, develop new information if necessary, and make firm recommendations on a promised schedule." This requires an extremely flexible organization, as clients' problems come in assorted shapes, sizes, and degrees of difficulty. It is not unknown for such organizations to hire or consult old-line professionals as well as various new whiz kids. This may not be the ideal, or only, answer to problems of coordination among specialists, but it will bear watching.

Chapter eight: The professional and
his peers: prestige

THE professional in private practice welcomes both the general prestige accorded to his status as a professional, the special prestige, if any, accorded to his particular occupation, and perhaps the differential *esteem*[1] in which he is held as a particularly exemplary practitioner of his specialty. Yet the judgments of the laity must always be suspect, even if ego-satisfying and occupationally useful, for the layman is in a poor position to judge competence, and his opinions are too conspicuously subject to false cues and to manipulation.

The professional does in principle accord the right to judge his relative competence and performance to his peers, though not to all of them equally—since he also makes judgments, and will not accord equal weight to the opinions of colleagues. A colleague who is an administrative superior will not be accorded automatic superiority in technical judgment nor will the professional most widely known and acclaimed by the laity.

The professional community, to which Goode refers,[2] does indeed behave as a fairly cohesive collectivity in its direct dealing with lay clients and indeed in its fairly indirect dealing with the undifferentiated public. Yet within itself, it is almost as differentiated as an "ordinary" community, both in terms of functional specialization and in terms of invidious distinctions by rank, status, authority, influence, and esteem for performance. In this relatively brief discussion of still another dimension of the relations of a professional to his colleagues, we shall explore the sources of manifestations of prestige in the way professionals deal with one another. It may be well to add that we are using the term pres-

[1] Kingsley Davis, "A Conceptual Analysis of Stratification," *American Sociological Review*, 7:309–321, June 1942.

[2] William J. Goode, "Community Within a Community: The Professions," *American Sociological Review*, 22:194–200, April 1957.

tige elliptically to encompass the differential recognition and awards that accrue to a *position* in a fairly organized social system (*prestige* proper), and to the deference accorded to superior role performance in a position (properly speaking, *esteem*[3]).

The sources of prestige

The standing of a professional with his nominal peers is, not surprisingly, a mixture of various overt and informal criteria, not infrequently mixed with personal judgments verging on the professional—"He seems to show promise"—and those verging on the particularistic—"He seems to be able, but I should not want him in my [department, unit, firm, division]." Professionals do not quite spend their lives judging colleagues—after all, they do have clients, and, mostly, families, friends, neighbors, and the usual run of lay organizations and involvements. Yet it remains true that they do make comparative judgments of their nominal peers, ranking those peers in relative competence and always, anxious as they typically are, compare themselves to ideal and actual fellow practitioners.

KNOWLEDGE AND POWER

Those occupations that have a high scale-value on our cumulative index of professionalism are sometimes known as the "learned professions," which, by our criteria, would be a redundant expression. There are no others. Yet the aspiring professional, during his training period, is systematically graded and ranked according to his mastery (or simple recall) of a body of information. Cutting-points vary by institution and curriculum, but perfection is rarely demanded. Thus, demonstrated competence for oral, written, or manual demonstration that the information or technique has been acquired is likely to result in grading scales. The probability of success but the potentiality of failure, we have earlier suggested, is an important element in developing a professional commitment. Yet success is rarely unitary; it is still

---

[3] Davis, reference cited in note 1.

differentiated, and yields a possibly grudging respect for the proficient.

No competitive system is free from envy, from rationalization for failure and "undeserved" success, or from plaints about the fairness of the competition. Nevertheless, a fairly well-established competitive system yields differential results, and that kind of system pervades both training and practice in the professions, despite their genuine communality.

It may be true, as frequent and badly conceived studies seem to have demonstrated, that school performance and career performance have no relationship.[4] The studies have failed to parcel out the "guaranteed successes," such as having inherited wealth; have failed to take adequate account of selective procedures for admission to "guaranteed" success mechanisms; and have failed to sequester the influence of "connections." In fact, after one has sorted out various important, nonprofessional considerations, it remains true that those who best demonstrate their abilities in competitive situations do fare well, and do indeed command the respect of those who just get by.

We are making here a sharp and necessary distinction between the prestige of a professional among his peers and that accorded by the laity. The two may often coincide, and this circumstance is somewhat more than a coincidence, that is, an unexplained accident. Yet one encounters with sufficient frequency the doctor's doctor, the lawyer's lawyer, the professor's professor to be wary of assuming a nice symmetry between prestige with the laity and prestige with the professions.

The reluctance of those who are adequate, and therefore members of the fraternity, to proclaim the superior knowledge of the highly proficient members of the club is counterbalanced by external signs of recognition of competence. Yet even without this kind of external confirmation, which is an extremely sophisticated and subtle form of lay control, the

---

[4] Donald P. Hoyt, "The Relationship Between College Grades and Adult Achievement: A Review of the Literature," *ACT Research Reports*, No. 7, September 1965, American College Testing Program, Iowa City.

professionals in fact recognize that knowledge is power. The review mechanisms vary by field; in the learned (and aspiring) professions, the practitioners submit their data, their new techniques, and their theories to criticism by the written word in technical journals. That is one way of building a reputation among colleagues, and a means whereby youngsters may score off their more successful elders. Each party to this kind of impersonal transaction is at risk. The man who has subjected his work to review may be caught short. The reviewer (more often junior than senior, but that, too, varies) may also seek to score points that in effect show his own lack of comprehension. (The Europeans do things differently, as the author attempts to manipulate the assignment of critics, and the whole reviewing process is rather overtly recognized as the political process that it is. On balance, the results, being totally suspect, are not to be believed. American professional scholarship has nothing to learn from European practice in this respect; *au contraire*.)

The differential command over the techniques of solving human problems universally results in a prestigious position for the supplier of that knowledge or skill. The Davis-Moore theory of stratification—the controversy over which could not be usefully reviewed here—is clearly authenticated in this respect.[5]

RELATIVE POSITION

The professional world abounds in distinctions, some of which make a difference. The salaried professional may be judged by his relative rank in the hierarchy of the organization where he is employed, and further by the relative status or reputation of the organization itself. Thus a senior engineer in a major aircraft company outranks not only many other engineers employed by the same firm, but also probably a person with a similar title employed by a hosiery manufacturer. College teachers have formal ranks, and are also ranked somewhat informally in terms of the

---

[5] Kingsley Davis and Wilbert E. Moore, "Some Principles of Stratification," *American Sociological Review*, 10:242–249, April 1945.

reputation of the college or university in the academic universe. The Roman Catholic church provides an elaborate hierarchy of positions for clergymen, but the parish priest, like his Protestant colleague, may also be informally judged according to the size and prosperity of his parish or congregation.

Even professionals in private practice have differential positions. A physician may be known by the size or wealth of his practice, and possibly by the reputation of the group with which he practices and by the teaching hospital with which he is affiliated. An attorney may be known by the individuals or firms numbered among his clients and by his relative position in a law firm.

In a completely "fair" competitive system, individuals would achieve the more prestigious and highly rewarded positions on the basis of merit by demonstrated professional performance. Thus there would be a virtual symmetry between the esteem accorded to meritorious performance of professional roles and the prestige accorded to professional positions. Since professional positions are not filled at random and merit is the norm for placement, there is a normal relationship between the respect given the individual and that deriving from his position, but there are likely to be exceptions.

THE TAINT OF DEXTERITY

The tradition of learning in the professions, the possession of abstract knowledge of principles which may be applied to particular cases, results in some ambiguity in the position of specialists whose performance depends principally on the manipulation of tools and instruments. The most conspicuous example is that of surgeons. The surgeons emerged in Europe from a craft guild, where they were allied with or were themselves barbers. Lacking a university base and excluded from the medical fraternity, the surgeons in England formed their own "Royal College." By the time specialization overtook American medical practice, surgery was well within the scope of medicine. The circumstance that the American surgeon must have basic medical training gives him standing as a learned man, but does not entirely remove the taint of being "a mere craftsman."

Engineering, too, is often associated with manual skills, though training in the physical sciences and mathematics is a substantial part of the engineer's education. Even in physics, specialists in theory are at least slightly derogatory in their view of experimentalists.

We are not suggesting that the requirement of dexterity or mechanical aptitude is a serious impairment of professional status, but rather a nuance, a slight impairment of relative standing, which may be overcome by sheer virtuosity of performance.

The manifestations of prestige

The way that prestige among professionals is symbolized and displayed ranges from very subtle and informal deference to elaborate and ceremonial behavior. Deference is implied in asking the advice of a fellow professional, although of course the relationship may be reciprocal. Deference is also implied in the informally developed consensus among professionals concerning unusual skill or judgment. The choice among specialists for referral of clients may reflect the original man's judgment of relative merit, but it may also rest on merely personal relationships between the professionals.

Professionals are not above a bit of pomp and circumstance. Recognition is given to originality or to cumulative success by election to honorific offices in professional associations, by election to honorific bodies with restricted membership, by citations and awards, testimonial dinners, book dedications, and the like. Although it is rare for the professional to be alive to enjoy the honor, he may eventually have a building or a wing of one called by his name, a plaque installed marking his birthplace or former workplace, or perhaps an endowed professorship named in his honor. If he is a British subject, the professional may appear on the monarch's honors list.

Aside from a general proclivity of human beings to be invidious, what do these manifestations of prestige mean? Their positive function, and often explicit purpose, is to encourage the professional in excellence. Recognition of outstanding merit by those best able to judge is unlikely to be scoffed at. Some of those not widely honored may do the scoffing, or deride the judgment, but their motives are not above suspicion. More than incidentally for the professional in private practice, display of certificates of membership, citations, and awards on the office walls is a legitimate form of advertising one's honorable position in his fraternity.

Prestige patterns may actually serve as part of the control mechanisms in professional practice. In his study of the medical profession, Hall found a basic process of "sponsorship," which operates to select young physicians for eventual admission to what he calls the "inner fraternity."[6] This inner fraternity controls access to hospital positions, to inclusion in well-established medical practices, and to participation in mutual referrals.[7] Coleman and his colleagues found that the diffusion of a medical innovation was much more rapid among physicians characterized as "profession-oriented" than among those characterized as "patient-oriented."[8] Although their study did not include a prestige-ranking of physicians, it appears consistent with Hall's inner fraternity.

Formal specialization within a profession is likely to multiply the total number of honors available for distribution, and increase the chance that any given meritorious practitioner will come to the attention of those most likely to appreciate his work. Indeed, the formation of highly specialized associations, either as adjuncts of more inclusive professional societies or independently of them, is usually

[6] Oswald Hall, "The Informal Organization of the Medical Profession," *Canadian Journal of Economics and Political Science*, 12:30–44, February 1946.

[7] *Ibid.* See also, Oswald Hall, "The Stages of a Medical Career," *American Journal of Sociology*, 53:327–336, March 1948.

[8] James Coleman, Elihu Katz, and Herbert Menzel, "The Diffusion of an Innovation Among Physicians," *Sociometry*, 20:253–270, December 1957.

promoted on the grounds that too little attention is given to the specialty by the general organization. This may well have technical justification in the desire of specialists to communicate with one another, but it is also likely to mean that too little distribution of prestige and its symbols is being accorded the specialty.

Public and professional prestige rankings need not coincide, as we have noted. Indeed, within the profession any individual's relative rank may not be consensual, for both his position and his performance may be differently appraised by various portions of the relatively informed constituency of judges. Matters are still more complicated in that professional roles are in some degree multiple. Thus a physician may be known for his diagnostic skill but generally poor relations with patients and colleagues. An attorney may be known for his negotiating skill but not for his forensic ability in court. And university faculties are claimed to be thickly populated by renowned researchers who are poor teachers and possibly even disagreeable colleagues. Yet status inconsistency within a profession should scarcely surprise us, since it is widely characteristic of modern complex societies. There are so many criteria of judgment and so many distinct constituencies of judges that a high degree of consistency in outcomes would be surprising.

SPECIAL-INTEREST associations proliferate in modern industrial societies, and there seems to be no finite limit to the kinds of interests that induce those sharing them to form formal organizations. The *Encyclopedia of Associations*[1] lists information on some 13,600 American associations having a national scope or interest. Since some distinctly local or regional groups are included, the criteria for listing are not absolutely clear; in any event, the number of national groups is still very large. Although recreational and expressive interests command a goodly share of organized attention, it is scarcely surprising that a great many of the associations reflect the diverse interests in a complex economic network—especially trade associations and occupational associations. Of course many of the occupational associations are labor unions in the strict sense, but the distinction between a labor union and a professional association is not sharp. Generally speaking, labor unions expect to engage in collective bargaining with employers on behalf of the union membership, and professional associations do not. Yet it would be naive to suppose that professionals have no interest in their economic well-being, or that their organizations are not used to maintain and enhance the level of salaries and fees.

Early professional associations in the United States, Gilb notes,[2] were local and often more social and exclusive than either intellectual or professional in the strict sense of controlling and improving technical standards. Yet professional interests did emerge, and organizations were established or expanded to further them.

---

[1] Frederick G. Roffner *et al.* (eds.), *Encyclopedia of Associations*, Vol. I, *National Organizations of the United States*, 5th ed. (Detroit: Gale Research Co., 1968).

[2] Corinne Lathrop Gilb, *Hidden Hierarchies: The Professions and Government* (New York: Harper & Row, 1966), pp. 28–33.

The utility of organization

Precisely because the professional is strongly oriented toward his peers, even when he competes with them for clients and for public and professional prestige, there exists a high potential for formalizing professional relations in organizations.

COMMUNICATION

Although professional associations are likely to be instigated by small groups of very active practitioners for whom a formal organization might seem least necessary,[3] formalization has the advantage of putting the stamp of legitimacy on setting meetings, having conferences, and presenting papers on intellectual and professional concerns, and, as we shall see, taking unified action on matters of common interest.

Whatever else a professional association does as a collectivity, it provides formal (and persistently informal) means of communication among its constituents. Conventions or annual meetings are organized, and the programs commonly afford opportunity both for presentation of new technical information and for panels or symposia on professional training, standards, ethics, regulation, and other matters involving the relations of professionals to clients, peers, and the community. In addition, one or more periodic publications may be sponsored, again possibly affording both intellectual and professional exchange.

It would be too cynical to argue that the formal programs of professional meetings constitute excuses rather than reasons for assembling the fraternity. Yet anyone who has participated in a professional convention or, worse luck, has been an ordinary guest in a convention hotel, is aware of the conviviality that makes it difficult to distinguish between the meetings of leading intellectuals and those of war veterans. Conventions provide opportunities for old friends and colleagues who have become geographically separated to get together, and for everyone, particularly

---

[3] *Ibid.*, pp. 37–40.

for those who do not have extensive professional contacts in the ordinary course of their work, to pick up the latest gossip. And for the honorably ambitious and those alert to possibilities for professional improvement through shifting locations, partners, or employers, the convention affords the means to explore new openings. Youngsters have the opportunity to see the acknowledged leaders in their chosen field, and perhaps even meet them informally. The lone practitioner from a small community, the salaried adviser who has no colleagues in his company, or the one-man department from a small college may reaffirm his professional identity as a representative of a high calling.

All this is true, and important. Yet at the professional meeting some portion of the constituency is involved in presenting, listening to, or discussing technical papers; sitting in committee meetings to draft resolutions or organize a new specialty that may seek official recognition from the general organization; or conducting the business of the organization in meetings of delegates or directly elected officers and representatives comprising the formal government of the association.

Technical communication is of course inhibited by specialization. Large professional associations thus tend to become increasingly a kind of umbrella or holding company for specialized sections or affiliates. What unites the membership, if anything, then becomes common professional interests in the narrow sense and not common intellectual interests. This tendency gives significance to Gilb's comment, with regard to physicians, that "In 1957 it was estimated that 90 per cent *of all private practitioners* belonged to the AMA."[4] It has been especially the ideology and economic interests of physicians in fee-for-service practice that the medical association spokesmen have stridently represented.[5]

Specialization increases the chances for the specialist to communicate with at least part of his colleague. This is also a principal function of regional, state, and local associations,

---

[4] *Ibid.*, p. 118. Emphasis added.

[5] Richard Harris, *A Sacred Trust* (New York: New American Library, 1966), pp. 11–19.

for these multiply the total number of chances of getting a
place on the program, and thus may secure participation by
those who might not fare well in national competition, either
because their possible contributions may be less sophisticated or because they lack contacts with program chairmen
and other gatekeepers at the national level.

THE UNITED FRONT

Perhaps the major rationale for formal professional organization is precisely in dealing with various interests and
publics outside the professional group, as distinct from
maintaining communications within a self-contained community. Gilb argues that the transformation of local and
rather exclusive clubs of the more successful professionals
into state and national associations professing to speak for
the common interests of the occupation was primarily an
effort to establish jurisdiction and self-regulation.[6] This
placed professional leaders in the awkward position of sharing out power and influence with those less highly regarded,
or at least to do so nominally. Yet only by incorporating
all or most practitioners in a common organization was there
any chance of exercising both internal controls over competence and performance and external influence over legislatures, training centers, and other relevant components of the
professional environment. Inclusiveness of course does not
assure equality, and we shall see that oligarchy in fact persists in formally democratic organizations.

Partly because professional associations are at least nominally voluntary, the claim to inclusiveness has been incomplete in American practice. We have observed that the AMA
apparently has a greater appeal to the physician in private
practice than to other medically trained professionals. In
1960 less than half of the lawyers in the United States were
members of the American Bar Association.[7]

These failures in total representation, which also prevail
in varying proportions in other fields, must be interpreted
in the light of the American political system. Since the ma-

---

[6] Gilb, work cited in note 2, pp. 34–81.

[7] *Ibid.*, p. 122.

jor collective concerns of professional associations have been those closely related matters of control of training and admission to practice and the attempt to establish and maintain preemptive jurisdictions, the effective controls are primarily effective at regional, state, and local levels. College and professional school accrediting agencies are commonly regional in character. Licensing requirements and the establishment of examination or review boards are usually the prerogative of state legislatures. If medicine, unlike law, knows no political boundaries—and it is interesting that medical schools are accredited nationally—it remains true that the control of medical practice may be very local. City and county medical societies may effectively control access to hospitals; nonmembers may thus be at a serious disadvantage except in the practice of "office medicine."

The American college teacher is by no means required to join the American Association of University Professors, which attends to common professional concerns, or indeed his appropriate disciplinary association, which may pay at least some attention to professional concerns proper to the discipline. Again, however, practical professional matters are likely to be local in their incidence and local in their resolution. This accounts for the great variability in the size and activity of chapters of national associations and the uneven appearance of separate local associations.

The notion of a united front is subject to several strains. Specialization, again, impairs intellectual commonality, and the nostalgia of survivors of shared ordeals in training may be an insufficient basis for current cohesion. This strain is intensified if a common interest in what Gilb calls "bread-and-butter professionalism"[8] is also missing. Thus groups such as the National Educational Association that include both professional workers and their administrators may find that the genuine differences in occupational orientation threaten the presumed common interest in promoting education as a high calling.[9] Nursing and librarian associations face similar problems.

---

[8] *Ibid.*, Chap. I.
[9] See, for example, *ibid.*, pp. 161, 167.

Some discord in actual professional interests may be patched up or papered over by attempting to secure offices for those in what might be called rank-and-file professional positions, by separate sections for special interests, or, very usefully, by reiterated emphasis on common dangers and common enemies—hostile legislation, jurisdictional competitors, the challenge of untrained amateurs.

Professionals may simply be excluded from local or national associations by overt discrimination by race and sex,[10] or covert discrimination through the actions of committees on credentials.

The united front may be impaired from still another source, and that is overinclusiveness. The older associations of practicing professionals only reluctantly, and still partially, opened membership to all fully qualified practitioners. The officers of associations were not tempted to enlist interested amateurs, though they were not averse to regaling the laity with professional accomplishments when public support was thought to be advantageous. Many of the disciplinary associations, however, though primarily university-based, welcomed to membership anyone professing an interest in the subject. As professional concerns inevitably came to supplement intellectual ones, and particularly as questions of authentication and standards came to be troublesome, the "affiliated laity" often came to be more embarrassing than advantageous. By simple payment of annual dues, the layman could claim authentication as a mathematician, economist, or psychologist, for whatever personal interests he was trying to pursue. As a consequence of such difficulties, most disciplinary associations now have established restrictive criteria for membership, or have set up classes of members so as to distinguish between those qualified and those merely interested.

Whether officers and other spokesmen for professional associations do in fact represent a consensus of professionals, or even of the association's membership, is open to question.

---

[10] *Ibid.*, pp. 46–50.

We shall note below that professional associations share some characteristics with other formal voluntary organizations: they are democratic in form and oligarchic in operation. The genuine differences in professional interests may be inadequately represented in the composition of associational leadership, and especially in the interests represented by professional staffs. Successful practitioners may be concerned about performance standards of their less successful colleagues, for fear of discredit to the profession as a whole. The less successful practitioners may be concerned about jurisdictional protection or protection of employment continuity, subjects that need not worry those who are secure. Although Garceau's study of the American Medical Association before World War II indicated a disproportion of urban specialists and medical school professors in the leadership,[11] the professional as distinct from intellectual concerns of organized medicine—and particularly the opposition to the extension of publicly supported medical care—seems to have put both the intellectuals and those interested in standards and reputation into a subordinate position.[12]

Precisely because detailed professional interests may differ, it is not surprising that the united front partially disintegrates. The result, however, is not an end of organization, but a proliferation of associations with more narrowly defined objectives. In some instances the interests of salaried professionals may result in an outright labor union, such as the American Federation of Teachers. In other instances some mixture of substantive specialty and practical concerns leads to the formation of specialized, but still professional groups—for example, the Industrial Medicine Association or the Association of Insurance Attorneys. The one thing that is most difficult, and not very rational, for modern man to do is to avoid organization altogether, since potentially adverse interests are not similarly reticent.[13]

[11] Oliver Garceau, *The Political Life of the American Medical Association* (Cambridge: Harvard University Press, 1941), pp. 54–55.

[12] Harris, work cited in note 5, pp. 20–21.

[13] Wilbert E. Moore, *Order and Change: Essays in Comparative Sociology* (New York: John Wiley & Sons, Inc., 1967), p. 224.

The range of interests promoted by professional associations is precisely that represented by the variety of professional concerns, processes, and role-relationships that constitute our principal preoccupations in this book. Professional bodies are concerned with the selection and training of new recruits, criteria of admission to professional practice; the economics, politics, and ethics of dealing with clients and other employers; problems of competence, performance, and prestige, in dealing with peers; and, above all, questions of jurisdiction over a field of knowledge and practice.

Certainly the most extensive and careful analysis of the tactics of American professional associations in enhancing the collective status of occupational groups is the study by Corinne Gilb,[14] to which frequent previous references have been made in this chapter. Viewing professional associations as private governments with a principal aim of dealing with public governments, Gilb traces the steps from achieving a measure of occupational solidarity and then taking the common case to legislatures to secure public authorization for essentially private regulation. At times the association itself may be recognized as the regulating agency. More commonly, review and examining boards are established, which are only nominally public, being comprised of recognized professionals (who may be nominated by the association). Training is usually controlled by the recognition of accrediting agencies, which in turn may represent various mixtures of public and private representation and control.

Direct efforts to affect the course of legislation— usually through licensing regulations, but occasionally through attempts to block legislation regarded as harmful, such as the American Medical Association's opposition to medical care as a part of social security coverage—take the standard American form of "lobbying." Either a member of the association's regular administrative staff or a special public relations consultant attempts to testify before legislative

---

[14] Gilb, work cited in note 2.

committees and persuade individual legislators. (Some of this activity is of dubious propriety in the legal sense, aside from broader questions of public policy. Professional associations are usually tax-exempt. Such organizations are not supposed to devote a substantial amount of their resources or activities to attempts to influence legislation. "Substantial" is one of those wondrous words beloved of legislative draftsmen, for the meaning can only be determined by litigation.) Large and powerful associations such as the American Medical Association have used other tactics: encouraging the personal physicians of legislators and congressmen to act as unofficial lobbyists; carrying on national advertising campaigns; and operating through "cover" organizations, the sponsorship of which is not difficult to discover. That organizational tactics are not always successful is demonstrated by the failure of the AMA to defeat the introduction of Medicare as an adjunct of the federal social security system. The blatant distortions in the propaganda campaign, and the image-destroying revelation that organized medicine seemed indifferent to the extensity and quality of medical care, resulted in a major setback in the political power of the AMA.[15] As Gilb remarks—not with reference to the case just cited—"The established association cannot afford to stress narrowly and manifestly self-interested legislation."[16] Past successes induced the policy-makers of the AMA to overlook that principle.

Aside from influencing legislation and gaining state-supported autonomy, professional associations may carry on public relations campaigns of various degrees of formality. Members of the association may simply be reminded of the honorable traditions of community service in the profession, or the association as such may seek to inform the laity of its good works, professional and otherwise. The more public and official a professional group's claim to conspicuous virtue, the more hazardous the operation, for some portion of the relevant public may suspect the possibility of ulterior motives. Above all, some identification with the public inter-

---

[15] Harris, work cited in note 5, pp. 123–208.
[16] Gilb, work cited in note 2, p. 153.

est is as important in dealing with the general public as it is in dealing with their elected representatives in legislatures.[17]

Internal structures: the ambiguity of oligarchy

Every formally organized voluntary association is under the effective control of a minority.[18] This extension of the famous "iron law of oligarchy" of Robert Michels[19] is continuously reaffirmed in the organization of professional associations. Within the association there is a differential distribution of prestige—though often by several competing criteria—and of mere acquaintanceship. Professionals get known and evaluated by their colleagues by conduct that reflects well on the trade, and, somewhat separately, by conduct that exemplifies loyalty to the profession itself, and its constituted organization. Yet it must not be assumed that every person who, for whatever reasons of collective loyalty or personal advantage, becomes an authentic member in an association is thereby anxious to participate in all of its activities or to be an eager candidate for leadership. One can distinguish, crudely, between the "active center" and the "passive periphery" in associations, and with finer observations of man-hour inputs of organizational time, derive a fairly clear-cut "exponential wastage rate" curve of organizational participation.[20]

OLIGARCHY AND DEMOCRACY

There is no necessary and inherent inconsistency between effective organizational control by a minority and the formal principles of democracy established in the legal structure of professional associations. Apathy, after all, is a form of consent, and can be converted into active dissent if the constituted authorities conspicuously and grievously fail to conform to the wishes of the potential electorate that otherwise

---

[17] *Ibid.*

[18] Wilbert E. Moore, *Man, Time, and Society* (New York: John Wiley & Sons, Inc., 1963), p. 110.

[19] Robert Michels, *Political Parties,* trans. by Edcon Paul and Adar Paul (New York: Free Press, 1949).

[20] Moore, work cited in note 18, p. 111.

is not deeply engaged. The essential dilemma of organizational leadership is a more subtle one:

The stage is now set for a paradox. The leaders of the association are likely to be identified with the organization and its goals and thus seek to extend the participation of members both as an indication of group loyalty and as a basis for effectiveness in the pursuit of the interests for which the association was founded. At the same time, from the point of view of power or administration, increased participation is likely at best to delay decisional processes and at worst may threaten the whole structure of leadership.[21]

The dilemma of the rank-and-file membership of professional associations is no less severe. The member's rationale for affiliation may be precisely that of securing the authentication of being a member of the group, of being in "good standing." Good standing depends upon the reputation of the officers and other identifiable leaders of the association. And those leaders, we have observed, may not in fact share the problems and anxieties of the rank-and-file, and may indeed have permitted (and encouraged) members' participation only for limited purposes of a unified front, or to bring them under a measure of collective control. The leaders may not be genuine spokesmen for the rather distinctive interests of ordinary members.

Selectivity in democratic governments should not surprise us. If the system were truly equalitarian, positions should be determined by lot. The problem, rather, is that the criteria of organizational advancement tend to be mixed, and, as in all representational systems, the very attributes that distinguish a man from his colleagues may set him apart from their interests, rather than representing them with exceptional skill.

The view of professional associations as private governments, adopted by Gilb[22]—a view equally appropriate to corporations, universities, hospitals, and the like—picks up some of these nuances, and not others. Particularly, Gilb

---

[21] *Ibid.*

[22] Gilb, work cited in note 2, Chap. 4.

misses the point that democracies are not equalitarian bodies, and especially emphasizes the point of overrepresentation by professional status. Yet the latter, too, may be an exaggeration, for some status figures may have scant need for, or interest in, professional associations.

The ordinary dues-paying, voting, and possibly convention-attending member of a professional association is likely to have a limited choice in the selection of officers from a slate picked by a nominating committee not of his choosing. He may make his voice heard in a business meeting that conducts no essential business, and he might be selected for some secondary committee assignment if he seems especially earnest and not unduly disruptive of decorum and predominant ideology. Even if he is at odds with "the establishment," and speaks for a detectable and possibly fractious segment of opinion, he may be coopted rather than outlawed. He is made a minority member of a committee, reasoned with, and if necessary voted down, but he has not been turned loose as the leader of a secessionist faction.

The history of professional associations abounds with examples of successes and failures in the containment of divergent views and the organizational splintering of intransigent positions. The rules for success are relatively easy in principle, somewhat difficult to put into practice: (a) Do not rely on narrow majorities of voters, with widespread nonparticipation; keep negotiating and seek a compromise. (b) Do not leave a cohesive and somewhat dedicated minority; compromise and "marry the opposition." (c) With regard to a small and concerted minority, decentralize and specialize, with an area of unquestioned autonomy for the minority, which cannot commit the association as a whole. This will usually entail a formally organized and titled group. If necessary, disavow the group—nicely—by assuring that it is not a recognized section or chapter of the general association.

Organizations of substantial and growing size exhibit uniformly another intrinsic strain in the conduct of their internal affairs. The need to face the possibly hostile environment as an entity or collectivity, plus all the economies of scale in providing administrative staffs, common billings, and all the expensive trivia of operating an organization, push strongly for *centralization*. But, as all experienced inhabitants of work-doing bureaucracies and of large voluntary associations know from experience, there is almost a perfect correlation between centralization and standardization. From the point of view of the ordinary client, employee, or member of such coordinated organizations, there is another and grimmer correlation between standardization and idiocy—or at least the failure to attend to rationally and intellectually defensible differences. Organizational *decentralization* then sets in, either because a consensus is no longer possible, or because it is no longer sensible in terms of the particular needs of members of the trade in varying political jurisdictions, with varying interprofessional relations, and with varying standards of what is just and prudent.

Decentralization does not end oligarchy; it only dissipates and therefore in a sense extends it. For those who are fearful of power concentrations, some comfort may be taken from the fact that petty oligarchs are more likely to be competitive than a set of feudal fiefs owing allegiance to a common monarch. And though the rule, historically, is by no means certain, it may be easier to influence local chiefs than the lords of the kingdom.

Lest the metaphors carry us away, what we are analyzing here is the way that common professional interests somehow get exemplified, represented, and articulated differentially by outstanding exemplars of the profession and its interests; how common interests turn out to be differentiated, and thus represented in somewhat less exclusive hierarchies of influence; and how organizations adapt or fail to adapt to the contrary pressures of centralization and decentralization. We are still dealing with the role relations of a professional with his peers. But in the organizational context, as in others, we keep rediscovering that "some are more equal than others."[23]

---

[23] Wilbert E. Moore, "But Some Are More Equal Than Others," *American Sociological Review,* 28:13–18, February 1963.

From time to time, particularly in this chapter, we have had occasion to distinguish within professional associations an orientation to common *intellectual* interests and an orientation to common occupational or *professional* interests. Professional associations appeal to one or another of those interests in varying degrees, and there may be a more or less precise fit between official programs as enunciated, planned, and carried through by constituted officers, staffs, and committees, on the one hand, and the appeal of the association on the other. For assembled conclaves, intellectual exchange may be emphasized by program committees, to the possible boredom of prospective attendants at the festivities. For the dedicated professionals among the officers, the welfare of the profession in face of seen and unseen enemies may be paramount, but that is a little more likely to lead to committees, small discussion groups, and forays by trusted scouts than it is to a general membership discussion. (Here, again, the officers and staff of the AMA sometimes have been inept. Mistakenly thinking that constituent support for extreme ideological positions was important, the ideologists enlisted and gained the support of the somewhat benighted constituency. A vicious circle set in, by which the constituency goaded the officers and salaried staffs into increasingly extreme positions.[24] It is not an unknown phenomenon in public politics. It could scarcely be more devastating to the image of the physician as a member of a high calling, with professional responsibility.)

We must now add to the *intellectual* and *professional* interests of professional associations (and possibly of their constituents) the distinctly *organizational* interests of individual professionals.

Almost every authenticated professional with better-than-average ability or achievement has alternative career paths open to him. We are here attending only to professional organization, and that narrows but does not eliminate the alternatives. Professional associations occasionally do reward

---

[24] Harris, work cited in note 5, pp. 206–208.

(as a judging but not as a placing organization) outstanding service to the laity.[25] More reliable awards, or at least honors and deference, go to those who represent the claims of professionals to jurisdiction, the victors over presumptuous adversaries, the spokesmen for professionals before legislative committees and legislative bodies. Those victories are not likely to be absolute and untainted by compromise. Thus it is a little unseemly, and a little impolitic, to advertise them widely. What ordinarily happens is that the heroes are unsung publicly, but privately known to those who matter. Associationally, they will be rewarded with responsible positions that may not require popular (membership) acclaim, but will command the respect of more widely known members of the organization. Since the oligarchy of an association has few rewards to offer other than prestige, and the judgment of prestige is not always shared by ordinary members and the inner fraternity, there arises the political problem of getting public recognition, of some sort, for those whom the gods have favored. It does not always happen: the "old pro" may have an extremely limited, select constituency which cannot be converted into a popular one. He remains the trusted adviser, but not the elective officer.

It is not unknown for distinctly *professional* types to rise to eminence in occupational associations. As a political body, the AMA has repeatedly turned up honorific officers who represent the narrowest professional interests of the association's membership.[26]

Professional associations exceptionally anxious about their claims to competence—and contrary to the position of say, physicians, who are properly anxious about their claims to trust—are likely to produce elective officers that represent some segment of the intellectual pretensions of the electorate. These individuals have added to the substantive dimensions of their field, else they could not have got identified and recognized. They get selected by nominating bodies and

---

[25] Gilb, work cited in note 2.

[26] See Report of Inaugural Address by American Medical Association President Milford O. Rouse in *The New York Times*, June 21, 1967, p. 24.

constituent assemblies as individuals who show forth to their colleagues and the laity those manifest advantages of encouraging an intellectual discipline.

Surprisingly, the older the established professional or disciplinary association, the more difficult it is to get an intellectual into high office. The reason for this is that the steady course of specialization makes it difficult for even very able contributors to be known outside the relatively limited group of those who share their specialty. The person who has received the accolades available to specialists is likely to get wider recognition only by attention to professional interests widely shared, or by displaying *organizational* interests and talents that will bring him to the attention of precisely that segment of the profession that is organizationally involved and committed.

Administrative staffs and doubtful constituencies

The elective officers of professional associations normally serve a single, relatively short (usually annual) term in any office. Moreover, the duties are performed while the officer continues in his regular employment or practice. In other words, the positions are chiefly honorific. The president or executive committee may have some patronage to distribute, but perhaps little additional power. From an organizational standpoint the principal reasons for the relative weakness of elective officials are two: (1) brief tenure in an unsalaried and part-time position does not permit either the knowledge or other resources necessary to have a substantial impact on the organization; (2) the governing statutes and operating procedures are virtually certain to have evolved in such a way as to protect the organization from annual oscillations in policies and practices.

Some continuity in elective officialdom is maintained by having governing bodies (houses of delegates, senates, councils, executive committees) the membership of which has overlapping terms. Occasionally an elective secretary serves for a longer term than the nominal chief officer.

The principal source of continuity, and therefore a major center of power, in professional associations rests with the salaried secretariat or administrative staff. Salaried executive officers tend to be principal representatives of the association, and often its spokesmen in dealing with professional matters. These officers have the requisite time and knowledge; elective officials often have neither.

Salaried officials are of course selected by and responsible to some elective governing body. But since members of such bodies come and go, and are in any event organizational amateurs, the supervision of the administrative staff is not likely to be close. It is not even always necessary for the salaried officers to have been trained in the profession that they now serve. (Thus, it should surprise no one that there is a National Association of Association Executives, the members of which undoubtedly regard themselves as professionals.)

The question inevitably arises as to whether the salaried officers of professional associations do in fact correctly represent their respective constituencies. It is an unanswerable question from available evidence, and the answer would certainly differ by association and circumstance. The ways of oligarchy are such, however, that even if the answer were strongly negative, much time and effort would be necessary for an association's membership to rectify the situation. This is not exactly power without responsibility, but the responsibility is greatly attenuated by organizational complexity.

THE specialization of occupations that involve rendering
problem-solving services for clients does not stop at the
claimed or effective jurisdictional boundaries of the principal professions. Several processes account for specialized
occupations that are complementary to the services of the
established professions. The process most closely related to
professional specialization itself is that of "subprofessionalization," that is, the spinning off to subordinates of professional duties that do not require full professional training.
Another process might be called "centrifugal specialization," in which new occupations of some degree of specialization appear or persist just beyond the *formal* control of
the established profession. A third process that may be of
growing significance arises from the growing technical sophistication in a great many areas of human activity; this
process we might call "independent invention and unintended complementarity."

The range of professional control

Given the forces creating complementary occupations, which
will presently be discussed in greater detail, a question arises
as to the degree that these are somehow integrated or controlled by the established professions. In American professional practice, it appears that physicians have the most extensive influence or control over paramedical personnel, but
even that control is by no means complete. Lawyers exercise
relatively slight control over the many occupations dealing
with legal processes. The teaching profession is fairly dis-
orderly in its own ranks. Teachers in public elementary and
secondary schools are generally highly organized, but little
influenced by the more highly educated and autonomous university professors, whose own common professional association commands less attention than do the subject-oriented

disciplinary associations. Neither of the major branches of the teaching profession exercises any effective control outside of formal educational organization. Independent art, music, and dancing teachers serve as complementary but uncontrolled occupations.

SUBPROFESSIONALIZATION

When the professional in private practice has a larger claim on his services than he can manage without assistance, he is likely to consider delegating part of his activities that do not in fact require his professional training. (The new member in some mode of group practice may get such assistance as a by-product of membership, although perhaps not essential to his own practice.) The business aspects of professional practice are first likely to be delegated: handling appointments, correspondence, record-keeping, and billing. A next significant step is the identification of useful skills, which the professional may or may not possess himself, but which in either case do not require his elaborate technical training to master. Thus a physician may use the services of a laboratory technician in diagnosis, and nurses, physical therapists, and occupational therapists in treatment. Although physicians in the ancient world compounded their own remedies, the apothecary or druggist has long been formally independent of the physician. The registered pharmacist is not supposed to practice medicine, however, but to respond to instructions in prescriptions issued by physicians. In a sense, he is therefore under a considerable measure of control.

Nurses were inserted in the list in the preceding paragraph despite their long and arduous attempt to achieve a fully professional and fully independent status. Leaders in the nursing profession assure each other and the general membership of their professional associations that their aims are achieved.[1] Unfortunately, in the offices of physicians, in clinics, and hospitals, the physicians have somehow failed to get the message that nurses are their equals. Occasionally

---

[1] Anselm Strauss, "The Structure and Ideology of American Nursing: An Interpretation," in Fred Davis (ed.), *The Nursing Profession: Five Sociological Essays* (New York: John Wiley & Sons, Inc., 1966), pp. 68–69.

the supervising nurse in a hospital will deal with physicians as equals, or perhaps even adopt a superordinate stance with young interns. The ordinary duty nurse has no such privilege.

Even the clergy has not been immune from subprofessionalization. Sunday school teachers are usually dedicated amateurs, but choir directors ("ministers of music") and organists may be technically trained. Historically, sextons attended to the ordinary nonprofessional duties of a parish, from bell-ringing to gravedigging.

Engineers may enlist the services of draftsmen, mechanics, glass blowers, or other skilled trades. Colleges, some schools, and some law firms and research laboratories provide librarians. To consider librarians as subprofessional is also to invite controversy, for they, too, have been at considerable pains to develop full professional status.[2] The wide range of training in the field, and the uncertainty of their relations with other professions, leads to a conclusion that some librarians do indeed represent complementary professionalism in the scholarly world, and some seem clearly subordinate to teachers and researchers.

Part of the process of subprofessionalization is a stage in professional training. Thus teaching and research assistants in colleges and universities are usually in training for their own professional independence, though some assistants in natural science laboratories are permanently subprofessional. The extern or intern in hospital medical practice lacks the autonomy of the full professional, but this is an extension of training. Some salaried lawyers in law firms, who also lack autonomy, may be expected to achieve full standing in the original firm, another firm, or in independent practice; but some will remain in a subordinate status.[3]

Law, indeed, provides an interesting example of extensive subprofessionalization without very extensive professional control. A great deal of the actual operation of

---

[2] William J. Goode, "The Librarian: From Occupation to Profession," *The Librarian Quarterly*, 31:306–320, October 1961.

[3] Erwin Smigel, *The Wall Street Lawyer* (New York: Free Press, 1964), Chap. 4.

the law is outside the hands of attorneys: for example, process servers, bail bondsmen, insurance adjusters, probation officers, and private investigators. These do not include an additional list of specialists who occupy some portion of territory that lawyers also claim, a problem to which we shall turn shortly. And we should not overlook the largest body of legal practitioners, the police. Recent court decisions have restricted the sphere of police action when the accused does not have legal counsel, but the policeman necessarily continues to make legal and even judicial decisions. And the police, too, are attempting to improve their professional status.[4]

The control of subprofessional occupations is easiest in an administrative setting. Thus it is especially in hospital practice that physicians exercise the most effective control over paramedical specialists. Colleges and universities afford something comparable, but here many of the services that are ancillary to education are not in fact controlled by the professors. Medical, custodial, and "hotel" services are of slight professorial responsibility, power, or, in fact, concern. Engineers in a consulting firm or the salaried engineers in industrial research and development units generally control the subprofessionals. The most complete control is of course provided in the military services, where all specialties are laid out by duty, and by rank. The courts provide the closest approach to administrative control of legal services, but that is still very partial, and a great deal of legal business is outside the purview of courts. If lawyers are nervous about legal work not under their supervision, they might try to emulate the situation in medical schools and teaching hospitals, where training in ancillary services is provided under the auspices of the established profession. It is perhaps fair to say that lawyers have been more concerned with protecting their claimed jurisdiction, on the whole unsuccessfully, than they have been with exercising effective professional controls.

Subprofessionalization is bound to increase in the future,

---

[4] See James Q. Wilson, *Varieties of Police Behavior* (Cambridge, Mass.: Harvard University Press, 1969).

at various levels of approximation to the professional's position. We now have nurses' aides and teachers' aides, salaried or otherwise, and meter maids to help the traffic police. It can be fully expected that various subordinate and ancillary occupations will attempt to seek a status of complementary equality. Some will achieve that goal.

CENTRIFUGAL SPECIALIZATION

One prominent reason for attempted control of specialized and complementary services surrounding the more or less established domains of the established professions is to avoid jurisdictional disputes. Yet such disputes abound and proliferate, for it is rarely possible for a professional group to delineate a neat territory, keep its boundaries intellectually intact in view of burgeoning new knowledge and skills, and to capture or control new specialties, particularly if they (often properly) challenge the currently accepted orthodoxy.

Let us start, once more, with medicine. Despite the notable success of physicians in instigating or capturing a variety of paramedical services that command less than full professional prestige, the claims of the physician to own man's anatomy, physiology, and psyche do not go unchallenged. Druggists and even drug-inventing pharmaceutical chemists have generally seen fit to work cooperatively with drug-prescribing physicians. Yet pharmacists often still serve as poor-man's physicians, and they are commonly retail merchants as well: in the United States, drug stores fill physicians' prescriptions and sell patented remedies under trade names, but also run soda fountains and lunch counters, and sell merchandise having little if anything to do with health.[5] Apothecaries, or pharmacists, have indeed fallen on evil days as independent professionals, for they have been squeezed between the physicians, who assert their greater knowledge concerning the efficacy of particular inorganic or organic compounds, and the manufacturing drug concerns, who make

---

[5] Bernard Barber, *Drugs and Society* (New York: Russell Sage Foundation, 1967), pp. 105–114. Walter I. Wardwell, "Limited, Marginal and Quasi-Practitioners," in Howard Freeman, Sol Levine, and Leo G. Reeder (eds.), *Handbook of Medical Sociology* (Englewood Cliffs, N.J.: Prentice-Hall, Inc., 1963), pp. 215–219.

local compounding of prescriptions unnecessary by centralized manufacturing and even prepackaging.

Other, and sometimes more effective, challenges to the physician's sole surveillance of man's body and mind also exist.
For reasons that must be set down as historical accident, both
surgery and dentistry—having guild origins—remained distinct from medical practice in England, but only dentistry
retained its independent status in the United States. The
dentist is, in his early training and orientation, a physician
manqué. It is not quite accurate to view dentists as a medical
subprofession. The oddity is that it is now a controlled medical specialty rather than an independent profession, a
profession not conspicuous for its prestige among either
professionals or the laity.[6]

If physicians abandoned the mouth, or at least teeth, they
seem also to have abandoned most of their interest in feet.
Thus podiatry flourishes, particularly in caring for the relatively minor disorders of those who are on their feet a great
deal.

The fitting of corrective glasses was never held as a secure
jurisdiction by physicians. In effect, until specialized training and internships were developed in ophthalmology—a
very recent development indeed—optometrists were manifestly superior in equipment and technique to the medically
trained eye, ear, nose, and throat specialists whose capacity
for fitting corrective glasses owed nothing to medical training, and rested mainly on the buying or renting of corrective
lenses supplied by the appropriate manufacturers; the patient made the diagnosis, and determined the therapy. Contemporary ophthalmologists probably know more about the
physiological structure of the eye and its pathologies than
does the separately certified optometrist. Yet it is extremely
unlikely that most ophthalmologists can do any better than
the standard optometrist in diagnosing and prescribing for
ordinary visual disorders.

If the physicians have paid scant attention to mouths and
feet, and proved extremely laggard in the ordinary problems

---

[6] Wardwell, pp. 219–220.

of vision, they have placed strong but contested claims in other areas of human anatomy and function, and in the organization of medical practice. Chiropractors are licensed in many American jurisdictions, and osteopaths in most. In fact, there is now a considerable movement to assimilate osteopaths into the medical fraternity as recognized specialists, since they do in fact learn general medicine and are, perhaps, no more exaggerated in their true belief in the efficacy of their specialty than are, say, surgeons, internists, and psychiatrists.[7] Medically trained psychiatrists have to contend for jurisdiction with clinical psychologists. The latter have been very active in licensing efforts, as we have previously observed. The medical psychiatrists may have some sympathy with either physiological explanation of mental disorders or with physiological remedies (psychopharmacology), or they may have none. The clinical psychologist is likely to place greater reliance on (poorly authenticated) standard tests of mental disorders, and to share with some psychiatrists the techniques of therapy that do not involve direct changes in physiological states.[8]

The spinoffs from medicine seem almost boundless, for physiological and emotional states engage everyone, at some time. Man's physiological functioning is disputed among professional physicians, druggists and manufacturers of chemical compounds, recreational directors, dieticians, chiropractors, and masseuses. His psychic and emotional state is disputed by medically trained psychiatrists, clinical psychologists, social workers, clergymen, occasional teachers, and community do-gooders not elsewhere classified. Relations with professionals beyond one's control can get sticky; relations with amateurs can get very difficult indeed.

One very interesting development has been the contrast between physicians and "lay" administrators in the supervision of hospitals. We shall observe in Chapter 12 that one form of career tangent is the professional who becomes an

---

[7] *Ibid.*, pp. 224–225.

[8] *Ibid.*, pp. 223–224. William J. Goode, "Encroachment, Charlatanism, and the Emerging Profession: Psychology, Sociology, and Medicine," *American Sociological Review*, 25:902–914, December 1960.

administrator of professionals. In the instant case, for some decades there has been a controversy over the control of hospitals. Physicians claim that the purpose of the hospital is to cure and care for persons medically in need, and who could be better than a physician to organize the appropriate services? Lay hospital administrators claim that hospitals are multifunctional organizations that need a variety of services ranging from groundskeeping through feeding and custodial services, to and including medical skills: What could a physician know about that range of services? The balance is gradually shifting to the administrators' position. Again, since the chief and vocal antagonists are recognized professionals, it could surprise no one that the hospital administrators reject the term "lay." The American College of Hospital Administrators has existed since 1933.[9] It holds conventions, and tries to behave in a fashion that would gain public acceptance of specialized competence.

Centrifugal specialization also affects other professional fields. The claims of lawyers to "universal" jurisdiction have been at least as insistent as the claims of physicians, and with even less efficacy—this despite the fact that lawyers are accustomed to pursue what they regard as their authenticated, jurisdictional claims in the courts. The lawyer has long felt threatened by the Certified Public Accountant (Chartered Accountant in Britain), for the lawyer often dealt with tax cases and the complex law of taxation, but did not always command the elementary skills of a bookkeeping system—to say nothing of tax writeoffs, amortization rates, allowable capital accumulations, and other nuances of tax computations. Both banks and accountants offer to manage current assets as well as trust funds, and stock brokerage firms do not mind getting into that competition. Since fees are often set by state law as a percentage of assets, and not in terms of a kind of fee-for-service basis, the lawyer may be willing to waive a couple of professional principles in order to get into the act, but his credentials for doing so are no longer overwhelming. Generally, on the contrary.

---

[9] Corinne Lathrop Gilb, *Hidden Hierarchies: The Professions and Government* (New York: Harper & Row, 1966), pp. 102–103.

In addition to the handling of other people's money, in which the lawyer has a contested jurisdiction, there are serious jurisdictional problems in other areas that are strongly tinged with the law, but for which legal training may be irrelevant or absolutely disfunctional. In the area of marital counseling, for example, the lawyer's training in advocacy of adversaries may be totally disruptive. Similar situations develop in labor arbitration and in a variety of other negotiating circumstances involving diverse interests. The result is that other occupational specialists appear, essentially dealing with legal problems that are unlikely to come to full litigation in courts, and beyond the lawyer's formal training to handle.

The military deals with needed complementary professional skills either by using consultants or by adding them on at higher echelons in "staff" (which means advisory) positions. Engineering has almost never recognized its need for anything beyond subprofessionalization and, possibly, dealing with other qualified specialists.

The clergy, on the other hand, has been threatened from all sides: by social workers, psychiatrists and clinical psychologists, and by all sorts of well-meaning persons ranging from amateur neighbors to quasi-professional workers with youths, drug-addicts and alcoholics, and other odd types.

The principal threat to university professors in their role as innovators of new knowledge has come from research establishments that are governmentally supported, supported by profit-oriented business corporations, or supported from private foundations. In general, the extra-university research organizations have been able to lure and coopt university-based professionals into consulting arrangements, some of which may be very lucrative for the academic professional, and some not. Yet these arrangements have a common characteristic: the problems are being set by the pragmatists, who may regard the university-based experts simply as resources. The complementarity implied by consultations among professional equals is faintly impaired by the nominally subordinate, consultative position in which the technical consultant is placed.

The relations among specialists that we have been discussing have involved the division of labor within broad but recognizable areas of human concern : health, law, technology, military operations, and teaching. We have noted that the complementarity is not always frictionless, as claimed competences overlap; part of the difficulty arises precisely because the territory to be shared is finite.

There are other situations, however, where interdependence is surprising. One example that now has several decades of history is that of the relation between medical service and social work. Although medical students have been admonished to treat the "whole patient," the physician is scarcely qualified in either time or training to investigate the patient's family situation. Thus, particularly in the urban hospital setting, decisions on the release of patients for convalescence at home may be made in part not on strictly medical grounds, but on the report of a social service worker concerning the household and family situation.

Currently both law and medicine—not to mention certain kinds of humanistic scholarship in universities—are flirting somewhat gingerly with a distinctly exotic specialty, which we may call "computerology." Computerized diagnosis following the input of observable symptoms is a distinct possibility; so is computerized case-finding in law, and even computerized decisions based upon the net weight of precedents stored in the machine. As this development progresses, a new variety of specialist will develop: the liaison computer programmer who can link the professional's questions and machine-designer's capacities to produce answers.

It is perhaps improper to say that these complementarities are unintended, for definite decisions are made to establish the linkages. The point is, however, that the original development of the field of knowledge and practice was not to serve as an adjunct to one of the established professions or to claim jurisdiction in its general area. Thus, to take another example, the social sciences were not developed to aid in the practice of medicine, law, or even business administration, yet their relevance to these areas is increasingly recognized; again, new liaison specialists have appeared to bridge the distinct fields of competence.

Totalitarianism and pluralism

It is a matter of regret to many practicing professionals that their jurisdictions are not unchallenged, and that complementary occupations are not firmly under their control—or at least the control of the professional collectivity. Yet many of the occupations that we have been discussing have simply occupied territory actually left vacant by the older and established professions.

Partly because of the greater emphasis on "legal logic" in the highly codified Roman law system, together with a strictly national legal jurisdiction, the various professions in continental Europe have somewhat clearer jurisdictions than they enjoy in the Anglo-American system. The complete bureaucratization of the occupational structure in Communist regimes leads to a kind of syndical organization of complementary specialties.[10]

In sharp contrast, the multiple legal jurisdictions in the United States, and a general legal framework that minimized the tidiness of legislative codes, has permitted great diversity and some inevitable confusion. Any attempt now to organize and clarify both jurisdictions and relative ranks and degrees of control would threaten the independence and perhaps the livelihood of many. Moreover, an attempt to rationalize complementarities by redefining rights and privileges would require various "grandfather clauses" to protect at least the licensed professionals from what would amount to retroactive legislation.

Independently organized occupational groups are scarcely likely to welcome either extinction or subordinate affiliation with another group. Aside from the interests of salaried officers and those who have made the organization a promi-

---

[10] Mark G. Field, *Doctor and Patient in Soviet Russia* (Cambridge: Harvard University Press, 1957), esp. Chap. 4.

nent part of their occupational perspective, what is mostly at stake is the claim to autonomy. And it is autonomy that is correctly perceived as a critical component of the claim to professional standing. True, organizational independence does not guarantee autonomous judgment in actual practice —witness the situation of nurses. But practical autonomy is more likely to be improved through the collective efforts of an independent organization than by one that is already coopted by a "superior" professional group.

Specialization always poses the problem of coordination, and the two principal coordinating mechanisms in the modern world are the market and the bureaucratic organization, public or private. We have noted that the least confusion about the spheres of competence of complementary occupations occurs in such organizations as hospitals and schools and, to a lesser degree, in professional firms and courts. We should add another possible coordinating mechanism, which is inter-occupational negotiation, leading to private treaties.[11]

Reliance on the market as a way of allocating professional and related services has the dual disadvantage that the need for services may not coincide with ability to pay and the prospective client may not be able to judge among competing alternatives. Yet a somewhat open market and somewhat accessible and decentralized legal system has the distinct advantage of permitting new specialties to get established. Nothing in the history of the established professions leads to much optimism that a kind of syndical control of broad territories would result in the regular pursuit of novelty. Indefinite jurisdictions, only customarily or vaguely defined, probably permit a more favorable field for innovation than do attempts to set the outermost bounds of a claimed intellectual territory or of applications to service. The absence of any regulation is likely to result in terrible wrongs perpetrated on the uninitiated. The presence of total regulation may have the same effect, for the initial regulators will not have foreseen, and their followers will not allow, sensible changes of problems and therefore of their solutions.

---

[11] Gilb, work cited in note 9, pp. 162–164.

Any attempt on the part of established professionals to exercise leadership with respect to complementary occupations is likely to be viewed with some suspicion by those occupations threatened by leadership. Some of the taint of self-interest may be alleviated by an educational setting: university refresher courses for public school teachers on new developments in their subject-matter fields (*not* on pedagogy); medical school courses for (and perhaps by) rehabilitation specialists; law school courses for police officers. If complementarity is genuine, then the "leading" professional also needs to be led, by increased knowledge of what other specialists have to contribute to what might be, on occasion, a genuinely common enterprise. The notion that the led may instruct their constituted leaders is not new. It is always a little difficult for the leaders.

PERHAPS because the stereotype of the general medical practitioner serving individual patients has so colored popular
(and some scholarly) thought about the professions, a kind
of individual-to-individual relationship is often taken as the
norm of professional practice. It is accordingly well to re-
mind ourselves that the military serves a strictly collective
client, that only part of the services of clergymen and teachers are for particular individuals, that engineering rose to
a distinctive professional status primarily in the service of
public and corporate clients, and that lawyers have had
public clients for centuries and corporate clients for many
decades.

The probability is high that a collective client will seek to
regularize at least some of its relations with professionals
by placing them on salary rather than a fee-for-service basis
of payment. The rule is by no means invariant, as the great
importance of corporate clients of independent law firms
attests.

The absolute and relative increase of salaried professionals
is explained in part by the increasingly organized character
of the production of goods and services, in part by the multiplication of technical specialties for which there is little
individual demand (or capacity to pay) as compared to the
demand and resources of private and public administrative
organizations.

The professional bureaucratized

By the bureaucratized professional we mean, typically, the
salaried official in a public or private administrative organization who provides expert knowledge and counsel on behalf
of the employing organization. In 1960 over four-fifths
(about 82 per cent) of all male "professional, technical, and

kindred" workers in the United States were salaried.[1] Of
the older and major professions, only lawyers and physicians
were predominantly self-employed.[2] The salaried professional is, technically, in a staff (information-supplying)
position. Although this is the typical situation, we shall see
that there are at least two other situations in which the professional is in some degree "collectivized" even though he
may not be salaried, or may render his services to clients
outside the employing organization.

NEW DEMANDS FOR KNOWLEDGE

In the great world of corporate business and industry, the
demand for professional and quasi-professional services has
expanded rapidly over recent decades. Indeed, the function
of supplying information and advice has expanded disproportionately in comparison with production, sales, or administration. This expansion derives from several sources,
which are worth exploring.

For the most part technical inventions—new products and
new processes—no longer "just happen": they are planned,
organized, and supported by private or public funds. Physical and life scientists and engineers of many varieties in-
habit "basic" research laboratories and Research and
Development organizations in private industry and in governmental research units. These salaried professionals account for a fair proportion of the "knowledge industry."

Although Machlup's numerical data on knowledge-producing
occupations and their rapid growth in the United States do
not provide a neat distinction between salaried persons and
those in private practice, he does exclude some professional
workers from his category on grounds that they are carrying
out skilled activities but their product is not ". . . a message,
a piece of information, anything primarily designed to

---

[1] U.S. Bureau of the Census, *U.S. Census of Population, 1960; Subject
Reports: Occupation by Industry*, Final Report PC(2)–7C (Washington, D.C.: Government Printing Office, 1963), Table 1.

[2] *Idem, Subject Reports: Characteristics of Professional Workers*,
Final Report PC(2)–7E (Washington, D.C.: Government Printing
Office, 1964), Table 4.

create an impression on someone's mind . . ."[3] If we assume, with some hypothetical justification, that salaried professionals are more likely to be dealing with knowledge production in this broad sense than is the private practitioner dealing with clients at first hand, we have a basis for expecting at least a modicum of formal, bureaucratic organization of the productive process.

The organization of such research units has excited a considerable amount of sociological attention.[4] These studies demonstrate the importance—both as expressed values and as conditions of creativity—of relative autonomy and of colleagueship, the orientation to the good opinion of peers. That is, persons with professional levels of training wish to be treated as professionals in the way they conduct their occupational affairs. The realities of administrative supervision, of restrictions on what lines are to be pursued, and perhaps even on the procedures to be followed, impair in some degree professional autonomy.

It is not only in science and technology, narrowly conceived, that contemporary administrative organizations seek information and advice. To the problems of dealing with the nonhuman environment are added the multitude of problems of social relationships. We discussed in Chapter 5 the rise of the rational spirit as a cause of the continuous quest for new knowledge, with consequent specialization in old professional fields and the appearance of new ones. Nowhere is this more evident than in the attempts of bureaucracies to rationalize their decisional processes through improved informational inputs and improved procedures for using informational flows in determining courses of action. Mere experience is no longer an adequate basis for determining

[3] Fritz Machlup, *The Production and Distribution of Knowledge in the United States* (Princeton: Princeton University Press, 1962), esp. pp. 377–388; excerpt from p. 383.

[4] William Kornhauser, *Scientists in Industry: Conflict and Accommodation* (Berkeley: University of California Press, 1962); Simon Marcson, *The Scientist in American Industry: Some Organizational Determinants of Manpower Utilization* (Princeton: Industrial Relations Section, Princeton University, 1960); Warren O. Hagstrom, *The Scientific Community* (New York: Basic Books, Inc., 1965).

courses of action. Specialists are called upon to advise, and in some spheres even to determine policy.

A less-than-exhaustive set of illustrations will serve to underscore the extensity of high-level specialization in the attempts of bureaucracies to deal rationally with their complex social environment. The contemporary corporation must deal with suppliers of labor, that is, prospective and current employees. This is commonly a function under the jurisdiction of specially trained personnel administrators, concerned with "scientific" selection and placement, and with various services in the interests of morale and productivity (or to meet the standards of a competitive market). Attention to employee well-being may be shared with safety engineers, and perhaps with "human engineers" concerned with man-machine relationships.

Functional specialization and diversification within single organizations may lead to the employment of one or another type of communications expert, and possibly systems analysts. The prior training of new managerial recruits is often considered inadequate, and thus teachers for training programs are put on the payroll.

Bureaucracies also have complex external relations. The business corporation must deal with suppliers of raw materials, parts, and equipment (purchasing agents), with the financial community (treasurers or other financial officers), with investors (stockholder relations), with unions (industrial relations), with customers (economists and market analysts), with executive and administrative agencies of government (attorneys), tax collectors (accountants), and, it is thought, with the public at large (public relations).[5]

The specialists dealing with the external relations of administrative organizations are actually dealing with clienteles, but those clienteles are technically the clienteles of the company or agency, not of the specialists. The specialist's role is to *interpret* the employer's policy to the relevant interest group, and to interpret the current state of his

---

[5] Wilbert E. Moore, *The Conduct of the Corporation* (New York: Random House, Inc., 1962), Chaps. XIII and XV.

"constituency" for the decision makers in his employing organization. By so doing, he does in fact become the representative of "his" clients in the councils of the employing organization. He necessarily becomes a "two-faced expert."[6] Knowledgeable and clever members of collective clienteles may discover that they have a friend in court, and go directly to that friend for redress of grievances. It is a curious situation, for the professional's nominal client, the employer, cannot be properly served unless he, the professional, also adequately represents the interest group, or interested client, which can affect the capacity of the collectivity to maintain satisfactory relations with its environment. Yet, as a question of the norms of professional conduct (and we are dealing here with occupations of mostly dubious status, and therefore fairly anxious about it), there is no question that the salaried adviser owes his primary allegiance to his employer. This perception, if put crudely, misses the importance of representation of clienteles in corporate bodies. If the notion is expressed with overly exquisite subtlety, one misses the circumstance that the representative depends upon an accurate assessment of the appropriate clientele and some liaison with its leaders and reliable informants, but his loyalty still rests with his employers and his peers.

The level of professionalism represented by these specialists is variable, and on the whole not of the very highest. By employment customs in the American business and governmental sectors of the labor market, the "relations" specialists are extremely likely to have college degrees, and perhaps to have graduate degrees in business or public administration (with a somewhat variable probability of genuine intellectual content in their training). The people who drift into these specialties are extremely unlikely to have the requisite training in the social sciences, which would be essential for any claim to an intellectual basis for their practice.

There is a terrible truth about the market for special information and skills: If there is an insistent demand, the demand will be supplied, often by charlatans. Public relations,

---

[6] *Ibid.*, Chap. XIII.

opinion research, and other notably "soft" areas in terms of scientific techniques (or the willingness of the client to pay for correct as distinct from convenient findings) abound with off-grade and clearly dishonest practitioners. A shoulder-shrugging cynicism on the part of qualified practitioners does not quite discharge the honorable man's duties. Even if the client is corporate and accordingly invites no sympathy, the honest practitioner still deserves defense against the silly and venal creatures who profess to give advice on matters that could not yield responsible advice on the basis of expert knowledge. On many of the claimed areas of competence, there is no reliable knowledge, and it would be very expensive to produce.

The context of the preceding discussion has been that of the modern, mostly American, corporate community, a community that sees fit, in its combination of rational orientations and acute uncertainty, to get expert advice on everything—even if that advice is off-grade or self-serving. (It is commonly both.) We should attend, momentarily, to another type and context of salaried professional service. This is the situation in which the professional supervises the assembly and publication of information, which may serve the needs of agencies other than the immediate employer, and indeed may be intended primarily for relevant portions of the public. For example, the constitutional basis for the United States decennial census is to determine the apportionment of representatives in Congress. The census has developed a host of users of other information, with a professional staff to assure proper standards of reliability and also to do interpretive analyses. Indeed, virtually every agency of government has a research staff of greater or lesser size and diversity. In some instances, these staffs develop information for strictly internal use—typically the situation in the Department of State and Department of Defense. In other instances the information is made public, and partially identifiable external clients benefit. Clients in fact may influence the kinds of information available, by direct appeal, by serving on advisory committees of data users, or by appeals to congressmen for legislative authorization. The situation is not radically different in other modern and indeed in modernizing societies. One consequence is a considerable concentration of professionals in national capitals.

POOLS OF SPECIALIZED TALENT

The private practitioner is not immune to at least some of the forces that have given rise to the salaried professional in administrative organizations. The growth of specialized knowledge has affected old fields as well as produced new ones.

The typical pattern of group practice in medicine is an assembly of nominally independent practitioners, who, however, tax themselves for the support of nurses, laboratory assistants, receptionists and appointments clerks, business offices, and common facilities. Until relatively recently any form of group practice earned the American Medical Association's favorite opprobrium of "socialized medicine." The advantages to specialists were too great to resist, however. Nevertheless, group practice combined with prepaid medical insurance that would assure a full range of medical care when needed is still opposed by the AMA. (It is, perhaps, not too severe a comment on the American Medical Association that had the question of aspirin for the common cold— for which the intelligent sufferer should carefully avoid professional help—come before the governing board of the association, it would have been rejected as an anti-professional home remedy, and possibly as an unauthorized practice of medicine.) The national health system in England is a major target of criticism by American physicians, and is not universally loved by their English colleagues. It does have public and bipartisan political support. Of course, just as group practice may exist without prepayment or governmental support, so "socialized" medicine does not in effect require that medical specialists be assembled or incompetent.

Law is increasingly practiced in firms, which in legal form are partnerships. The larger and more affluent firms also have salaried assistants, known as associates, who are generally also qualified attorneys. This type of organization allows for surreptitious specialization, as we have already observed. The client is normally not referred; rather, the attorney whom he consults has the opportunity of consulting, in turn, with partners and associates. Incidentally, law partners do not normally take equal shares of fees collected, after payment of expenses. "Shares" are allocated in approximate proportion to the "business" attracted to the firm, *not* in proportion to time spent or the difficulty of cases. This is the reason that successful law firm partners can spend so little time practicing law.

Expert consultants in other fields have also found the advantages of combining. We therefore encounter firms of consulting engineers, and a host of new specialties with highly variable claims to professionalism: management, marketing, opinion surveys, personnel tests, and, perhaps now the fastest-growing, systems analysis.

The advantages of organization are several: the possibility of taking on tasks beyond the specialized competence of single individuals; correlatively, the possibility of offering the prospective client something like "one-stop service," rather than having to do his own assembly of specialized services; the possibility of pooling, and improving, such overhead items as assistants, books, and equipment.

It is true, of course, that some independence is lost through organization, which is the justification for discussing the professional in pooled practice in the same context as the professional employee. The law or engineering partner or the physician in group practice is likely to have to abide by various administrative rules, adopted for the maintenance of orderly routines in the interests of collectivity. The man who is sloppy with his accounts or in the use of communal equipment or facilities will be subject to reprimand—by his peers or even subordinates rather than an administrative superior, but that does not really soften the sanction. Both admission to a group and continuation with it are essentially determined by the collectivity. That collectivity resembles an employer.

Even the presence of subordinates is not an unmixed blessing. The privilege of having assistants is balanced by some responsibility to supervise them, and, above all, keep them constructively busy. The man who likes to keep odd hours or to work furiously but intermittently is likely to find assistants a powerful pressure for regularity.

The similarity of collectivized private practice to the situation of the salaried professional may be seen by attention to the major type of organization that pools the talents of specialists, the university. We have earlier observed that the university is less a community of scholars—since specialization minimizes common intellectual interests—than it is a community having common professional interests: quality of students and their performance, salary levels and teaching "loads," academic freedom, and an increased measure of faculty determination of both educational and administrative policies. At least in the better-known private universities and some public ones, all ranks of professors exercise considerable collective power in policy-making. The full professors in a department resemble the partners in a law firm, determining (in formal terms, recommending) who shall be admitted to the club. And, given the principle of academic freedom, every professor is king in his own domain, both as a teacher and as a scholar.

This is not to say that salaried employment makes no difference. University faculties do not control their own resources. Some are permitted to make some of the organization's administrative rules. Yet salaried administrators are generally not subject to faculty control (other than harassment) but rather to appointment by trustees or regents.

What we are suggesting is that professional autonomy may be somewhat impaired by collective practice or by being fully in an employee status, but need not be eliminated. College and university professors (and some clergymen) perhaps most closely approximate the private practitioner in having a great deal of discretion in their use of time. And whether salaried or supported by fees, the professional is subjected to constraint by subordinates as well as by peers and superiors.

Private practice is not equally appealing to all professionals, even in fields where that is the predominant mode of rendering services. Particularly for the newly-minted professional who has neither an outstanding record nor well-established connections with a well-to-do prospective clientele, a salaried position may be very attractive. Then too, the types of professional practice may differ for the salaried worker. The physician interested in medical research or medical administration or primarily in the teaching of medicine will seek a salaried position, with or without some additional private practice. Somewhat similar options are available to attorneys, who may also seek judgeships or other elective or appointive official positions. Judges are ordinarily not permitted any private clients. Other salaried attorneys may be. Some salaried positions are undoubtedly attractive precisely because the professional does not have to deal with ordinary clients.

Historically, the regularization of position and income affected the military, the soldier of fortune becoming the salaried officer and gentleman; the clergy, the pastor's income being made somewhat independent of the amount in the collection plate, except in extremely poor parishes; and even teaching, the salaried teacher more or less replacing the private tutor or the faculty member in a proprietary school who received a share of students' tuition payments. Salaried professionals generally have a narrower range of income levels than do those in private practice. In totalitarian regimes salaries are simply set by administrative fiat. Even so, it is difficult to avoid some operation of market principles, since a degree of occupational choice is likely to prevail, and rewards must be adequate to attract sufficient talent. In pluralistic systems with a considerable number of competitive employers, salary schedules will reflect supply and demand. Also, in such systems, if private practice is an alternative to salaried positions, the income from the two kinds of employment are likely to have some relationship. Nevertheless, some private practitioners with poor incomes are not likely to be attractive to corporate or other employ-

ers, either, and some with very high incomes are likely to
have priced themselves out of salaried positions. Thus physicians and lawyers show a wider income spread than do college teachers, though the median income of those established
professions with a majority of private practitioners is
higher than that of the high-level teachers and other normally salaried professionals (see Table 11.1).

Peers and superiors

For the executive of an administrative organization, professional employees are bound to be among the most difficult.
From the administrative viewpoint, professionals present
a series of awkward problems. First, the professional almost
certainly knows more than his administrative superior in
the professional's special field of competence. Were this not
true, the employing organization would scarcely need him.
Mere delegation of authority would suffice, not deference to
superior knowledge. Then too, the professional is likely to
belong to an occupational association. He may be the sole
member of the association on the employer's staff, and still

*Table 11.1: Median income of selected occupations, civilian
males, United States, 1959*

OCCUPATION	MEDIAN INCOME
Clergymen	$ 4,020
College presidents, professors, and instructors	7,207
Dentists	11,858
Engineers	8,361
Lawyers and judges	10,587
Physicians and surgeons	14,561
Social, welfare, and recreation workers	4,961
All professional and technical workers	6,619
All employed males	4,621

SOURCE: U.S. Bureau of the Census, *Statistical Abstract of the United
States, 1967* (Washington, D.C.: Government Printing Office, 1967),
Table 330, p. 232.

behave as though he were the bargaining representative for a union, which, in effect, he is. Moreover, the professional employee is doubtfully loyal to his employer, paying primary attention to his professional peers, wherever they are employed. All of these actual or potential violations of standard bureaucratic assumptions being true, it is remarkable that salaried professionals are increasing even more rapidly than the occupational class as a whole. What has happened is that the authority of knowledge (real or claimed without effective challenge) is so great that time-honored principles of administrative organization have had to be adjusted to accommodate the purveyors of expertise.

If the professional employee challenges the principles and practices of hierarchical organizations, in which, conventionally, wisdom gets disseminated and filtered as it emanates from high authorities to be absorbed and applied by lesser creatures, what of the role-relationships from the professional's viewpoint?

MARKET MECHANISMS

Outside of totalitarian regimes, where new assignments of professionals are likely to be made by administrative decision, professionals in the modern world operate in a more or less open market for their services. Our concern here is with the employed professional, and his role situation is slightly tainted in that he has given primary or exclusive claim on his services to his employer, represented by a salaried manager. The professional is subject to administrative rules and such supervision as a layman can exert over a professional. In pluralistic societies, however, the professional is free to change his employers, and this operates as a powerful restraint on the imposition of intolerable conditions on the professional employee. If the salaried professional finds his employment conditions unsatisfactory, he may threaten resignation as a bargaining strategy, or actually resign to accept what he (perhaps naively) hopes will be a better position.

The open-market principle is a safeguard for the professional employee in variable degrees. Generally speaking, professional skills are relatively scarce, and there are competing employers seeking to reallocate the supply. Also, generally speaking, professionals communicate with each other regardless of organizational affiliations, and thus may have a general sense of salary and other relevant standards and also of prospective employment opportunities.

These assumptions are of course not uniformly true. Open markets operate somewhat impersonally, and exhibit little respect for individual career decisions or for the capacity of demand to match supply. All special labor markets are especially "sticky," since necessary training time prohibits quick adaptation to changes in demand. Moreover, many career choices, again precisely because of training time, are essentially irrevocable. Specialization subsequent to formal education introduces a further impediment to easy transfer.

Let us attend to some examples. There are recurrent shortages or overages of engineers in the United States, the demand being mainly affected by the level of federal expenditures for one sort or another of research and development, and the supply being often an off-phase reaction to levels of demand when career choices are made. Within the broad field of engineering, aeronautical specialists tend to be in demand, because of the rapid change of the technology of flight, and so do electronics engineers, because of widespread interest in automatic electronic controls, and because of burgeoning computer technology. Mechanical engineers and so-called industrial engineers (otherwise known as "efficiency experts") face a declining demand, partly because some areas of their competence have been standardized and thus subprofessionalized.

The academic marketplace[7] was active indeed in the 1960's, as a joint product of birth-rate increases after World War II and a rapidly increasing proportion of secondary school graduates seeking higher education. Yet some fields of knowledge ran well ahead of the general trend, and some well behind. A shift in particular clienteles (they even exist in college populations) left classicists, philosophers, and

---

[7] Theodore Caplow and Reece McGee, *The Academic Marketplace* (New York: Basic Books, Inc., 1958).

some traditional language and literature specialists in a market position that was not improving, and often deteriorating. The physical, life, and social sciences were riding high. Bureaucratization actually helped the fields with a deteriorating relative position: The notion of some uniformity in salary schedules for those of formally equal position meant that those representatives of less popular fields who actually found or retained positions benefited from the superior market position of their more glamorous colleagues. We have yet to encounter a recognition of this consequence on the part of the unloved, not to mention any sign of gratitude. Yet it generally remains true in universities that those faculty specialists in the poorest market position are nearer the lower than the upper range of announced salary ranges by rank, move through the academic ranks more slowly, have a lower mobility rate between institutions, are less likely to have research grants or similar sources of assistance and of summer-salary supplements to the American standard ten-month salary, and are more likely than their more marketable colleagues to emphasize teaching rather than research and publication as the highest professional responsibility. Paradoxically, these absolute beneficiaries who are relatively underprivileged are more likely to be engaged in "political" behavior within their employing college or university to enhance their chances for retention or advancement, and more likely to be involved in strictly professional organizations such as the American Association of University Professors, in the hope that an inter-university, collective stance might enhance their poor bargaining position as individuals.

The employed professional who does not automatically assume that his initial employer is the best one, and does not rely solely on mere continuity of satisfactory service as an adequate basis for a career, sets about building a reputation. That reputation *may* be strictly internal to an organization, in which case the requirement is to produce results, not to be a star in excellence of intellectual or technical procedures, for none of his lay colleagues or superiors would understand those. Because he wants to be understood—a trait to which we shall attend presently—and not merely successful in the organizational sense, the professional is likely to try to establish himself with his peers.

For professionals with good mechanisms of communication, the procedures for notoriety are clear: manuscripts are successfully submitted for publication in technical journals; patents, though assigned to the employer, are taken out in the name of the innovator; papers are presented at professional associations. Lawyers are caught in a difficult situation. Most employers of lawyers would prefer to have their legal experts keep them out of litigation, rather than win and enjoy some dubious notoriety on a disputed issue. The attorney can scarcely establish an *external* reputation that way, though he may be able to get the word around among his fellows, if he can speak without an improper revelation of confidences.

The market for professionals is not always fair, as it conspicuously is not in the distribution of goods. Some highly competent people who lack certain elements of personal or professional appeal remain with their original employers, embittered or contented, but never able to use an external offer as a means of bargaining. Others, demonstrably competent but also highly visible, may secure unusually rapid advancement, staying or moving, because "everyone" wants such a talented person. This is in effect very like the bestseller phenomenon in book sales, where the ratio of sales of widely acclaimed books may be very high relative to almost equally good books that do not "take off." Professionals, it turns out, are no more immune to popularity and acclaim than are the supposedly less sophisticated laity. Brilliant careers are therefore somewhat accidental: talent is mixed with widespread, competitive recognition of talent, while other talent is left to find more ordinary career paths.

Mechanisms are not lacking for establishing professional marketplaces. Conferences, conventions, and seminars are increasingly common (the cost commonly borne by the employer in order to encourage the professional enrichment of the salaried expert, but often used by the latter as an informal informational mechanism to find out what is going on in his field, and where). In the academic disciplines chiefly associated with universities, annual meetings of the professional association have long since earned the designation of "slave markets." Most of these associations have formalized the whole procedure of the meeting between employers' representatives and prospective professional employees by easy recourse to state (usually federally financed) representatives of employment commissions in the convention hotel headquarters. This kind of development is almost exclusively true of those professions that are normally salaried, and their professional associations are also likely to run printed "employment bulletins" in associational house organs. It is also true that all such formal and quasi-formal mechanisms of establishing a market transaction generally serve newly-trained professionals, and, among them, those not finishing their work in highly reputed training centers. Thus, in effect, a multitude of markets operate, without real coordination.

Initial allocations of salaried professionals thus contain considerable elements of chance, and subsequent careers depend upon keeping a close liaison with peers, maintaining a marketable position, and thus improving career chances either by being in a favorable bargaining position with administrative superiors—who are by definition laymen—or by actually changing employers in the quest for career advancement.

PROFESSIONAL LOYALTY

The salaried professional clearly owes to his employer the loyal performance of the services for which he is hired. The employer, or his administrative representative, however, is in the position of any other lay client in that he cannot judge the competence of professional procedures but only results—and even there his judgment may be only approximate.

The professional is almost certain also to identify with his peers, wherever they may be employed.[8] Professionals in

---

[8] Alvin W. Gouldner, "Cosmopolitans and Locals: Toward an Analysis of Latent Social Roles—I & II," *Administrative Science Quarterly* 2:281–306, 444–480, December 1957–March 1958; Moore, work cited in note 5, pp. 133–136.

different fields working for the same employer are likely to recognize that they have more in common than any of them has with administrators. But it is the outward orientation that raises the most serious doubts about loyalty. The professional or other staff expert is much more likely to change employers than is the manager.[9] The latter's competence is likely to rest more heavily on experience than on abstract knowledge, and thus be less readily transferable than is the expertise of the staff specialist. The tension between the two types of careers and orientations is scarcely reduced if it turns out that the professional can command a higher salary than can his administrative superior. And if an overly bureaucratic wage and salary administration carefully prevents such inconsistencies between administrative rank and salary, the administrator's sensitivities may be alleviated, and the services of the professional lost to another employer.

Reduction of line-staff conflict by tours of duty in different functions is simply not feasible if the staff positions require genuinely professional levels of training. However, assigning a professional to a special task force with mixed occupational composition, or otherwise getting him identified with distinctive aspects of the employer's operations, may be a way of encouraging organizational loyalty.

Here and there one finds some faint signs of guilt among salaried professionals concerning duties to employers. The reputed reluctance of university professors to stay on their campuses and teach classes has probably been exaggerated, but widespread criticism seems to have caused a bit of soul-searching and actual modification of conduct. Universities have probably had greater difficulties in defining professional loyalties than have other employers, partly because university policy in "name hunting" has encouraged reputation-building at the possible expense of proper attention to other professional duties. Wherever professional talents are in

---

[9] Dwaine Marvick, *Career Perspectives in a Bureaucratic Setting*, University of Michigan, Michigan Governmental Studies No. 27 (Ann Arbor: University of Michigan Press, 1954), Chap. IV.

short supply, however, and therefore highly marketable, the autonomy of the professional is asserted and not always balanced by loyal responsibility.

Role conflict

Sorting out and properly allocating an employed professional's proper responsibilities is not always a matter of simple morality. The employer may, for example, expect behavior on the part of the employee that is contrary to professional norms. If the proposed violation is flagrant— for example, an attempt to bribe potential witnesses in a liability suit—the professional may simply refuse, on the grounds that he risks disqualification by his peers and would then be no longer valuable to the employer—not to mention his own risk of loss of professional recognition and livelihood.

Other situations may be more subtle. Professionals tend to be garrulous with their own kind, and particularly want to share the excitement of novelty. If the employed professional is in fact engaged in research on a new process not yet patented, he is under a dual restraint: not to reveal a trade secret, and perhaps not even to reveal that he is interested in the subject.

Perhaps the outstanding situations that are productive of role conflicts are those in which the employer and the client are not the same. This is clearly the situation in schools and colleges, in social welfare agencies, and in public-supported hospitals and clinics serving indigent patients. And it is in such situations that salaried employees may seek to take collective action against employers to improve salaries or work assignments, but at the expense of clients.

A teacher's union strikes in behalf of a better economic bargain with the school board, but the clients (students) miss classes. A union of social workers strikes, also as a bargaining maneuver, against private or public welfare agencies, but the welfare clients do not get their accustomed checks or personal counseling. Similar strikes have been called by hospital attendants. . . . All of these cases present clear-cut ambivalence in loyalties, yet all present certain additional ambiguities. Public school teachers, welfare workers (doubtfully fully qualified social workers), and hospital attendants would scarcely meet all of the rigorous tests of full professional position. The recognized professional is more likely to leave his position, perhaps unjustly and, on his part, cravenly, than to withdraw his service or to appear as a mere trade unionist.[10]

The ambivalence noted in the cited passage is more or less recognized within some occupational groups. The National Educational Association includes both teachers and school administrators (and some college professors of education) in its membership, and until recently opposed strikes as unprofessional.[11] The American Federation of Teachers, on the other hand, argues that professionalism does not bar collective action.[12] During the summer of 1967 part of the salaried welfare workers in New York City participated in a "work-in." They reported to their offices, but not for regular duty. Those who continued to report for ordinary, and probably extraordinary, duty regarded their colleagues' conduct as unprofessional.[13] The New York chapter of the American Federation of Teachers has conducted numerous, technically illegal, strikes—three during the autumn of 1968. That unhappy spectacle, and we shall not here review the racial overtones of the several issues, had one clear message of current interest: Public school teachers have no clear claim to professional status, and their collective actions confirm what our scale of professionalism would have told us: they are not very professional.

The client who is not the employer has very little control over professional services. We have no authentic information about the reaction of school children to the closing of schools by teachers' strikes. It requires no special feat of the

[10] Wilbert E. Moore, "Economic and Professional Institutions," in Neil J. Smelser (ed.), *Sociology: An Introduction* (New York: John Wiley & Sons, Inc., 1967), pp. 325–326.

[11] Corinne Lathrop Gilb, *Hidden Hierarchies: The Professions and Government* (New York: Harper & Row, 1966), p. 167.

[12] *Ibid.*

[13] *The New York Times*, June 20, 1967, pp. 1, 78; June 21, 1967, pp. 1, 35; June 22, 1967, pp. 1, 42.

imagination to distinguish between those few children who feel thereby deprived and the many who think that a (perhaps vacuous) vacation has been extended. Since schools are, somewhat more than incidentally, baby-sitting agencies, one can also imagine the reaction of parents.

For people "on welfare," failure of normal services can be somewhat more immediately serious, as are strikes by workers in hospitals and clinics.

All of these occupations, and others, have serious claim to importance and legitimacy within the value system of the society in which they operate, and none can lay serious claim to full professional rank. One cannot say that the case is automatically closed—since physicians' strikes against prepaid or state-determined fees are not unknown—but only that the failure of the normal presumption of primary service to the client puts in doubt the claims of professionalism by the groups involved. This harsh, objective judgment applies to any occupational group claiming professional status and failing to give service to clients a very high priority. If physicians or lawyers or professors choose to withhold services from needful clients in order to enforce economic demands, one is permitted to compare that behavior and their status with, say, plumbers and electricians; the result of such comparison would not be clearly favorable to the superior position of those who claim professional status.

Chapter twelve: Mixed roles: the professional as administrator

ONE of the anomalies of the modern professions is that some portion of those who go through the lengthy and difficult training and other qualifications for professional status end up in other occupational positions. Some of these simply discover, tardily, that they have chosen an unsuitable career, either because they do not do well or because they dislike it, or both. Others may have taken professional training as a steppingstone to a different career. A fair proportion of trained engineers end up as business managers, and some intended it that way. Some lawyers follow a comparable path, but perhaps more intend law as a way into politics or public administration.

These career dropouts or career deviants are not our primary present concern. Rather, our focus is on the career path that leads a professional to be an administrator of professionals. Again, we are not concerned with so-called professional administrators, meaning by that those who have been educated precisely for administrative positions, for we have expressed serious reservations about their claim to fully professional status. No, our "subject population" is restricted to that portion of persons who have achieved professional qualifications but then become supervisors or coordinators of their nominal peers. Since the "supervision of peers" seems to be a contradiction in terms, we already have a hint of the somewhat complex position of the administrative professional.

The discontinuous career

It is perhaps not totally accurate to refer to the qualified professional who "goes over into administration" as having a discontinuous career. The phrase "diagonal shift," which we use below, is perhaps more precise. Yet the curious circumstances of the positions we wish to examine do involve an anomaly : It is ordinarily necessary to have established professional qualifications to be eligible as an administrative professional, and yet there is nothing in the *formal* training of the professional to qualify him for administrative duties. To become a chief of medical services (and sometimes to become a general administrator) in a hospital, to become the dean of an arts college or professional school in a university, or to become the administrator of a Research and Development unit in industry, it is first necessary to have been a physician, a professor, or a laboratory scientist. This means that whatever administrative skills or talents the professional has acquired or displayed, leading to his selection for such a position, must have been acquired informally, perhaps by performing lesser administrative tasks as a by-product of more strictly professional duties.

THE ORGANIZATION OF KNOWLEDGE AND SERVICES

A principal reason for the assembly of professionals in organizations, as we noted in the preceding chapter, is that formal organization is one effective way of coordinating the activities of specialists. The problems presented by individual or corporate clients may be beyond the competence of any one specialist and thus require either sequential approximations by a succession of experts, or coordinated attention from the outset. The hospitalized patient may require the attention of several medical specialists, as well as those of various complementary occupations such as nurses, pharmacists, and laboratory technicians. Assuring that those services will be available and actually rendered is an administrative task. Similarly, the college student studies some combination of subjects with a variety of professors as well as, possibly, teaching and laboratory assistants. Staffing positions, scheduling courses, and supervising various curriculum alternatives are administrative tasks.

Scientific and technological developments especially exemplify coordinated specialization, for team research becomes essential for some large and complex problems. Even if a number of fully qualified professionals are not involved, a "project principal" may have several assistants. (Supervising assistants is of course one source of experience in administration.)

In addition to the advantages of specialization and problems of coordination, the organization of professionals derives from the importance of capital and equipment. Again, the hospital, the university, and the industrial research laboratory exemplify the importance of shared resources in professional activities. Assembling those resources and determining their allocation or use are scarcely professional tasks, though users will be extremely interested parties in the necessary administrative decisions.

We may distinguish several organizational types involving professionals and their administrators. The closest approximation to the "pure" administrative organization involves an hierarchical ordering of responsibility: a general superintendent, divisional chiefs, and rank-and-file professional employees. Some large engineering units in industry approximate this organization. Its principal difficulty is that the subordinate professional may be assigned his task rather than having some choice, and may have little discretion in its performance. In other words professional autonomy is seriously impaired, and the administrative professional may have to contend with poor morale, high turnover, and minimal performance.[1]

Close supervision of professional subordinates is likely to be tolerated only if they are clearly less professionally qualified, such as youngsters still undergoing training or specialists who cannot in fact claim full professional status. Thus many organizations employing professionals attempt to select on grounds of both competence and commitment, and then afford considerable autonomy in actual work.[2] This results in a relatively "flat" administrative structure, and a

---

[1] William Kornhauser, *Scientists in Industry: Conflict and Accommodation* (Berkeley: University of California Press, 1962), pp. 56–73. Simon Marcson, *The Scientist in American Industry: Some Organizational Determinants of Manpower Utilization* (Princeton: Industrial Relations Section, Princeton University Press, 1960), pp. 147–148. Warren O. Hagstrom, *The Scientific Community* (New York: Basic Books, Inc., 1965), Chap. 3.

[2] Hagstrom, work cited in note 1, pp. 216–222.

style of administration that emphasizes facilitating rather than supervising. (The realities of budgetary controls, decisions on continuing service or promotion, and similar elements of administrative authority still exist, of course.)

In some situations of organized professional activities, policy decisions are made by senior professionals, such as partners in a law firm, and their implementation essentially decentralized to individual members, with perhaps a lay business manager. This builds the administrative role into the professional position rather than separating it. It is a limiting case, and no longer interests us.

Leadership in professional teams may be based on rank and seniority, specialized competence for the particular task, or mere rotation. When none of these principles seems adequate, an official administrator with enduring responsibilities is likely to be chosen or appointed, and we then have the phenomenon of the administrative professional.

TYPES OF ADMINISTRATIVE FUNCTIONS

The principal task of the professional as administrator is that of "expert" coordination. That is, the administrator must be attuned to the range of organizational functions, the uses of various specialties, and how to get them put together for varying particular tasks. Since schools, hospitals, research laboratories, and consulting firms include subprofessionals and various supporting occupations, the administrator's task is not limited to the coordination of the work of his professional colleagues. The organization's store of human resources must be allocated, along with tools, equipment, supplies, and, not least, space. Since all of these resources have some scarcity value, they are likely to be viewed by organizational participants symbolically in addition to merely utilitarian criteria. However dedicated the professional employed in organizations, he is not immune to competitive status striving: an extra assistant, a private secretary, a more spacious office. The administrative professional must somehow balance utility against considerations of rank or prestige, and find a tolerable, if not wholly satisfactory, solution.

The principal administrator of an organization more or less dominated by professionals is in a representative position for the organization as well as its internal coordinator. The "relations" functions include dealing with sources of funds; attending to external control centers such as trustees or higher corporate management; and often placating clients and other interested laymen. If professionals have mixed feelings about administrative supervision by one of their own kind (or at least one formerly so), they are more likely to approve of representation by persons so qualified than by anyone viewed as an outsider. Despite the tensions between practicing professionals and their administrators, the manager who has some basis for understanding the problems intrinsic to the professional role and its organizational setting is likely to elicit somewhat greater confidence than would be accorded a mere layman.

THE DIAGONAL SHIFT

The professional employed by a corporation or public agency in a staff position or in a research unit renders expert services or provides expert information and advice relevant to decisions. In such situations neither the decision to employ professionals nor the determination of what relevance their services or advice may have for general policies is made by professionals themselves. Thus in all organizational settings except partnerships there are ceilings on professional careers. If the professional seeks administrative rather than merely advisory authority, he must give up some or all of his strictly professional performance and make the diagonal shift to an administrative position.

The curious feature of this situation is that the administrator *must have been* a professional, but his administrative authority is clouded by two circumstances: (1) by the act of becoming an administrator he has in some degree "gone over to the enemy," since he now represents organizational interests, which are possibly adverse to strictly professional interests; (2) given the rapid changes in knowledge and state of the arts, the administrative professional loses his professional authentication. Since administrators are commonly (although not always) paid more than their expert subordinates, two more doubts arise, and they are not mutually exclusive. Did the administrator sell out? Or did he choose an alternative path to success that he was not going to achieve on strictly professional grounds?[3]

We encounter, then, another anomaly. If professional standing is necessary to become an administrator of professionals, does the administrator's competence erode proportionally to his loss of professional currency? Or, if he is in fact an effective administrator, does this not derive from acquiring a broader perspective along with mastery of the arts of administration? And that question in turn suggests another: Is it possible that selecting administrators of professionals from their ranks is conventional rather than essential? University presidents do not uniformly come from academic positions, although deans commonly do. Hospital administrators often are not trained as physicians, although many are. Research laboratory directors seem uniformly to have had research experience themselves.

Note that the exceptions to the professional prelude to administration of professionals are in situations that normally have several administrative echelons. It appears therefore uniformly true that the immediate administrative superiors of professional groups come from the ranks of those or similar groups. The rational bases for this uniformity of practice would appear to be that professional orientations and perspectives are difficult to understand or acquire from the outside, and that such orientations and perspectives are relatively durable despite particular changes in knowledge and technique.

Role relations and conflicts

The newly appointed administrative professional is essentially entering a new occupation, not simply a new position.[4]

---

[3] Wilbert E. Moore, "Economic and Professional Institutions," in Neil J. Smelser (ed.), *Sociology: An Introduction* (New York: John Wiley & Sons, Inc., 1967), pp. 326–327.

[4] Logan Wilson, "Disjunctive Processes in an Academic Milieu," in Edward A. Tiryakian (ed.), *Sociological Theory, Values, and Sociocultural Change: Essays in Honor of Pitirim A. Sorokin* (New York: Free Press, 1963), p. 291.

This occupation will have its own set of job specifications, together with the unwritten precedents and expectations that he, wittingly or not, inherits from his predecessors. And in the performance of his duties he finds himself in a new set of role relations with his former peers and with his new administrative colleagues and superiors.

TYPES OF ROLE RELATIONS

To a remarkable degree the administrative professional, like any bureaucratic manager, lives in a world of paper. Reports reach him both from within the organization and from outside interests. Files must be kept, correspondence answered, and memoranda initialed and passed along. The problem is not simply that of coping passively, for the administrator also initiates additional flows of paper: reminders to subordinates that reports are due, memoranda announcing new policy interpretations (ranging from the important to the trivial), letters seeking information about possible candidates for appointment, and, possibly, writing a speech for *his* superior. In fact, many administrators complain that the routine duties of office are so absorbing of time and energy that little time is left for the plans and developments that seemed the principal attraction of the positions when they accepted appointment.

The administrative professional still owes duties to his former colleagues, such as respect for competence, but to these are added others: protection from improper outside interference, representing his sphere of responsibility, both by translating or interpreting activities to the laity and by protecting or enlarging the flow of resources in competition with other claims. Particularly in the administration of research units the manager has the difficult task of affording his subordinates the necessary time and resources to carry through large tasks, and at the same time generate a sufficient flow of results to justify the activity as a whole.

Whether the administrative professional owes his subordinates the formal duty of consultation is highly variable in different settings. On questions of technical information the administrator must ask the man who knows. On matters of general policy, practice varies from the nearly collegial to the almost autocratic. Wilson notes that in university administration this problem is one of the touchiest in relations with the faculty.[5] He goes on to observe that in getting decisions made and action started, the usual equation of "democratic" with "good" is subject to challenge.[6] For similar reasons, a popular administrator is not necessarily an efficient one, even from the point of view of the collective interests of the unit he is supervising.

ROLE CONFLICTS

Autonomy ranks high in the value schemes of professionals, and not simply in our scale of professionalism. Thus *any* administrative coordination may be resented in some degree, despite the rational recognition of its necessity. Nonetheless, physicians go through long schooling in subordination to professional superiors, and deference patterns, with or without administrative subordination, seem to persist where physicians work together. Other professionals stay in a formally subordinate position in training for a somewhat shorter period, and may not in fact be "under orders" in any professional relation outside the classroom. The college teacher or industrial scientist, professionally authenticated by his Doctor of Philosophy degree, is likely to regard himself as any man's equal, if not his superior. It is accordingly not surprising that college and research administration display the greatest degree of ambivalence and conflict in the administrator's relations with his professional subordinates.

Since the administrative professional comes from the professional community, some conflict within his own orientations may occur: between professional loyalty and administrative requirements (the latter, perhaps, not of his own choice). The longer the administrative professional stays in office, the higher the likelihood that he will see things from an administrative point of view and pay attention to all of the considerations and interests represented by his administrative superiors and various constituencies. With

---

[5] *Ibid.*, p. 292.
[6] *Ibid.*, p. 293.

reference to professional subordinates, he may thus act increasingly like a foreman and decreasingly like a shop steward.

There are, of course, restraints on this evolutionary trend. The realities of competitive labor markets mean that dissatisfied professionals will simply leave. Moreover, professionals are a notably articulate variety of human beings, not to mention their special sensitivity to restraints on autonomy. Thus the administrator's internal constituency is unlikely to permit a purely arbitrary autocracy, although a benevolent despotism may prove tolerable.

The administrative professional runs some other risks in dealing with his subordinates. If he has been chosen from their number, he is certain not to have been equally friendly with all of his colleagues. In his administrative position he runs the risk of being accused both of favoritism for his friends and unwarranted prejudice against his "enemies." And whether he comes from the local organization or another, he is identified with a specialty. His behavior must be very circumspect if he is to avoid the suspicion that his former colleagues in the narrow sense will be favored over others. Indeed, he may be so circumspect that he leans over backward, and first loses the support precisely of those peers. And, to add further subtlety to the relationships, for the professional to have one of his *own* kind in an administrative position may turn out to be a disadvantage, for the administrative professional may persist in claims to competence in his specialty and thus supersede the technical judgment of his former colleague—a practice he would not consider with regard to other areas.

Universities exemplify all of these ambiguities and somehow survive. Perhaps some small part of the tension is creative. As research units in industrial firms and independent research organizations grow and multiply, the demand for administrative professionals will increase at least proportionately. Many of these organizations attempt to emulate the university atmosphere, partly because they are in competition for some of the same talent. Whether an adequate supply of administratively ambitious and competent professionals to fill the coordinating positions will be found is difficult to predict, but the odds are not favorable. Among other attributes, the prospective administrators will need to be brave, for professionals are among the least manageable of workers.

IN an open-market system, anyone could offer any service and advertise it widely, attribute to himself any qualifications that someone (or a sufficient number of gullible clients) would find credible, award himself certificates and degrees, and charge any unsuspecting client what the market would bear. That set of conditions was almost a description of the situation in some countries until very recently, and of the United States well into the nineteenth century.

Licensing, we have seen, has represented an attempt on the part of more or less honorable practitioners of a specialty fraught with critical personal interest to avoid competition with charlatans, under the dual guise of protecting trained and honorable men and of protecting an unknowing clientele from fraud and deceit. It would be needlessly cynical to suppose that licensing to secure a protected monopoly was the sole purpose of professional claims to exclusive jurisdiction, and needlessly naive to suppose that the potential client's possible interests are exclusive or even paramount.

In his relations with the public, then, the professional seeks: *authentication* as a genuine and competent specialist; status and *prestige* in the invidious sense of enjoying a relatively high rank in the neighborhood and community; and a distinctive *style of life* which will both reflect and symbolize his claims to distinction.

Authentication

For the professional, the public is somewhat more than a residual category—what is left over after one has dealt with clients, peers, and, possibly, employers. The established professional is subject to threat by new claimants on his jurisdiction. The aspiring professional seeks both formal and informal recognition that he has indeed achieved a privileged and protected position.

Yet, under the somewhat dubious assumption of a reasonable world, why should the professional be concerned with the public? Aside from questions of somewhat informal prestige, to which we shall return, the reasonable view of the public would attend to questions of a *potential* clientele—directly or by reputation and lay referral—to potential challengers of jurisdiction, and to questions of political support for official public recognition.

By organization, by licensing, and by public relations campaigns ranging from the subdued to the blatant, various occupational groups seek to identify "warranted practitioners," and to encourage potential clients to think that self-help or assistance from less-than-adequate advisers or performers of services represents an inadequate substitute for authentic services. *Individual* advertising of either claims to competence or schedules of fees is strongly discouraged in American professional services, and, with variable exceptions, within countries sharing the historic traditions of the "free" or "learned" or "liberal" professions. Yet *collective* advertising, either to encourage patronage of the "genuine" practitioner or to promote what is claimed to be the common interests of practitioners, is apparently under no such restraint. The American Medical Association, for example, has pursued the short-run economic interests of what appears to be the politically effective component of its constituency, with ample recourse to misrepresentation, to such a degree that its political efficacy is at least temporarily in the shadows.[1] The public, and its political representatives, turn out to be gullible, but not endlessly so. Physicians have probably not suffered seriously, as individuals, from the gross political ineptitude of the AMA, but the organized medical fraternity has been revealed as distinctly anti-professional in its normative orientations to the public. This will accentuate the ambivalence with which the layman views the professional, a consideration to which we return a few paragraphs hence.

---

[1] Richard Harris, *A Sacred Trust* (New York: New American Library, 1966).

Licensing authenticates a professional (and a variety of other occupations) if indeed a client seeks him out. How is authentication otherwise established? To hang out a shingle is proper in private practice in Western Europe and the overseas heirs of European traditions. Such chaste street-side notices (perhaps supplemented by "professional cards" in local newspapers and by listing in telephone directories) are likely to carry only initials relating to earned degrees (for example, M.D.—practice restricted to ophthalmology) or to an honorable occupational title—Attorney at Law, Consulting Engineer.

In some instances the professional or quasi-professional displays his *personal* authentication—Doctor of Medicine, Osteopathy, Optometry, Podiatry; of Philosophy, Veterinary Surgery, Theology, Education, Jurisprudence or Juridical Sciences, and, possibly, Pharmacology. If the profession has not yet tried to have its practitioners addressed as "doctor" by the laity—the physicians tried to preempt the title and fortunately failed—certain initials still belong to the authenticated individual. The Certified Public Accountant—C.P.A.—has made his way in a business civilization with a sophisticated and appropriately suspicious set of tax collectors, and we have earlier noted the appearance of specialists seeking recognition as upgraded life insurance salesmen—Certified Life Underwriters—and as sophisticated stock salesmen—Certified Securities Analysts. Until relatively recent times in the United States the graduate of a college-level engineering curriculum seeking further, and more advanced, professional authentication, attempted to qualify (usually in a university setting, but not always) for the "professional" degree in his specialty: C.E. for the civil engineer, M.E. for mechanical engineering, E.E. for electrical engineering, Chem.E. for chemical engineering. These degrees or diplomas still persist widely. They now suffer competition from degrees that confer the Ph.D. in "engineering sciences."

One should distinguish fairly sharply among: (a) those authenticating symbols that refer to the individual's qualifications, and carry with them a special term of address to anyone at all knowledgeable in the system; (b) those authenticating symbols that are attributable to the individual, with suitable displays on his stationery or business card, but do not command anything more than the usual forms of courteous address; (c) those authenticating symbols that would not command any title of special respect, in personal or written communication, but would still identify the bearer of such an authentication as a recognized (and possibly licensed) practitioner of his specialty.

In the Western world, which shares medieval origins (with the penchant for ranks and titles) and also the rationalizing experience of the scientific and industrial revolutions, one encounters what seems to be a bizarre array of terms of office and terms of address. The Germans are notable for stringing together titles (as well as compound words) and then proceeding in a tedious and mouth-filling fashion to use the whole occupational identification as a term of address: *"Herr Beamten Geheimrat* Doctor Professor Schüller . . ."* The French are long on protocol and signs of deference, but not usually long in terms of oral or written address. The Italians have similar customs, but, in the university system, find it not enough to have a chief academic officer called a "Rector," but require a personage who is *Il Magnifico Rettore,* and, in oral address, is called, precisely, *"Magnifico Rettore."* Sadly, no one laughs.

The Latin American taste for titles is notorious. Aside from the courteous, and now informal, conferring of the title "Don" followed by the first name—a kind of knighthood without ceremony—the universities and various licensing powers confer titles upon successful candidates for specialized and honorific occupations. A lawyer, for example, is by occupational title an *abogado*—an advocate—but because of a publicly conferred license is commonly called by the title *"Licenciado,"* and addressed as *Señor Licenciado* Rodriguez. But other titles and terms of address also abound: an engineer is *Señor Ingeniero* Gonzalez or, in less formal discourse, *Ingeniero* Gonzalez. Architects and other technical occupations enjoy similar deference. It is interesting to note that physicians no more monopolize the title of Doctor in Latin

America than in the United States. Similarly, it is interesting to note that titles are subject to expansion and amendment. The professional title of an economist in Latin America is *Ingeniero Comercial,* a job description that fits some
economists there and elsewhere, and not others.

With or without university-based degrees and initials mean-
ingful to initiates, professional and quasi-professional organizations seek to organize and assert their claims. The
authenticating initials may not be peculiar to the individual,
but represent his admission to a presumably select group.
The English specialize in this sort of relatively harmless
nonsense, some of the initialed honors being relatively broad
in recognition, and some more specific: O.B.E. (Order of
the British Empire), K.C.B. (Knight Commander of the
Bath), F.R.S. (Fellow of the Royal Society—probably a
scientist), Q.C. (Queen's Counselor, almost certainly a lawyer—probably a barrister or possibly a solicitor).

The British and the Americans not only put the abbrevi-
ations for earned academic degrees after their names—
though to a hearteningly lesser degree in the United States,
since Americans are educated in far higher degree than
Britons—but also emulate the practice of identification with
selective and therefore exclusive groups. Membership in the
American Institute of Architects yields the initials A.I.A.
after a (prominently displayed) sign on a residential (or,
more probably, business) structure in process. The American Institute of Interior Designers (A.I.I.D.) gives interior
decorators some claim to be superior to furniture salesmen
—though, truthfully, not much, except that they are conspicuously more expensive.

It is the uniform custom of American physicians to place
the initials M.D. after their names, not only in technical
articles (where it is unnecessary) but also in quasi-personal
correspondence (where it is offensive to good manners).

Some professional and semi-professional occupational types
affect authenticating garb in dealing with the laity. The
Roman Catholic church has long understood (and exaggerated) the importance of setting apart the clergy by distinctly

authenticating dress. Many Anglican and Episcopalian clergy have emulated this practice, and other Protestant denominations in the United States have encouraged, or not positively discouraged, this symbol of professional position in the community. A distinctive uniform, whether of the military or the clergy—both occupations often lacking, historically, a really distinctive claim to genuine eminence—has served to alert the layman that he was dealing with a special person. Uniforms, indeed, abound in all post-industrial societies, and their purpose is not always to command deference, though, occasionally, reluctant respect.

Time was that the distinctive occupations—the older professions and the various ranks of the military—could be readily identified by articles of dress and adornment. Military organizations adhere to this practice, because of a rigid chain of command that has only a slight resemblance to scales of competence, and because of a high turnover in inhabitants that need to know whom to salute and whom to order about.

Why should specialized occupations seek special uniforms and insignia? Such behavior is not absolutely universal among the older established professions, has a dubious relation to the newer established professions, and gives rise to rather silly behavior among the aspiring occupational groups. One is tempted into the interesting hypothesis that those occupations that seek recognition by very conspicuous symbols, such as uniforms of office, are those to whom such recognition might not be otherwise accorded, because their services are not highly welcome—for example, the clergy and military; because their professional status is not fully authenticated—for example, the white laboratory coat commonly affected by optometrists fitting glasses or clinical psychologists in a university or hospital setting where such garb is affected by experimentalists; or, most mischievously of all, because the mass media have led people to believe that working professionals of high prestige, such as physicians and laboratory scientists, normally wear clothing that is only occasionally functional in the proper conduct of their proper affairs. White coats do not a professional make.

As usual, matters are not quite that simple. The habits—we

are using this term with deliberate ambiguity—of some
traditional professions do indeed bespeak tradition rather
than current, rational function. (We shall not debate, but
rather concede, the functions of traditionalism.) It is true
that in British judicial practice the opposing attorneys and
the presiding judge wear wigs. Well, it's a cool climate and
a social order that reveres tradition, not always wisely. Yet
one should note the robed judge or Supreme Court justice
in the United States, and the rather severe—but not uni-
formed—attire in American legal practice. In situations of
specific and explicit client relations, physicians are more
than likely to wear white coats and surgeons green ones.
And in the never-never homeland of the professions, in the
universities, American practice requires informal dress in
the classroom for the professor, British practice is somewhat ambiguous, and continental European (and therefore
Latin American and African) practice requires rather formal "business" attire or even the medieval gowns of the
status-conscious faculty. And, lest tradition die too hard, the
nominally rational academic community is replete with opportunities or command performances for the display of
vivid, esoteric, and uncomfortable academic regalia for the
possible entertainment of the concerned laity and certainly
for the mildly hostile reactions of the professionals to one
another.

We are thus in no position to take a purely cynical view of
symbols of authentication. Once symbols are established,
we should evince no surprise that other, aspiring groups
should seek to emulate them—witness the colorful glories
of the academic gowns and hoods of those bearing off-grade
degrees in silly subjects from unlikely colleges or universities. The easy notion that conspicuous symbols of authenticity are especially sought, or practiced, by those anxious
to establish their claims has a certain ring of truth, but turns
out to be true only around the edges. The "old pros" do in
fact practice such authenticating behavior. It remains true
that one can certainly win money on even bets that among
those "categorically blessed"—that is, recognized by their
professonal position—those most attentive to the symbols

of authentication before the laity are the less well regarded by their peers, and, quite probably, are less professionally successful.

Professional prestige

The professions differ in many ways among themselves in criteria of training and organization of practice. These differences are greatly compounded if we compare the precise situations of professionals in various countries. Yet despite these differences, and despite some related difficulties in establishing exactly comparable boundaries for the occupational category, that labor-doing category universally commands the highest prestige ranking among occupations. The repeated studies of occupational prestige in the United States[2] and such international comparisons as similar observations permit[3] confirm this uniformity.

The prestige that professionals command is of course somewhat differentiated by specific professions. This is partly a result of genuine differences in social valuation, partly the result of problems of precise identification on the part of laymen. Thus physicians are uniformly ranked higher than attorneys,[4] no doubt because physicians are commonly seen as "doing good," whereas attorneys encounter some distrust as perhaps being more clever than honorable. The identification problem especially affects technical specialties not widely known to the laity, and this gives added reason for efforts spent at authentication not simply for the occupation as such but also for membership in the honorable company of professionals. The layman ranks a scientist above any

[2] Robert W. Hodge, Paul M. Siegel, and Peter H. Rossi, "Occupational Prestige in the United States, 1925–1963," *American Journal of Sociology*, 70:286–302, November 1964.

[3] Alex Inkeles and Peter H. Rossi, "National Comparisons of Occupational Prestige," *American Journal of Sociology*, 61:329–339, January 1956; Robert W. Hodge, Donald J. Treiman, and Peter H. Rossi, "A Comparative Study of Occupational Prestige," in Reinhard Bendix and Seymour Martin Lipset (eds.), *Class, Status, and Power*, 2nd ed. (New York: Free Press, 1966), pp. 309–321.

[4] See references cited in notes 2 and 3.

given variety of professional named in the scale,[5] thus generalizing the stereotype of the brilliant creator without requiring specific knowledge of particular fields of competence.

Professional prestige is reflected in rewards. Some of those rewards are financial. Money, however, is useful for whatever goods and services are available in the market; an interest in money is thus not to be confused with mere materialism.[6] The style of life maintained by a professional and his family is supposed to display at least moderate comfort and unquestionable respectability. True to the traditions of membership in a "high calling," at least part of the family's discretionary expenditures is supposed to reflect "cultural" interests—books and magazines; patronage of symphonies, the theater, and the arts; travel; charitable contributions; and support for education. And since these expectations are widely shared by the laity, there is no danger of the professional forgetting his proper position and behavior. He is high on the list for support or sponsorship of every allegedly worthy cause.

THE SOURCES OF PRESTIGE

The professional's claim to high prestige rests essentially upon his differential command over scarce values, a universal characteristic of systems of social inequality.[7] The professional's particular sector of scarce values is that of "useful knowledge," as distinct, say, from command over economic capital or political coordination. Such wealth or political influence as the professional may have is in principle a derivative of his primary function, and is in no way supposed to interfere with or supersede that function.

Knowledge, of course, is a source of power in the broad sense. Yet it is the utility of knowledge to those who do not share it that makes those unfortunates dependent on those who have it. In the "pure" case the only sanctions available

---

[5] See Hodge and others, article cited in note 2.

[6] Wilbert E. Moore, *The Conduct of the Corporation* (New York: Random House, Inc., 1962), pp. 152–155.

[7] Kingsley Davis and Wilbert E. Moore, "Some Principles of Stratification," *American Sociological Review*, 10:242–249, April 1945.

to professionals in dealing with clients is the clients' self-interest in accepting information and following advice. There are, it is true, situations of mixed role relationships in which professional advice is buttressed by formal administrative authority, but that should not dissuade us from identifying the analytic essentials of professional prestige.

The possession of advanced and esoteric knowledge represents a kind of property right, which carries with it responsibilities for honorable use. The exceptional educational levels attained by professionals may be a partially independent source of high social rank, but if the education is not put to professional purposes, such nonperformance is likely to be negatively valued. The proprietorship of knowledge may legally include the right of nonuse, but there is a considerable ethical basis for both the resentment of waste and for the feeling that the withholding of scarce and valuable services represents a failure in personal responsibility. Even in traditional societies where the selection to professional positions is largely ascriptive, exceptional effort on the part of the practitioner is still implied, and in return for the prestigious position a kind of *noblesse oblige* in performance is expected.

One component of the prestige accorded the possessors of scarce but useful knowledge is precisely its unintelligibility to the layman. We have already noted that the technical language of the professionals serves to identify peers and simultaneously to exclude the laity. Some technical language is genuine in the sense of precision and in the sense that there are no common synonyms in the ordinary vocabulary; other uses represent "jargon" in the exact sense that esoteric terms are substituted for ordinary ones without any increment in information. Along with the use of unintelligible language, at least some professionals also are able to "work wonders." It is not alone the clergyman who deals with "awful mysteries." The physician uses mysterious procedures in diagnosis and therapy; the engineer uses elaborate formulas in calculating stresses; the chemist or physicist performs experiments of mystifying complexity; attorneys produce writs, briefs, and bases of appeal from a trial court judgment that could not be derived from "common sense"; and social scientists, perhaps most vulnerable to the charge of deliberate mystification, are at considerable pains to demonstrate the sophistication of their results and not simply of their procedures.

It is thus not surprising that professional performance that promotes prestige with the laity may include some components of magic—the claim to produce observable results by nonobservable means. At least the status of the performance may take on the qualities of magic so far as the understanding of the laity is concerned. Both because the professional has a real interest in protecting his claim to differential knowledge and because he may not be immune to the temptation to foster the layman's credulity, he may feel no need or responsibility for explaining the exact components and procedures, except to his peers.

AMBIVALENCE IN PROFESSIONAL PRESTIGE

We should not assume that the prestige accorded to professionals is always and unstintingly elicited. It is certainly true that no system of social inequality is so perfectly institutionalized and incorporated into the attitudes of participants that the lower orders always give willing deferences to the higher ones.[8] Naturally not.

Aside from complaints about incompetence of professionals, of various degrees of legitimacy, there are problems of distrust of professional integrity, status, and authority in particular relationships with clients. Merton and Barber identify four "structural sources of ambivalence" in the layman's view of the professional[9]: (1) the norm of continuity, which, contrary to free-market principles, constrains the client to persist with his orginal choice among possible professionals, even though dissatisfied; (2) the attribute of

[8] Wilbert E. Moore, "But Some Are More Equal Than Others," *American Sociological Review*, 28:13–18, February 1963.

[9] Robert K. Merton and Elinor Barber, "Sociological Ambivalence" in Edward A. Tiryakian (ed.), *Sociological Theory, Values and Sociocultural Change: Essays in Honor of Pitirim A. Sorokin* (New York: Free Press, 1963), pp. 110–115.

authority, which requires of the client to reveal his "private" life to his professional adviser, and, if conscientious, to take advice that he will not uniformly enjoy; (3) the perception that professionals are dependent on clients, and "live off" them, even though clients also depend upon professionals; and (4) the circumstance that professionals, with their peers, tend to judge performance in terms of technical proficiency, but the client has an inveterate concern with results.

The context of the Merton-Barber discussion is that of the private practitioner and his clients, and in that context might well have been part of our analysis in Chapter 5. We have deferred the subject to this point, for we think its implications are of primary significance to the broader aspects of social status in the general community and society. For example, the deference that a professional commands from a client, who, after all, needs him, is perhaps simultaneously less assured and less salient on the part of the neighbor or chance acquaintance. The high prestige of physicians is envied, emulated, and derogated by others high on the scale of professionalism. It is not unquestioned by others who scarcely view their own social position as that of tribal natives.

The rising proportion of college graduates in the population has had mixed consequences for professional prestige. (The proportion of persons with four years or more of college education among Americans aged twenty-five and older was 4.6 per cent in 1940, and 7.7 per cent in 1960.[10]) The professionals with substantial claim to their designation are numbered among that population, and have much in common with it. Additionally, the demand for professional services is disproportionately high among that segment of the population, for a variety of not very subtle reasons beyond ability to pay or the occupancy of positions where the services are provided pretty much as a matter of course. Yet that "highly participating" portion of the total potential clientele is precisely the part of the laity that will include professionals of

[10] U.S. Bureau of the Census, *Statistical Abstract of the United States, 1967* (Washington, D.C.: Government Printing Office, 1967), Table 155, p. 114.

possibly lower public prestige; representatives of occupations that are only pretentious in their claims to professionalism; those whose college education is in some degree fraudulent in that the course followed was considerably less demanding than their athletic-field performance; those who have gone into business (more commonly as private bureaucrats than as truly independent enterprisers) who resent and eschew the intellectualism that is part of the professional's social garb.

We have previously observed (Chapter 11) that there are intrinsic tensions in the relations between the professional employed to render authoritative information and advice to administrators and the administrators who are supposed to combine possibly discordant professional inputs for a rather concrete output (which, again, is judged by results and not by virtuosity). What we are arguing here is that there is no ideal—to say nothing of practical—resolution of this problem. It is intrinsic to specialization and interdependence.

A very substantial time has elapsed, now, since Durkheim conclusively argued through the point that mere interdependence—such as that exemplified in pure market transactions—does not assure "solidarity" in a social system.[11] Such solidarity requires, most crucially, subscription to common and overriding values, and thus also to the roles that will govern exchanges. And it is the differing weights assigned to values, as well as the outright disagreement on some of them, that together account for the clear facts that the prestige of the professionals in contemporary society is high but qualified, uniform but reluctant, admiring but envious, and even deferential but angry. How could it be otherwise?

---

[11] Emile Durkheim, *The Division of Labor in Society*, trans. by George Simpson (New York: Free Press, 1960).

Part three: Social responsibilities

THE prized position of the professional in contemporary societies and the relative autonomy he is accorded in the performance of his work rest upon the assumption that he possesses such criteria of professionalism as commitment to a calling, a high level of education in abstruse mysteries, and a service orientation toward the use of his knowledge and skills. Although we argued in Chapter 1 for a scale of professionalism, and have not abandoned our conviction that it is a useful approach, we are in this concluding chapter particularly concerned with an important component of that scale : education or knowledge. Questions regarding the uses and abuses of differential knowledge afford us an opportunity for a selective summary of the special norms governing professional role relationships.

Knowledge is power

Some people know things and how to do things that others do not. If the knowledge that is not universally shared is at all useful or important for those who do not have it, then those who do possess it have a relative advantage. These simple truisms provide one basis for social inequality in general and for the position of professionals in particular. We have observed that some degree of specialization based on differential knowledge or skills is virtually universal in human societies ; it is an outstanding feature of post-industrial societies.

If we were to assume that there were no genetic differences in ability, no sources of difference in aspiration, and perfect equality of opportunity for educational achievement, one might imagine an adult population with a virtually uniform educational level. If all possessed the same knowledge, education would be irrelevant to the assignment of occupational positions, which might be filled by lot and rotation. Amateurism would reign supreme. Note, however, that without specialization of knowledge, the society so organized would sacrifice this principal source of accumulation in the collective store of knowledge. The scientific, technological, and informational basis for the production of goods and services would be relatively low and subject to little growth. Were specialization permitted, the society's productive system would either have to reflect somehow the uniformly high but specialized competence of the population, or a way still be found to secure the performance of the more elementary tasks—perhaps by assigning them to the young as a duty prior to admission to more advanced positions. Note that among specialists of presumably equal levels of qualification, each would be superordinate in his sphere of competence and subordinate in all others, leading to a symmetrical distribution of that aspect of power deriving from differential knowledge.

It is because the assumptions underlying this small utopian fantasy are unrealistic that we are permitted to examine the way unequal command over knowledge is displayed and controlled.

THE UTILITY DIFFERENTIAL

Clearly there is wide variability in the utility of knowledge, ranging from the strictly cultural to the highly utilitarian. The distinction, however, is not easy to establish. The mature scholar expanding knowledge about classical civilizations is commonly paid a salary to convey this information to students, and may earn additional income from speeches and publications. His students may be moderately interested in truth and somewhat more interested in receiving degrees and in gaining employment where a liberal education is valued, perhaps for reasons poorly perceived.

What we have called the utility differential in knowledge has three important components: (1) the importance of the goals pursued, (2) the necessity of advanced knowledge in their achievement, and (3) the number of people affected. Thus we have seen that matters of health and life affect everyone, have a high salience, and nearly universally are thought to require skills not commonly shared. Priests or similar religious functionaries have a comparable position in some situations, but not in all. The priest's superior competence in achieving supernatural goals rests upon faith rather than demonstration. Moreover, this faith may not be uniformly accorded. In many Protestant denominations and sects the clergyman is either regarded as superfluous or as not critically essential to individual salvation. In the contemporary world teaching is supported by the common confidence in the utility of education; however, the utility ranking of the occupation as a whole is tainted by some doubts as to the level of knowledge necessary to perform satisfactorily.

Although law is ubiquitous, legal services are not. Most citizens go through their lives without brushes with the criminal law sufficiently serious to require legal counsel. Much of the remainder of legal practice involves money and property, and many people have too little of either to need, or perceive that they need, expert assistance. Yet particularly for the businessman and corporate manager, and for others of sufficient wealth to be accumulating an estate, the lawyer's services have a high salience.

The differential utility of knowledge should not be confused with mere public recognition. Specialization makes difficult public understanding of what the nature of the service is, even among those professions with wide public contact. The effect of others is indirect, even if widespread. The military has a variable visibility and contact with the public, but presumably serves collective goals of some importance. Scientists and technologists constantly alter the productive system and the character of the environment, sometimes spectacularly but in the main quietly.

We should also note that not all segments of the public are equally significant in judging the utility of knowledge. For that portion of the legal fraternity that serves individual and corporate wealth, the utility of the services is highly regarded and highly rewarded. For those who do the "dirty work" of the law for less affluent clients, the services may be less highly regarded and, in fact, performed with less skill and less ethically.[1] Similarly, social workers may be serving the announced social welfare goals of the society, but their disadvantaged clients may be in no position to judge or influence their performance.

Indeed, one of the serious problems in judging the utility of knowledge and assuring that the development and use of knowledge be socially responsible is precisely the incompetence of the lay public. This incompetence is not just in information and techniques, which is intrinsic to differentiation, but even in determining which kinds of knowledge should be promoted and put to application. To an increasing degree such decisions are made by *fiduciaries* for the public or some segment of it: by political representatives, by governmental agencies, by custodians of public or private Research and Development funds, by corporate managers. One would have to be an extreme optimist in order to believe that the outcome of these decisions is uniformly consistent with the public interest.

THE ABUSES OF POWER

The power deriving from differential knowledge, like any other form of power, is subject to abuse. The most clear-cut situation in professional practice is in relationships with clients, which we have discussed in Chapter 5. An essential feature of this relationship is that the professional is in a position of trust, and therefore in a situation in which he may violate the confidence that the client has placed in his competence or integrity.

The ways in which a professional or pseudo-professional may take advantage of misplaced confidence are legion. We have added "pseudo-professional" because one of the oldest and most persistent forms of irresponsibility is that of charlatanism or quackery. Bogus knowledge is claimed, bogus remedies purveyed, bogus solutions to problems proffered. Because of the salience of health concerns, it is not surprising that charlatanism has long been a problem in medicine, and, as fake cancer cures testify, not exclusively

---

[1] See Jerome E. Carlin, *Lawyers' Ethics: A Survey of the New York City Bar* (New York: Russell Sage Foundation, 1966).

a characteristic of our less sophisticated past. It is possible that at least in modern American society the highest incidence of charlatanism is among those who claim to be expert in various kinds of applied social science: complex organization, attitude measurement, market research.

Compared with something firm like machine design or cost accounting, these more subjective or ephemeral features of human conduct constitute mysteries, and mysteries that threaten.

When there is a great demand for answers, answers are likely to be provided even if they are not right. . . . In many instances the basic theory and fundamental research that would form the groundwork for practical application simply do not exist. This situation invites the appearance of the charlatan who persuasively offers the simplifying "gimmick," the dandy little problem solver for all occasions. . . .

Where basic knowledge is uncertain the honest man can only say so, but the dishonest one is the more attractive because he exudes confidence and promises answers.[2]

The fully competent and authenticated professional may still abuse his power. For those dealing with clients in more or less intimate circumstances, sexual exploitation is a possibility. An attorney may be in a position to exercise undue influence on a wealthy client in the preparation of wills and trusts, with a sharp eye to his own financial interests. All professionals who receive privileged communications from clients may violate that confidence in ways ranging from the more or less inadvertent indulgence in gossip to outright blackmail. If teachers have any influence at all on character formation of the young—the evidence is mixed[3]—they are in a position to do (perhaps unwitting) damage as well as good.

There are also a variety of ways of taking money or advancing reputations under false pretenses. The attorney

---

[2] Wilbert E. Moore, *The Conduct of the Corporation* (New York: Random House, Inc., 1962), pp. 245–246.

[3] See John C. Glidewell and others, "Socialization and Social Structure in the Classroom," in Lois Wladis Hoffman and Martin L. Hoffman (eds.), *Review of Child Development Research* (New York: Russell Sage Foundation, 1966), Vol. II, pp. 221–256.

does so when he simultaneously represents adverse interests. The college professor may exploit his employers by treating his position mainly as a front and form of authentication for his much more lucrative consulting practice, or, for that matter, by using his position to advance causes having little or nothing to do with the subject he is supposed to be teaching. (Academic freedom, like any other, is subject to abuse.) And professors, as well as other scientists and scholars, may be in a position to exploit subordinates by taking credit for work actually done by others.

The professional outside his field of competence is a layman. True, the level of his preprofessional education and a kind of rational, problem-solving orientation to the world of experience may give him some advantages over the stupid and the poorly educated. It does not do so with others with comparable, but different, claims to expertise. Yet the practice of authority is habit-forming, and the professional is especially prone to indulge his habitual tone of authoritative pronouncement on any occasion that gives him opportunity. There was a time when professionals—and particularly physicians, lawyers, and clergymen—almost solely represented civilization and were therefore "thought leaders" in the communities in which they practiced their exotic arts. In an urbanized, fairly highly educated and highly specialized community typical of contemporary post-industrial societies, there are many claims to eminence, though all of them may be irrelevant to the issue at hand. The clergy has responded to the loss of influence fairly sedately, with an exception here and there. The physicians, being conspicuously incompetent outside their own area of claimed jurisdiction, have commonly failed to perceive the radical change in their environmental situation. Through their professed representatives in the United States, the American Medical Association, they have taken ridiculous stances on matters of public policy and on their own claims to professional respectability.[4] It is not difficult to understand the sources of the physicians' sense of relative deprivation, for they have

---

[4] See Richard Harris, *A Sacred Trust* (New York: New American Library, 1966).

lost their position of almost unchallenged priority in the hierarchy of pompous incompetence on public issues. Many physicians are angry because laymen (which includes a rising proportion of other professionals) do not take them seriously. Given their rather uneducated views on anything beyond their specialty, who could?

RESTRAINTS ON POWER

We have noted in the course of the argument in this book, and particularly in Chapter 6, that the professional's claim to legitimate power, and particularly his claim to the autonomous and therefore discretionary exercise of authority based on competence, have rested on a combination of normative principles and practices that are virtually unique to that segment of the labor force.

The man of knowledge will accord competent judgment only to his peers. Through attempts to control education for and access to the occupation, and organizational mechanisms to maintain professional discipline and competence, high-level occupational specialties seek self-regulation. By now a reiteration of the ambiguous rationale for protection of professionals against competitors and of prospective clients against incompetents would be tiresome. The fact remains that men of knowledge, including professional practitioners, try to keep control of both competence and conduct among those to whom, exclusively, they accord the competence to do so: their own kind.

This orientation raises some interesting, if somewhat esoteric, problems. Given a high degree of specialization, and the emphasis on creative originality in at least some fields, the originator of new knowledge or skills may have literally *no* peers. Those most closely approximating the technical criteria for professional judgment still rely on a mixture of technical competence and the layman's approach: Does it work?

Individual and collective self-restraint on the part of possessors of useful knowledge may be buttressed by a measure of client control. Clients may withdraw their trust, and potential clients may withhold it—both on grounds that may be irrational. For serious failures or misdeeds, the victim may have grounds for civil suit or a criminal charge. Even captive clienteles such as relief recipients or students may have sources of appeal if they have grievances. Licensing and certification offer some protection, although examinations and inspection of credentials remain firmly in control of members of the favored occupation. Yet legislators are at least nominally representative of the general public, and by recognizing some claims to competence and excluding others may be right part of the time.

Wider responsibilities[5]

The privileged position of the professional is ideally balanced by a set of duties and restraints in dealings with clients, peers, administrators, and the general public. The rules of competence and honorable conduct are likely to be specific to particular professional fields, although we have emphasized the commonalities in types of role relationships among the various specialties. These common responsibilities are particularly evident with respect to some general obligations of the man of knowledge. These may be summarized as a set of admonitions.

(1) *Preserve and enhance the "image."* The professional's conduct is taken by his peers and by at least part of the laity as reflecting not only his personal standards, or lack of them, but also those of his profession. All professionals suffer a sense of shame or chagrin at the conspicuous misconduct of a fellow; conscientious ones feel aggrieved at misconduct that does not become public. It is arguable, though not clearly demonstrated by existing evidence, that the sense of anxiety and collective guilt will be even greater among members of occupational groups striving for assured public acceptance as fully qualified professionals. Physicians, attorneys, and clergymen can, as a collectivity and individually, probably withstand publicly revealed misdeeds by

---

[5] For a more general discussion, see Florian Znaniecki, *The Social Role of the Man of Knowledge* (New York: Columbia University Press, 1960).

nominal members of the fraternity more readily than could, say, accountants or insurance adjusters or computer programmers. Silly and stupid historians and professors of English abound in universities, and negative reviews of their published pieces only moderately threaten the fraternity. Social scientists (and especially those not dealing with the neoscholastic or other inpenetrable mysteries performed by economists) have been admitted into the select circles of the American academy only recently, and, it is feared, tentatively. Silly attacks lead to silly defenses of silly positions.

(2) *Respect the public interest.* The professional owes the public not only his own honorable conduct, but also, in return for the claim of collective self-control, responsibility for the discipline of wayward brethren. At times this may be at variance with the first admonition, for there is strong temptation to cover up incompetence or dereliction in order to preserve the collective reputation of the profession.

Another problem worthy of note is the availability of professional services. Availability may be a question of simple adequacy of supply, with professional groups attempting to restrict access in order to maintain high earnings. It may also be a question of financial availability. Despite protestations of service to the community, some professional groups in private practice have operated on the market principle of ability to pay. As adequate medical care, and perhaps even legal counsel, comes to be regarded as a common right of citizenship rather than a differential privilege of the middle and upper income groups, attention to the public interest may be enforced by the public when not voluntarily accorded by the professionals.

(3) *Respect the duty to learn.* The rapid growth of technical knowledge in virtually all fields of specialization implies that the acquisition of competence is no longer properly terminated with the competion of formal education and acceptance into the fraternity. Just as tenure for university professors is an important element in the quest for professional autonomy but may be a shield for growing incompetence with age, so licensing may be a grant of perpetual immunity from having to keep abreast of developments in the field.

Although licensing may restrict charlatanism and reduce the uncertainty of the laity in the identification of authoritative knowledge, it may also be a source of stultification, preventing new approaches with possibly superior claims. Among the older licensed professions in the United States, law has been much less open to change than has medicine. We think that the primary explanation for this difference is the much stronger emphasis on new research in medicine, an emphasis conspicuously lacking in most law schools. Indeed, one of the strongest arguments for close university affiliation for professional schools goes beyond the maintenance of somewhat comparable standards in training neophytes; it is the university's mission as a producer of new knowledge that both challenges the aging professional and provides means for keeping pace.

(4) *Respect the duty to perform.* The investment that an individual or his family makes in acquiring an advanced state of knowledge in a specialty may be substantial. It is almost certainly exceeded by the contributions of others: donors of the past who have established endowments, current donors, and taxpayers, national or state. All of these contributors in combination cannot guarantee successful completion of the full, formal course of studies necessary to be an acknowledged professional. Once that acknowledgment is received, however, the trained person is expected to use that training in appropriate ways. In the eyes of both the qualified members of the honorable fraternity and of interested laymen, nonuse of knowledge is misuse.

The duty to perform is supposed to spring from the professional's commitment to a calling, with the associated norm of service. We have seen that calculation enters into this orientation, however. In the absence of a salary or fee, the professional may actually withhold his service, or perform perfunctorily. Yet commercialism, though rampant in current professional practice, is not universal. Unrewarded performance does occur. It is perhaps, mischievously, more often in the service to a professional association or to a colleague than on behalf of the laity.

The man of knowledge is in great demand for all sorts of

causes claimed to be worthy. Whether as a calculating ca-reer-builder, a conscientious professional, or merely as a good citizen, the professional is likely to succumb to some of these temptations. One can hope, but not confidently expect, that he knows the difference between an expert judgment and one that simply reflects the views of an educated layman, that he can properly distinguish between actions that further only professional interests and those that further the public interest, and even that he can distinguish between notoriety and esteem.

The self-confidence that professionals display is either a pretense or a mark of self-delusion. If a little learning is a dangerous thing, then most of us must live with virtually ubiquitous danger, for most of us do have a little, and the great learning of men of knowledge is still paltry, and still dangerous.

Selected bibliography

The sources listed here are by no means exhaustive of a truly tremendous literature; the references are particularly incomplete with respect to studies or reviews of particular occupations.

For references having a special relevance to particular chapters of this book, the appropriate chapter numbers are added to the reference in brackets. Annotations are limited to those references with titles that are not self-explanatory.

ABEL-SMITH, B. *A History of the Nursing Profession.* London: William Heinemann, Ltd., 1960. [2]

ADAMS, S. N. "Origins of American Occupational Elites," *American Journal of Sociology*, 62:360–368, January 1957. [4]

ADDISON, WILLIAM. *The English Country Parson.* London: J. M. Dent and Sons, 1947.

AKERS, RONALD L. "The Professional Association and the Legal Regulation of Practice," *Law and Society Review*, 3:463–482, May 1968. [6, 7]

ALBEE, GEORGE W., AND MARGUERITE DICKEY. "Manpower Trends in Three Mental Health Professions," *American Psychologist*, 12:57–70, February 1957.

ALLEN, PHILIP J. "Childhood Backgrounds of Success in a Profession," *American Sociological Review*, 20:186–190, April 1955. [4]

ALLEN, RAYMOND B. *Medical Education and the Changing Order.* New York: The Commonwealth Fund, 1946. [4]

ALLEN, RUSSELL. "The Professional in Unions and his Educational Preparation," *Industrial and Labor Relations Review*, 16:16–29, October 1962. [4]

ALLSOP, PETER. *The Legal Profession.* London: Sweet and Maxwell, Ltd., 1960.

ALONSO, WILLIAM. "Cities and City Planners," *Daedalus*, 92:824–839, Fall 1963. Reprinted in Kenneth S. Lynn (ed.), *The Professions in America.* Boston: Houghton Mifflin Company, 1965. [7]

AMERICAN ASSOCIATION OF UNIVERSITY PROFESSORS. "Academic Freedom and Tenure: Statements of Principles," *American Association of University Professors Bulletin*, 38:116–122, Spring 1952. [11]

AMERICAN BAR ASSOCIATION, SPECIAL COMMITTEE ON EVALUATION OF PROFESSIONAL STANDARDS. *Code of Professional Responsibility.* Preliminary Draft, September 15, 1969. [6]

AMERICAN BAR FOUNDATION. *The Legal Profession in the United States.* Chicago: American Bar Foundation, 1965.

AMERICAN INSTITUTE OF ARCHITECTS. *Architect's Handbook of Professional Practice.* Washington, D.C.: The American Institute of Architects, 1963. [6]

———. *Architecture: A Profession and a Career.* Washington, D.C.: The American Institute of Architects, 1945.

AMERICAN OCCUPATIONAL THERAPY ASSOCIATION. *Occupational Therapy—1952.* New York: The Association, 1952.

AMERICAN OPTOMETRIC ASSOCIATION, COMMITTEE ON ETHICS AND ECONOMICS. *Professional Standards for the Practicing Optometrist.* Minneapolis, Minn.: The Association, 1953. [6]

AMERICAN PSYCHOLOGICAL ASSOCIATION, EDUCATION AND TRAINING BOARD. "Anticipations of Developments During the Next Decade Which Will Influence Psychology," *American Psychologist,* 11: 686–688, 1956. [4]

———. "Ethical Standards of Psychologists," *American Psychologist,* 18:56–60, January 1963. [6]

——— AND CONFERENCE OF STATE PSYCHOLOGICAL ASSOCIATIONS. "Joint Report of the A.P.A. and C.S.P.A. Committees on Legislation," *American Psychologist,* 10:727–756, February 1955. [6]

AMERICAN SOCIOLOGICAL SOCIETY, COMMITTEE ON THE IMPLICATIONS OF CERTIFICATION LEGISLATION. "Legal Certification of Psychology as Viewed by Sociologists," *American Sociological Review,* 23:301, June 1958. [6]

AMERICAN STATISTICAL ASSOCIATION. *Careers in Statistics.* Washington, D.C.: American Statistical Association, 1962.

AMERICAN VETERINARY MEDICAL ASSOCIATION, COMMITTEE ON ETHICS. "Principles of Veterinary Medical Ethics," *American Veterinary Medical Association Directory.* Chicago: American Veterinary Medical Association, 1956. [6]

ARMOR, DAVID J. *The American School Counselor: A Case Study in the Sociology of Professions.* New York: Russell Sage Foundation, 1969. [1, 3]

ARGYRIS, CHRIS. "Explorations in Consulting-Client Relationships," *Human Organization,* 20:121–133, Fall 1961. [5]

ARMSTRONG, W. EARL. "The Teaching Profession: Retrospect and

Prospect," in Lindley J. Stiles (ed.), *The Teacher's Role in American Society*. New York: Harper & Row, Publishers, 1957, pp. 276–291.

ARMSTRONG, W. EARL, AND OTHERS. *The College and Teacher Education*. Washington, D.C.: American Council on Education, 1944. [4]

ARMYTAGE, WALTER H. G. *Civic Universities: Aspects of a British Tradition*. London: Ernest Benn, 1955. [2]

————. *A Social History of Engineering*. New York: Pitman Publishing Corporation, 1961. [2]

ASHER, CASH. *Your Life Is in Their Hands*. Washington, D.C.: The Dalaun Press, 1938. Chiropractic versus medicine. [7]

ASSOCIATION OF AMERICAN LAW SCHOOLS. *Selected Readings on the Legal Profession*. St. Paul, Minn.: West Publishing Company, 1962.

ASSOCIATION OF AMERICAN MEDICAL COLLEGES. *Admission Requirements of American Medical Colleges, Including Canada*. Evanston, Ill.: Association of American Medical Colleges, 1962. [4]

————. *Medical School Admission Requirements 1964–1965: U.S.A. and Canada*. Evanston, Ill.: Association of American Medical Colleges, 1964. [4]

————. COMMITTEE ON THE RESURVEY OF PROFESSIONAL EDUCATION IN THE LIBERAL ARTS COLLEGE. *Preparation for Medical Education: A Restudy*. New York: McGraw-Hill, Inc., 1961. [4]

ASTIN, ALEXANDER. "The Functional Autonomy of Psychotherapy," *American Psychologist*, 16:75–78, February 1961. [7]

ATKINSON, DONALD T. *Magic, Myth and Medicine*. New York: The World Publishing Company, 1956. [2]

ATWATER, REGINALD M. "Public Health Becomes a Profession," in James Stevens Simmons (ed.), *Public Health in the World Today*. Cambridge, Mass.: Harvard University Press, 1949, pp. 34–42. [3]

AUSUBEL, DAVID P. "Relationships Between Psychology and Psychiatry: The Hidden Issues," *American Psychologist*, 11:99–105, February 1956. [7]

BABCHUK, NICHOLAS, AND ALAN P. BATES. "Professor or Producer: The Two Faces of Academic Man, *Social Forces*, 40:341–348, May 1962. [7]

BACK, KURT W., AND OTHERS. "Public Health as a Career of Medicine: Secondary Choice Within a Profession," *American Sociological Review*, 23:533–541, October 1958. [7]

BAKKE, E. WIGHT, AND OTHERS. *Labor Mobility and Economic Opportunity.* New York and Boston: John Wiley & Sons, Inc., and Technology Press of M.I.T., 1954. [4]

BANERJEE, DEBARBRATA, AND RAMNATH KUNDU. "A Study of the College Teachers' Attitude Towards Their Authorities," *Indian Journal of Social Work,* 21:81–85, June 1960. [11]

BARBEAU, MARIUS. "Medicine-Men on the North Pacific Coast," *National Museum of Canada Bulletin,* 152, Anthropological Series No. 42, 1958. [2]

BARBER, BERNARD. *Drugs and Society.* New York: Russell Sage Foundation, 1967, Chap. 4, "Professional Specialists: Their Functions and Problems," pp. 76–114. Discusses medical doctors and pharmacists. [10]

————. "Is American Business Becoming Professionalized?" in Edward A. Tiryakian (ed.), *Sociological Theory, Values, and Socio-Cultural Change.* New York: Free Press, 1965, pp. 121–145. [1, 3]

————. "Some Problems in the Sociology of the Professions," *Daedalus,* 92:669–688, Fall 1963. Reprinted in Kenneth S. Lynn (ed.), *The Professions in America.* Boston: Houghton Mifflin Company, 1965. [1]

BARZUN, JACQUES. *Teacher in America.* Boston: Little, Brown and Company, 1945.

BEATMAN, FRANCES L. "How do Professional Workers Become Professional?" *Social Casework,* 37:383–388, October 1956. [4]

BECKER, HOWARD S. "Against the Code of Ethics," *American Sociological Review,* 29:409–410, June 1964. [6]

————. "The Career of the Chicago Public School Teacher," *American Journal of Sociology,* 57:470–477, March 1952. [4]

————. "The Nature of a Profession," in *Education for the Professions,* Sixty-first Yearbook of the National Society for the Study of Education, Part II. Chicago: University of Chicago Press for the Society, 1962, pp. 27–46. [1]

BECKER, HOWARD S., AND JAMES W. CARPER. "The Development of Identification With an Occupation," *American Journal of Sociology,* 61:289–298, January 1956. [4]

————. "The Elements of Identification with an Occupation," *American Sociological Review,* 21:341–348, June 1956. [4]

BECKER, HOWARD S., AND BLANCHE GEER. "The Fate of Idealism in Medical School," in E. Gartly Jaco (ed.), *Patients, Physicians and Illness.* New York: Free Press, 1958, pp. 300–307. [4]

———. "Medical Education," in Howard E. Freeman and others (eds.), *Handbook of Medical Sociology*. Englewood Cliffs, N.J.: Prentice-Hall, Inc., 1963, pp. 169–184. [4]

———. "Student Culture in Medical School," *Harvard Educational Review*, 38:70–80, Winter 1958. [4]

BECKER, HOWARD S., BLANCHE GEER, EVERETT C. HUGHES, AND ANSELM M. STRAUSS. *Boys in White: Student Culture in Medical School*. Chicago: University of Chicago Press, 1961. [4]

BECKER, HOWARD S., AND ANSELM L. STRAUSS. "Careers, Personality, and Adult Socialization," *American Journal of Sociology*, 62:252–263, November 1956. [4]

BEER, JOHN J., AND W. DAVID LEWIS. "Aspects of the Professionalization of Science," *Daedalus*, 92:764–784, Fall 1963. Reprinted in Kenneth S. Lynn (ed.), *The Professions in America*. Boston: Houghton Mifflin Company, 1965. [3]

BEN-DAVID, JOSEPH. "The Professional Role of the Physician in Bureaucratized Medicine: A Study in Role Conflict," *Human Relations*, 11:255–274, 1958. [11]

———. "Professions in the Class System of Present-Day Societies," *Current Sociology*, 12:247–330, 1963–64. (Vol. 12, No. 3 entire.) [13]

———. "The Rise of a Salaried Professional Class in Israel," in *Transactions of the Third World Congress of Sociology*. London: International Sociological Association, 1956, Vol. III, pp. 302–310. [2]

———. "Roles and Innovations in Medicine," *American Journal of Sociology*, 65:557–568, May 1960. [2]

———. "Scientific Endeavor in Israel and the United States," *The American Behavioral Scientist*, 6:12–16, December 1962. [2]

———. "Scientific Productivity and Academic Organization in Nineteenth Century Medicine," *American Sociological Review*, 25:828–843, December 1960. [2]

BEN-DAVID, JOSEPH, AND AWRAHAM ZLOCZOWER. "Idea of the University and the Academic Market Place," *European Journal of Sociology*, 2:303–314, 1961. [2]

BENDIX, REINHARD. *Higher Civil Servants in American Society*. Boulder: University of Colorado Press, 1949.

BENNIS, WARREN G. "The Effect on Academic Goods of Their Market," *American Journal of Sociology*, 62:28–33, July 1956. [5]

———. "The Social Scientist as a Research Entrepreneur: A Case Study," *Social Problems*, 3:44–49, July 1955. [12]

BENNIS, WARREN G., AND OTHERS. "Reference Groups and Loyalties in the Out-Patient Department," *Administrative Science Quarterly*, 2:481–500, March 1958. [11]

BEREDAY, GEORGE Z., AND JOSEPH A. LAUWERYS (eds.). *The Education and Training of Teachers*. London: Evans Brothers, 1963. [4]

——. *The Yearbook of Education, 1959: Higher Education*. London: Evans Brothers, 1959. [4]

BERELSON, BERNARD. *Graduate Education in the United States*. New York: McGraw-Hill, Inc., 1960. [4]

BERENDA, CARLTON W. "Is Clinical Psychology a Science?" *American Psychologist*, 12:725–729, December 1957. [7]

BERGER, PETER L. (ed.). *The Human Shape of Work: Studies in the Sociology of Occupations*. New York: The Macmillan Company, 1964. [4]

BERKOWITZ, DAVID S. *Inequality of Opportunity in Higher Education: A Study of Minority Groups and Related Barriers to College Admission*. Albany, N.Y.: State of New York, 1948.

BERLE, A. A., JR. "Legal Profession and Legal Education: Modern Legal Profession," in *Encyclopedia of the Social Sciences*. New York: The Macmillan Company, 1933, Vol. 9, pp. 340–345.

BERMAN, HAROLD J. *On the Teaching of Law in the Liberal Arts Curriculum*. Brooklyn, N.Y.: The Foundation Press, 1956. [4]

BERNAYS, EDWARD L. "American Public Relations: A Short History," *Gazette*, 2:1–9, No. 2, 1956.

BERRIAN, ALBERT H. "The Formation of Professional and Technical Cadres in the Congo," *Journal of Human Relations*, 11:31–42, Autumn 1962. [3]

BIDWELL, CHARLES E. "The Administrative Role and Satisfaction in Teaching," *Journal of Educational Sociology*, 1:41–47, September 1955. [12]

BLANK, DAVID M., AND GEORGE J. STIGLER. *The Demand and Supply of Scientific Personnel*. New York: National Bureau of Economic Research, Inc., 1957.

BLANK, LEONARD, AND HENRY P. DAVID. "The Crisis in Clinical Psychology Training," *American Psychologist*, 18:216–219, April 1963. [4]

BLAU, PETER M. "Orientation Toward Clients in a Public Welfare Agency," *Administrative Science Quarterly*, 5:341–361, December 1960. [5]

BLAU, PETER M., AND OTIS D. DUNCAN. *The American Occupational Structure*. New York: John Wiley & Sons, Inc., 1967. [4]

BLAU, PETER M., AND W. RICHARD SCOTT. *Formal Organizations: A Comparative Approach*. San Francisco: Chandler Publishing Co., 1962. A subsection, "Professional and Bureaucratic Orientation," pp. 60–74, is particularly relevant to the situation of the employed professional. [11]

BLAUSTEIN, ALBERT P., AND CHARLES O. PORTER. *The American Lawyer: A Summary of the Survey of the Legal Profession.* Chicago: University of Chicago Press, 1954.

BLOOM, SAMUEL W. "Some Implications of Studies in the Professionalization of the Physician," in E. Gartly Jaco (ed.), *Patients, Physicians and Illness*. New York: Free Press, 1958, pp. 313–321. [4]

BLOOM, SAMUEL W., AND OTHERS. "The Sociologist as Medical Educator: A Discussion," *American Sociological Review,* 25:95–101, February 1960.

BOGART, GEORGE G. "Faculty Participation in American University Government," *American Association of University Professors Bulletin*, 31:72–82, Spring 1945. [12]

BOKSER, BEN Z. "Codes of the American Rabbinate," *Annals of the American Academy of Political and Social Science*, 297:59–63, January 1955. [6]

BORGATTA, EDGAR F. "The Certification of Academic Professions: The Case of Psychology," *American Sociological Review*, 23:302–306, June 1958. [6]

BORGATTA, EDGAR F., AND OTHERS. *Social Workers' Perceptions of Clients: A Study of the Caseload of a Social Agency*. New York: Russell Sage Foundation, 1960. [5]

BOROW, HENRY. "Development of Occupational Motives and Roles," in Lois W. Hoffman and Martin L. Hoffman (eds.), *Review of Child Development Research*, Vol. II. New York: Russell Sage Foundation, 1966, pp. 373–422. [4]

BOSWORTH, FRANCKE H., JR., AND ROY C. JONES. *A Study of Architectural Schools*. New York: Charles Scribner's Sons, 1932. [4]

BOTTOMORE, THOMAS B. "Higher Civil Servants in France," in *Transactions of the Second World Congress of Sociology*. London: International Sociological Association, 1954, Vol. II, pp. 143–152.

BOWEN, ROBERT O. *The New Professors*. New York: Holt, Rinehart and Winston, Inc., 1960.

BOWEN, WILLIAM G. "University Salaries: Faculty Differentials," *Economica*, 30:341–359, November 1963.

BRANDEIS, LOUIS. "Business—A Profession," in Louis Brandeis (ed.), *Business—A Profession*. Boston: Small, Maynard and Company, 1914, pp. 1–12. [1]

BRAUDE, LEE. "Professional Autonomy and the Role of the Layman," *Social Forces*, 39:297–301, May 1961. [5]

BREWSTER, ROYCE EDWIN. *Guidance Workers' Certification Requirements*. Washington, D.C.: U.S. Department of Health, Education, and Welfare, Office of Education, 1960. [6]

BRIDGMAN, MARGARET. *Collegiate Education for Nursing*. New York: Russell Sage Foundation, 1953. [4]

BROCK, ARTHUR J. *Greek Medicine*. London: J. M. Dent and Sons, Ltd., 1929. [2]

BRODY, EUGENE B. "Interprofessional Relations, or Psychologists and Psychiatrists Are Human Too, Only More So," *American Psychologist*, 11:105–111, February 1956. [7]

BROGAN, JAMES M. *Ethical Principles for the Character of a Nurse*. Milwaukee, Wisc.: The Bruce Publishing Company, 1924. [6]

BROWN, ESTHER LUCILE. *Lawyers and the Promotion of Justice*. New York: Russell Sage Foundation, 1938. [14]

———. *Lawyers, Law Schools and the Public Service*. New York: Russell Sage Foundation, 1948.

———. *Newer Dimensions of Patient Care*. New York: Russell Sage Foundation, 1965. [5]

———. *Nursing as a Profession*. New York: Russell Sage Foundation, 1936.

———. *Nursing for the Future*. New York: Russell Sage Foundation, 1948.

———. *Physicians and Medical Care*. New York: Russell Sage Foundation, 1937.

———. *The Professional Engineer*. New York: Russell Sage Foundation, 1936.

———. *Social Work as a Profession*. New York: Russell Sage Foundation, 1936.

———. *The Use of Research by Professional Associations in Determining Program and Policy*. New York: Russell Sage Foundation, 1946. [6]

BROWN, J. DOUGLAS. *The Role of Engineering as a Learned Profession*. Presented at the Conference on Engineering Education at the Dedication of the New Engineering Quadrangle, Princeton University, October 1962.

BROWN, J. H. U. "The Science Administrator: A New Profession," *Journal of Medical Education,* 43:33–35, January 1968. [12]

BROWN, WILLIAM ADAMS. *The Case for Theology in the University.* Chicago: The University of Chicago Press, 1938. [4]

BROWNE, EDWARD G. *Arabian Medicine.* Cambridge, Mass.: The University Press, 1921. [2]

BRUNO, FRANK J. *Trends in Social Work, 1874–1956.* New York: Columbia University Press, 1957.

BRYAN, ALICE I. *The Public Librarian.* New York: Columbia University Press, 1952.

BUCHER, RUE. "Pathology: A Study of Social Movements Within a Profession," *Social Problems,* 10:40–51, Summer 1962. [7]

BUCHER, RUE, AND ANSELM STRAUSS. "Professions in Process," *American Journal of Sociology,* 66:325–334, January 1961. [9]

BURCHARD, WALDO W. "Role Conflicts of Military Chaplains," *American Sociological Review,* 19:528–535, October 1954. [11]

BUREAU OF SOCIAL SCIENCE RESEARCH. *Two Years After the College Degree.* Washington, D.C.: National Science Foundation, 1963. [4]

BURNAP, GEORGE W. *The Professions: An Oration, Delivered Before the Literary Societies of Marshall College, Mercersburg, Pennsylvania, at Their Anniversary, September 27, 1842.* Baltimore: John Murphy, 1842.

BUTLER, JOHN J., AND EDNA M. O'HERN. "Medical Education and Research in Catholic Medical Schools and Hospitals," *American Catholic Sociological Review,* 19:224–237, October 1958. [4]

BUTLER, PIERCE. "Librarianship as a Profession," *Library Quarterly,* 21:235–247, October 1951.

CABOT, RICHARD C. *Social Work: Essays on the Meeting-Ground of Doctor and Social Worker.* Boston: Houghton Mifflin Company, 1919. [10]

CADZOW, DONALD A. "The Vanishing American Indian Medicine-Man," *Scientific American,* 140:418–420, May 1929. [2]

CALHOUN, DANIEL H. *Professional Lives in America, Structure and Aspiration, 1750–1850.* Cambridge, Mass.: Harvard University Press, 1965. [2]

CAMBELL, DONALD. *Arabian Medicine.* London: Routledge and Kegan Paul, 1926. [2]

CAMPBELL, ERNEST Q., AND THOMAS F. PETTIGREW. "Racial and Moral Crisis: The Role of Little Rock Ministers," *American Journal of Sociology,* 64:509–516, March 1959. [14]

CANADA, DEPARTMENT OF LABOUR. *Employment and Earnings in the Scientific and Technical Professions.* Ottawa: Queen's Printer and Controller of Stationery, 1963.

———. *Report on Organization in Industry, Commerce and the Professions in Canada.* Ottawa: Department of Labour of Canada, 1947. Chap. 13, pp. 124–130, gives information on professional associations. [6]

CANADA, ROYAL COMMISSION ON CANADA'S ECONOMIC PROSPECTS. *Skilled and Professional Manpower in Canada, 1945–1965.* Ottawa: Economics and Research Branch, Department of Labour, July 1957.

CAPLOW, THEODORE, AND REECE J. MCGEE. *The Academic Marketplace.* New York: Basic Books, Inc., 1959. [11]

CAREY, JOHN L. "The Ethics of Public Accounting," *Annals of the American Academy of Political and Social Science,* 297:1–8, January 1955. [6]

———. *Professional Ethics of Certified Public Accountants.* New York: American Institute of Accountants, 1956. [6]

CARLIN, JEROME E. *Lawyers' Ethics: A Survey of the New York City Bar.* New York: Russell Sage Foundation, 1966.

———. *Lawyers on Their Own: A Study of Individual Practitioners in Chicago.* New Brunswick, N.J.: Rutgers University Press, 1962.

CARLIN, JEROME E., JAN HOWARD, AND SHELDON L. MESSINGER. *Civil Justice and the Poor: Issues for Sociological Research.* New York: Russell Sage Foundation, 1967. [5]

CARLSON, RICHARD O. "Succession and Performance Among School Superintendents," *Administrative Science Quarterly,* 6:210–227, September 1961. [4]

CARPER, JAMES W., AND HOWARD S. BECKER. "Adjustment to Conflicting Expectations in the Development of Identification with an Occupation," *Social Forces,* 36:51–56, October 1957. [4]

CARR-SAUNDERS, ALEXANDER MORRIS. "Metropolitan Conditions and Traditional Professional Relationships," in Robert M. Fisher (ed.), *The Metropolis in Modern Life.* New York: Doubleday & Company, Inc., 1955, pp. 279–287. [13]

———. *Professions: Their Organization and Place in Society.* Oxford: The Clarendon Press, 1928.

CARR-SAUNDERS, ALEXANDER MORRIS, AND P. A. WILSON. "Professions," in *Encyclopedia of the Social Sciences.* New York: The Macmillan Company, 1934, Vol. 12, pp. 476–480.

———. *The Professions.* Oxford: The Clarendon Press, 1933.

CARTER, RICHARD. *The Doctor Business.* New York: Doubleday & Company, Inc., 1958.

CARTTER, ALLAN M. *An Assessment of Quality in Graduate Education.* Washington, D.C.: American Council on Education, 1966. [4]

CASQUET, CARDINAL. *Parish Life in Medieval England.* London: Methuen & Co., Ltd., 1906.

CHAPMAN, BRIAN. *The Profession of Government: The Public Service in Europe.* London: Allen and Unwin, Ltd., 1959.

CHAPMAN, STANLEY H. "The Minister, Professional Man of the Church," *Social Forces,* 23:202–206, December 1944.

CHARLESWORTH, JAMES C. (ed.), *Theory and Practice of Public Administration: Scope, Objectives, and Methods.* Philadelphia: American Academy of Political and Social Science, 1968. See especially Dwight Waldo, "Scope of the Theory of Public Administration," pp. 1–26, and Fred W. Riggs, "Professionalism, Political Science, and the Scope of Public Administration," pp. 32–62. Both papers discuss professionalization. [3]

CHEATHAM, ELLIOTT E. (ed.). *Cases and Materials on the Legal Profession,* 2nd ed. Brooklyn, N.Y.: The Foundation Press, Inc., 1955.

———. *A Lawyer When Needed.* New York: Columbia University Press, 1963. [5]

CHEEK, NEIL H., JR. *The Professions: A Paradigmatic Approach.* New York State School of Labor and Industrial Relations, November 1965.

CHICAGO UNIVERSITY LAW SCHOOL. *Conference on the Profession of Law and Legal Education.* Chicago: The University of Chicago Law School, 1952. [4]

CLAPHAM, ANTHONY. "A Short History of the Surveyor's Profession," *Journal of the Royal Institute of Chartered Surveyors,* 29: 16–54, December 1949.

COGAN, MORRIS L. "The Problem of Defining a Profession," *The Annals of the American Academy of Political and Social Science,* 297:105–111, January 1955. [1]

———. "Toward a Definition of Profession," *Harvard Educational Review,* 23:33–50, Winter 1953. [1]

COLE, G. D. H. *Studies in Class Structure.* London: Routledge and Kegan Paul, Ltd., 1955. Contains information on the process and extent of professionalization in Britain.

COLEMAN, JAMES, AND OTHERS. "The Diffusion of an Innovation Among Physicians," *Sociometry*, 20:253–270, December 1957. [7]

COLLINS, SYDNEY. "Social Mobility in Jamaica, with Reference to Rural Communities and the Teaching Profession," in *Transactions of the Third World Congress of Sociology*. London: International Sociological Association, 1956, Vol. III, pp. 267–276.

COLVARD, RICHARD. "Foundations and Professions: The Organizational Defense of Autonomy," *Administrative Science Quarterly*, 6:167–184, September 1961. [9]

CONANT, JAMES B. *The Education of American Teachers*. New York: McGraw-Hill, Inc., 1963. [4]

CONGALTON, A. A. "Social Grading of Occupations in New Zealand," *British Journal of Sociology*, 4:45–55, March 1953. [13]

COOK, STUART, W. "The Psychologist of the Future: Scientist, Professional, or Both," *American Psychologist*, 13:635–644, November 1958. [7]

COPE, OLIVER. *Man, Mind and Medicine: The Doctor's Education*. Philadelphia: J. B. Lippincott Company, 1968. [4]

COPE, ZACHARY. *The Royal College of Surgeons of England*. London: Anthony Blond, Ltd., 1959. A historical study. [2]

CORIN, GENEVIÈVE. "Une Profession Feminine: L'Assistance Sociale," *Bulletin de L'Institut de Recherches Economiques et Sociales*, 19:749–783, November 1953.

CORWIN, RONALD G. "Militant Professionalism, Initiative and Compliance in Public Education," *Sociology of Education*, 38:310–331, Summer 1965. [3, 11]

———. "The Professional Employee: A Study of Conflict in Nursing Roles," *American Journal of Sociology*, 66:604–615, May 1961. [11]

CORWIN, RONALD G., AND MARVIN J. TAVES. "Nursing and Other Health Professions," in Howard E. Freeman and others (eds.), *Handbook of Medical Sociology*. Englewood Cliffs, N.J.: Prentice-Hall, Inc., 1963, pp. 187–212. [10]

COSER, ROSE LAUB. "Authority and Decision-Making in a Hospital: A Comparative Analysis," *American Sociological Review*, 23:56–63, February 1958. [11]

COUNCIL OF STATE GOVERNMENTS. *Occupational Licensing Legislation in the States*. Chicago: The Council of State Governments, 1952. [6]

COUTU, WALTER. "The Relative Prestige of Twenty Professions as Judged by Three Groups of Professional Students," *Social Forces,* 14:522–529, May 1936. [13]

COWLEY, W. H. "Professional Growth and Academic Freedom," *Journal of Higher Education,* 21:225–236, May 1950. [7]

CRAWFORD, NELSON A. *Ethics of Journalism.* Boston: Little, Brown and Company, 1918. [6]

CREEGAN, ROBERT F. "Concerning Professional Ethics," *American Psychologist,* 13:272–275, 1958. [6]

CROATMAN, WALLACE, AND PAUL B. SHEATSLEY. *The Prescription Pharmacist Today: A Factual Study of his Role in the Health Field.* New York: Health Information Foundation, 1958, Research Series No. 3. [10]

CULMANN, HENRI. *Les Principes de l'Organisation Professionnelle.* Paris: Presses Universitaires de France, 1945. [9]

CUMMINGS, GEORGE B. "Standards of Professional Practice in Architecture," *Annals of the American Academy of Political and Social Science,* 297:9–16, January 1955. [6]

CUTTS, EDWARD L. *Parish Priests and Their People in the Middle Ages in England.* London: Society for Promoting Christian Knowledge, 1898. [2]

DALTON, MELVILLE. "Conflicts Between Staff and Line Managerial Officers," *American Sociological Review,* 15:342–351, June 1950. [11]

DANIELS, MORRIS J. "Affect and Its Control in the Medical Intern," *American Journal of Sociology,* 66:259–267, November 1960. [4]

DARNELL, T. W. "Is the Preacher a Professional?" *Scribner's Magazine,* 81:361–365, April 1927. [1]

DAVIS, ARTHUR K. "Bureaucratic Patterns in the Navy Officer Corps," *Social Forces,* 27:143–153, December 1948. [11]

DAVIS, F. JAMES, AND OTHERS. *Society and the Law: New Meanings for an Old Profession.* New York: Free Press, 1962. [14]

DAVIS, FRED (ed.). *The Nursing Profession.* New York: John Wiley & Sons, Inc., 1966.

DAVIS, FRED, AND VIRGINIA L. OLESEN. "Initiation into a Woman's Profession: Identity Problems in the Status Transition of Coed to Student Nurse," *Sociometry,* 26:89–101, March 1963. [4]

DAVIS, HAZEL, AND AGNES SAMUELSON. "Women in Education," *Journal of Social Issues,* 6:25–37, 1950.

DAVIS, JOHN DENIS. *The Moral Obligations of Catholic Civil Judges.* Washington, D.C.: The Catholic University of America Press, 1953. [14]

DAVIS, MILTON S. "Variations in Patients' Compliance with Doctors' Orders," *Journal of Medical Education,* 41:1037–1048, November 1966. [5]

DAWSON, WARREN R. *The Beginnings: Egypt and Assyria.* New York: Paul B. Hoeber, Inc., 1930. Historical work on medicine. [2]

DEMERATH, NICHOLAS J., RICHARD W. STEPHENS, AND R. ROBB TAYLOR. *Power, Presidents, and Professors.* New York: Basic Books, Inc., 1967. [11]

DENNISON, CHARLES P. *Faculty Rights and Obligations.* New York: Teachers College, Columbia, 1955. [11]

DERTHICK, MARTHA. "Militia Lobby in the Missile Age: The Politics of the National Guard," in Samuel P. Huntington (ed.), *Changing Patterns of Military Politics.* New York: Free Press, 1962, pp. 190–234. [9]

DEUTSCHER, IRWIN. *Public Images of the Nurse.* Kansas City, Mo.: Community Studies, Inc., 1955. [13]

DEVEREUX, GEORGES, AND FLORENCE R. WEINER. "The Occupational Status of Nurses," *American Sociological Review,* 15:628–634, October 1950. [8]

DEWITT, NICHOLAS. *Education and Professional Employment in the U.S.S.R.* Washington, D.C.: Government Printing Office, 1961.

———. "Professional and Scientific Personnel in the U.S.S.R.," *Science,* 120:1–4, July 1954.

———. *Soviet Professional Manpower.* Washington, D.C.: National Science Foundation, 1955.

DIBBLE, VERNON K. "Occupations and Ideologies," *American Journal of Sociology,* 68:229–241, September 1962. [6]

DIEKHOFF, JOHN S. *The Domain of the Faculty in our Expanding Colleges.* New York: Harper & Row, Publishers, 1956. [11]

DITCHFIELD, P. H. *The Old-Time Parson,* 2nd ed. London: Methuen and Co., Ltd., 1909. [2]

DIX, GREGORY. *Le Ministère Dans l'Église Ancienne.* Paris: Delachaux et Niestlé, 1955. [2]

DOERSCHUK, BEATRICE. *Women in the Law: An Analysis of Training, Practice and Salaried Positions.* New York: The Bureau of Vocational Information, 1920.

DOHERTY, ROBERT E. *The Development of Professional Education.* Pittsburgh, Pa.: Carnegie Institute of Technology, 1950. [4]

———. "Education for Professional Responsibility," *Journal of Engineering Education*, 39:76–80, October 1948. [4]

———. "Professional Development and Responsibility," *Mechanical Engineering*, 64:10–12, January 1942. [6]

———. "Value Judgments in Professional Education," *Journal of Engineering Education*, 40:159–165, November 1949. [4]

DONHAM, WALLACE B. "The Emerging Profession of Business," *Harvard Business Review*, 5:401–405, July 1927. [3]

———. "The Failure of Business Leadership and the Responsibility of the Universities," *Harvard Business Review*, 11:418–435, July 1933. [4]

———. "Some Recent Books on Business Ethics," *Harvard Business Review*, 5:245–250, January 1927. [6]

DORNBUSCH, SANFORD M. "The Military Academy as an Assimilating Institution," *Social Forces*, 33:316–321, May 1955. [4]

DRESSEL, PAUL L., AND MARGARET F. LORIMER. *Attitudes of Liberal Arts Faculty Members Toward Liberal and Professional Education*. New York: Bureau of Publications, Teachers' College, Columbia University, 1960. [4]

DRINKER, HENRY S. *Legal Ethics*. New York: Columbia University Press, 1953. [6]

———. "Legal Ethics," *Annals of the American Academy of Political and Social Science*, 297:37–45, January 1955. [7]

DUBARLE, DANIEL. "The Scientist and His Responsibilities," *Bulletin of Atomic Scientists*, 7:253–257, September 1956. [14]

DUMMETT, CLIFTON ORRIN. *The Growth and Development of the Negro in Dentistry in the United States*. Chicago: Stanek Press, 1952.

DUNCAN, OTIS DUDLEY. "Social Origins of Salaried and Self-Employed Professional Workers," *Social Forces*, 44:186–189, December 1965. [4]

DURKHEIM, EMILE. *The Division of Labor in Society*. New York: The Macmillan Company, 1933; reissued, New York: Free Press, 1949. See especially Preface to the 2nd ed. for a theoretical discussion of the functions of occupational groups. [6, 14]

———. *Professional Ethics and Civic Morals*. London: Routledge and Kegan Paul, Ltd., 1957. [6]

DVORAK, ELDON J. "Will Engineers Unionize?" *Industrial Relations*, 2:45–65, May 1963. [9]

EATON, JOSEPH W. "A Scientific Basis for Helping," in Alfred J. Kahn (ed.), *Issues in American Social Work*. New York: Columbia University Press, 1959, pp. 271–292. Theoretical discussion of "helping professions" (clinical psychologists, psychiatrists, home economists, vocational counselors, social workers). [10]

———. "Social Processes of Professional Teamwork," *American Sociological Review*, 16:707–713, October 1951. [9]

———. "Whence and Whither Social Work? A Sociological Analysis," *Social Work*, 1:11–26, January 1956. [3]

EBAUGH, FRANKLIN G., AND ROBERT H. BARNES. "Psychiatric Education," *American Journal of Psychiatry*, 112:561–564, January 1956. [4]

ECKSTEIN, HARRY H. *The English Health Service: Its Origins, Structure and Achievements*. Cambridge, Mass.: Harvard University Press, 1958.

———. "The Politics of the British Medical Association," *The Political Quarterly*, 26:345–359, October–December 1955. [9]

EDELSTEIN, LUDWIG. *The Hippocratic Oath*. Baltimore: The Johns Hopkins Press, 1943. [6]

EDGEWORTH, RICHARD LOVELL. *Essays on Professional Education*. London: J. Johnson, 1809. [2]

EDUCATION AND WORLD AFFAIRS, COMMITTEE ON THE PROFESSIONAL SCHOOL AND WORLD AFFAIRS. *Report of the Task Force on Agriculture and Engineering*. New York: Education and World Affairs, 1967. [4]

———. *Report of the Task Force on Business Administration and Public Administration*. New York: Education and World Affairs, 1967. [4]

EDWARDS, G. FRANKLIN. *The Negro Professional Class*. New York: Free Press, 1959.

EIDUSON, BERNICE T. *Scientists: Their Psychological World*. New York: Basic Books, Inc., 1962.

ELGOOD, CYRIL. *Medicine in Persia*. New York: Paul B. Hoeber, 1934. History from mythical times to twentieth century. [2]

ELIAS, NORBET. "Studies in the Genesis of the Naval Profession," *British Journal of Sociology*, 1:291–309, December 1950. [2]

Encyclopedia of Associations, National Organizations of the U.S. Published biennially by Gale Research Company, Detroit, Michigan.

ERON, LEONARD D. "Effect of Medical Education on Medical Students," *Journal of Medical Education*, 10:559–566, October 1955. [4]

ETZIONI, AMITAI (ed.). *The Semi-Professions and Their Organization*. New York: Free Press, 1969. On teachers, nurses, and social workers. [3, 9]

EVANS, A. A. "Correctional Institution Personnel: Amateurs or Professionals?" *Annals of the American Academy of Political and Social Science*, 293:70–78, May 1954. [3]

EVANS-PRITCHARD, E. E. *Witchcraft, Oracles, and Magic Among the Azande*. London: Oxford University Press, 1937. [2]

FEIN, RASHI. *The Doctor Shortage: An Economic Analysis*. Washington, D.C.: The Brookings Institution, 1967.

FERGUSON, R. S. "The Doctor-Patient Relationship and 'Functional' Illness," in E. Gartly Jaco (ed.), *Patients, Physicians and Illness*. New York: Free Press, 1958, pp. 433–439. [5]

FICHTER, JOSEPH H. *Social Relations in the Urban Parish*. Chicago: University of Chicago Press, 1954, especially Chap. 10, "Social Roles of the Parish Priest." [5, 14]

FIELD, MARK G. *Doctor and Patient in Soviet Russia*. Cambridge, Mass.: Harvard University Press, 1957.

———. "The Doctor-Patient Relationship in the Perspective of 'Fee for Service' and 'Third-Party Medicine,'" *Journal of Health and Human Behavior*, 2:252–262, Winter 1961. [5]

———. "Doctors and Patients," in Alex Inkeles and Kent Geiger (eds.), *Soviet Society*. Boston: Houghton Mifflin Company, 1961, pp. 361–381. [5]

———. "Structured Strain and the Role of the Soviet Physician," *American Journal of Sociology*, 58:493–502, March 1953. [11]

FITTS, WILLIAM T., AND BARBARA FITTS. "Ethical Standards of the Medical Profession," *Annals of the American Academy of Political and Social Science*, 297:17–36, January 1955. [6]

FLETCHER, JOSEPH. *Morals and Medicine*. Princeton, N.J.: Princeton University Press, 1954. [5, 14]

FLEXNER, ABRAHAM. *Medical Education: A Comparative Study*. New York: The Macmillan Company, 1925. [4]

———. *Medical Education in Europe*. Boston: D. B. Updike, The Merrymount Press, 1912. [4]

———. *Medical Education in the United States and Canada*. Boston: D. B. Updike, The Merrymount Press, 1910. [4]

FLORO, GEORGE K. "Continuity in City-Manager Careers," *American Journal of Sociology*, 61:240–246, November 1955. [11]

FLOUD, JEAN, AND W. SCOTT. "Recruitment to Teaching in England and Wales," in A. H. Halsey and others (eds.), *Education, Economy, and Society.* New York: Free Press, 1961. [4]

FOLEY, ALBERT S. "The Status and Role of the Negro Priest in the American Catholic Clergy," *American Catholic Sociological Review,* 16:83–93, June 1955.

FORD FOUNDATION, THE. *Careers in Teaching Engineering.* New York: The Ford Foundation, 1965. [4]

FORD, JAMES L. C. "Women 'Arrive' in Journalism," in George F. Mott (ed.), *New Survey of Journalism.* New York: Barnes and Noble, Inc., 1950, pp. 133–137.

FORD, P. *The Government Lawyer: A Survey and Analysis of Lawyers in the Executive Branch of the U.S. Government.* New York: Prentice-Hall, Inc., 1952. [11]

FOSTER, WILLIAM D. *A Short History of Clinical Pathology.* London: E. & S. Livingstone Ltd., 1961.

FOX, RENÉE C. *Experiment Perilous: Physicians and Patients Facing the Unknown.* New York: Free Press, 1959. [5]

———."Medical Scientists in a Château," *Science,* 136:476–483, May 1962.

———. "Physicians on the Drug Industry Side of the Prescription Blank: The Dual Commitment to Medical Science and Business," *Journal of Health and Human Behavior,* 2:3–16, Spring 1961. [10]

———. "Training for Uncertainty," in Robert K. Merton and others (eds.), *The Student Physician.* Cambridge, Mass.: The Commonwealth Fund, 1957, pp. 207–241. [4]

FRANCIS, E. K. "Toward a Typology of Religious Orders," *American Journal of Sociology,* 55:437–449, March 1950.

FRAZIER, E. FRANKLIN. *Black Bourgeoisie.* New York: Free Press, 1957.

FREDERICKS, MARCEL A., AND PAUL MUNDY. "The Relationship Between Social Class, Stress-Anxiety Responses, Academic Achievement and Internalization of Professional Attitudes of Students in a Medical School," *Journal of Medical Education,* 42:1023–1030, November 1967. [4]

FREEMAN, HOWARD E., SOL LEVINE, AND LEO G. REEDER (eds.). *Handbook of Medical Sociology.* Englewood Cliffs, N.J.: Prentice-Hall, Inc., 1963.

FREIDSON, ELIOT. "Against the Code of Ethics," *American Sociological Review,* 29:410, June 1964. [6]

———. "Client Control and Medical Practice," *American Journal of Sociology,* 65:374–382, January 1960. [5]

———. "The Impurity of Professional Authority," in Howard S. Becker and others (eds.), *Institutions and the Person.* Chicago: Aldine Publishing Company, 1968, Chap. 3, pp. 25–34. [1]

———. "Medical Personnel. I. Physicians," in David L. Sills (ed.), *International Encyclopedia of the Social Sciences.* New York: Free Press, 1968, Vol. 10, pp. 105–114.

———. "Medical Personnel. II. Paramedical Personnel," in David L. Sills (ed.), *International Encyclopedia of the Social Sciences.* New York: Free Press, 1968, Vol. 10, pp. 114–120. [10]

———. *Patients' Views of Medical Practice: A Study of Subscribers to a Prepaid Medical Plan in the Bronx.* New York: Russell Sage Foundation, 1961. [5]

FREIDSON, ELIOT, AND JACOB J. FELDMAN. *Public Attitudes Toward Health Insurance.* New York: Health Information Foundation, 1958, Research Series No. 5. [5]

———. *The Public Looks at Dental Care.* New York: Health Information Foundation, 1958, Research Series No. 6. [5]

———. *The Public Looks at Hospitals.* New York: Health Information Foundation, 1958, Research Series No. 4. [5]

FREIDSON, ELIOT, AND BUFORD RHEA. "Processes of Control in a Company of Equals," *Social Problems,* 11:119–131, Fall 1963. [6]

FREUND, PAUL A. "The Legal Profession," *Daedalus,* 92:689–700, Fall 1963. Reprinted in Kenneth S. Lynn (ed.), *The Professions in America.* Boston: Houghton Mifflin Company, 1965.

FRIED, MORTON H. "Military Status in Chinese Society," *American Journal of Sociology,* 57:347–355, January 1952. Historical. [2]

FRIEDMAN, MILTON, AND SIMON KUZNETS. *Income From Independent Professional Practice.* New York: National Bureau of Economic Research, 1945. [5]

FUCHS, RALPH F. "A Profession in Quest of Itself," *American Association of University Professors Bulletin,* 48:104–109, Summer 1962. The roles of faculty members in U.S. colleges. [11]

FUJIKAWA, YU. *Japanese Medicine.* New York: Paul B. Hoeber, 1934. Historical account from "The Mythical Period" to the present. [2]

FULTON, ROBERT L. "The Clergyman and the Funeral Director: A Study in Role Conflict," *Social Forces,* 39:317–323, May 1961. [7, 10]

FURFEY, PAUL HANLEY. "The Code of the Catholic Clergy," *Annals of the American Academy of Political and Social Science*, 297:64–69, January 1955. [6]

GARCEAU, OLIVER. *The Political Life of the American Medical Association*. Cambridge, Mass.: Harvard University Press, 1941. [9]

GEISER, PETER, AND EDWARD C. MCDONAGH. "Decision-Making Within a Professional Association," *Social Work*, 7:33–40, July 1962. [9]

GELINAS, AGNES. *Nursing and Nursing Education*. New York: The Commonwealth Fund, 1946. [4]

GERVER, ISRAEL, AND JOSEPH BENSMAN. "Toward a Sociology of Expertness," *Social Forces*, 32:226–235, March 1954. [1]

GETZELS, JACOB W., AND EGON G. GUBA. "The Structure of Roles and Role Conflict in the Teaching Situation," *Journal of Educational Sociology*, 29: 30–40, September 1955.

GILB, CORINNE L. *Hidden Hierarchies: The Professions and Government*. New York: Harper & Row, Publishers, 1966. Especially concerned with professional associations. [9]

GILLIN, JOHN. "The Making of a Witch Doctor," *Psychiatry*, 19:131–136, May 1956. [2]

GILPIN, ROBERT. *American Scientists and Nuclear Policy*. Princeton: Princeton University Press, 1962. [14]

GLASER, BARNEY G. "The Local-Cosmopolitan Scientist," *American Journal of Sociology*, 69:249–259, November 1963. [8]

———. "Variations in the Importance of Recognition in Scientists' Careers," *Social Problems*, 10:268–276, Winter 1963. [8]

GLASER, WILLIAM A. "Doctors and Politics," *American Journal of Sociology*, 66:230–245, November 1960. Primarily concerned with political attitudes and behavior of individual medical practitioners rather than the political policies of the American Medical Association. [14]

———. "Internship Appointments of Medical Students," *Administrative Science Quarterly*, 4:337–356, December 1959. [4]

———. *Pretrial Discovery and the Adversary System*. New York: Russell Sage Foundation, 1968.

GLASS, BENTLEY. "The Academic Scientist, 1940–1960," *Science*, 132:598–603, September 1960.

GLAZER, MYRON. "El Proceso de Socialización Profesional en Cuatro Carreras Chilenas," from *Revisita Latino Americana de Sociología*, 3:333–367, 1966. [4]

GLICK, PAUL C., AND HERMAN P. MILLER. "Educational Level and Potential Income," *American Sociological Review*, 21:307–312, June 1956.

GOLDMAN, ERIC F. *Two-Way Street: The Emergence of the Public Relations Council*. Boston: The Bellman Co., 1948. [3]

GOLDSTEIN, BERNARD. "The Perspective of Unionized Professionals," *Social Forces*, 37:323–327, May 1959. [9]

———. "Some Aspects of the Nature of Unionism Among Salaried Professionals in Industry," *American Sociological Review*, 20:199–205, April 1955. [9]

GOLDSTEIN, SIDNEY I. "The Roles of an American Rabbi," *Sociology and Social Research*, 38:32–37, September–October 1953.

GOODE, WILLIAM J. "Community Within a Community: The Professions," *American Sociological Review*, 22:194–200, April 1957. [1]

———. "Encroachment, Charlatanism, and the Emerging Profession: Psychology, Sociology, and Medicine," *American Sociological Review*, 25:902–914, December 1960. [3, 7, 10]

———. "The Librarian: From Occupation to Profession?" *The Library Quarterly*, 31:306–320, October 1961. [3]

GOODSON, MAX R. "Teacher and Educational Standards," in Lindley J. Stiles (ed.), *The Teacher's Role in American Society*. New York: Harper & Row, Publishers, 1957, pp. 146–163. [6]

GORDON, BRUCE F., AND IAN C. ROSS. "Professionals and the Corporation," *Research Management*, 5:493–505, November 1962. [11]

GORDON, GERALD, AND OTHERS. "Freedom and Control in Four Types of Scientific Settings," *American Behavioral Scientist*, 6:39–43, December 1962. [11]

GORDON, ROBERT A., AND JAMES E. HOWELL. *Higher Education for Business*. New York: Columbia University Press, 1959. [4]

GOSS, MARY E. "Administration and the Physician," *American Journal of Public Health*, 52:183–191, February 1962. [11]

———. "Influence and Authority Among Physicians, in an Out-Patient Clinic," *American Sociological Review*, 26:39–50, February 1961. [8, 12]

GOSS, MARY E., AND GEORGE G. READER. "Collaboration Between Sociologist and Physician," *Social Problems*, 4:82–89, July 1956. [10]

GOULD, JAY M. *The Technical Elite*. New York: Augustus M. Kelley, 1966.

GOULDNER, ALVIN W. "Cosmopolitans and Locals: Toward an Analysis of Latent Social Roles," *Administrative Science Quarterly*, 2:281–306, December 1957; and 2:444–480, March 1958. [11]

GOWER, L. C. B., AND LEOLIN PRICE. "The Profession and Practice of the Law in England and America," *Modern Law Review*, 20:317–346, July 1957.

GRAHAM, HARVEY (pseud.). *The Story of Surgery*. Garden City, N.Y.: Doubleday & Company, Inc., 1939. Historical. [2]

GRAMBS, JEAN D. "Roles of the Teacher," in Lindley J. Stiles (ed.), *The Teacher's Role in American Society*. New York: Harper & Row, Publishers, 1957, pp. 73–93.

GRANICK, DAVID. *The European Executive*. Garden City, N.Y.: Doubleday & Company, Inc., 1962.

———. *The Red Executive*. Garden City, N.Y.: Doubleday & Company, Inc., 1960.

GREENWOOD, ERNEST. "Attributes of a Profession," *Social Work*, 2:45–55, July 1957. [1]

GREENWOOD, GLENN, AND ROBERT K. FREDERICKSON. *Specialization in the Medical and Legal Professions*. Mundelein, Ill.: Callaghan and Co., 1964. [7]

GROFF, PATRICK J. "The Social Status of Teachers," *Journal of Educational Sociology*, 36:20–25, September 1962. [13]

GROPPER, GEORGE L., AND ROBERT FITZPATRICK. *Who Goes to Graduate School?* Pittsburgh, Pa.: American Institute for Research, 1959. [4]

GROSS, EDWARD. *Work and Society*. New York: Thomas Y. Crowell Co., 1958, Chap. 4, "The Occupational Status and Authority System"; Chap. 5, "The Career"; and pp. 77–82 on "the axis of professionalization."

GROSS, MARTIN L. *The Doctors*. New York: Random House, Inc., 1966.

GROSS, NEAL. *Who Runs Our Schools?* New York: John Wiley & Sons, Inc., 1958.

GROSS, NEAL, AND OTHERS. *Explorations in Role Analysis: Studies of the School Superintendency Role*. New York: John Wiley & Sons, Inc., 1958. [12]

GULLAHORN, JOHN T., AND JEANNE E. GULLAHORN. "The Role of the Academic Man as a Cross-Cultural Mediator," *American Sociological Review*, 25:414–417, June 1960. [14]

GUSTAD, JOHN W. "Policies and Practices in Faculty Evaluation," *Educational Record,* 42:194–211, July 1961. [6]

GUSTAFSON, JAMES M. "An Analysis of the Problem of the Role of the Minister," *Journal of Religion,* 34:187–191, July 1954.

——. "The Clergy in the United States," *Daedalus,* 92:724–744, Fall 1963.

GUTHRIE, DOUGLAS. *A History of Medicine.* Philadelphia, Pa.: J. B. Lippincott Company, 1946. [2]

GUTTMACHER, MANFRED S., AND HENRY WEIHOFEN. *Psychiatry and the Law.* New York: W. W. Norton & Company, Inc., 1952.

HABENSTEIN, ROBERT W. "Conflicting Organizational Patterns in Funeral Directing," *Human Organization,* 22:126–132, Summer 1963. [9]

——. "Critique of 'Profession' as a Sociological Category," *Sociological Quarterly,* 4:291–300, Autumn 1963. [1]

HACKET, JOHN WINTHROP. *The Profession of Arms.* London: The Times Publishing Co., 1963.

HAGGARD, HOWARD W. *Devils, Drugs and Doctors: The Story of the Science of Healing from Medicine-Man to Doctor.* New York: Harper & Row, Publishers, 1929. [2]

——. *The Doctor in History.* New Haven: Yale University Press, 1934. [2]

HAGGERTY, M. E. "Occupational Destination of Ph.D. Recipients," *Educational Record,* 9:209–218, October 1928. [4]

HAGSTROM, WARREN O. "The Protestant Clergy as a Profession: Status and Prospects," *Berkeley Publications in Society and Institutions,* 3:1–12, Spring 1957.

——. *The Scientific Community.* New York: Basic Books, Inc., 1965.

HAIMSON, LEOPOLD. "Three Generations of the Soviet Intelligentsia," in Alex Inkeles and Kent Geiger (eds.), *Soviet Society.* Boston: Houghton Mifflin Company, 1961, pp. 619–626.

HALL, JOHN, AND D. CARADOG JONES. "Social Grading of Occupations," *British Journal of Sociology,* 1:31–55, March 1950. [13]

HALL, OSWALD. "Half Medical Man, Half Administrator: A Medical Dilemma," *Canadian Public Administration,* 2:185–194, December 1959. [12]

——. "The Informal Organization of the Medical Profession," *Canadian Journal of Economics and Political Science,* 12:30–44, February 1946. [9]

————. "The Stages of a Medical Career," in E. Gartly Jaco (ed.), *Patients, Physicians and Illness.* New York: Free Press, 1958, pp. 289–300. [4]

————. "Types of Medical Careers," *American Journal of Sociology,* 55:243–253, November 1949. [4]

HALL, RICHARD H. "Professionalization and Bureaucratization," *American Sociological Review,* 33:92–104, February 1968. [11]

HALL, ROBERT KING, AND OTHERS (eds.). *The Yearbook of Education, 1953.* London: Evans Bros., 1953. [4]

HALPIN, ANDREW W. *The Leadership Behavior of School Superintendents.* Columbus, Ohio: The Ohio State University Press, 1956. [12]

HAMMER, D. P. "Legal Education in the U.S.S.R.," *Soviet Studies,* 9:20–27, July 1957. [4]

HANSEN, W. LEE. "Professional Engineers: Salary Structure Problems," *Industrial Relations,* 2:33–44, May 1963.

HARDBECK, GEORGE W. "Occupational Trends in the United States 1900 to 1960 and Their Implications," *Labor Law Journal,* 13:361–373, May 1962.

HARMON, LINDSEY R. "High School Backgrounds of Science Doctorates," *Science,* 133:679–688, March 10, 1961. [4]

————. "Production of Psychology Doctorates in the U.S.," *American Psychologist,* 16:716–717, November 1961. [4]

HARMON, NOLAN B. "Ethics of the Protestant Ministry," *Annals of the American Academy of Political and Social Science,* 297:70–75, January 1955. [6]

HARPER, ROBERT A. "Should Marriage Counseling Become a Full-Fledged Specialty?" *Marriage and Family Living,* 15:338–340, November 1953. [3, 7]

HARRIS, RICHARD. *A Sacred Trust.* New York: New American Library, 1966. Historical account of the American Medical Association. Lobby against federal health insurance. [9]

HARRIS, SEYMOUR E. *The Economics of American Medicine.* New York: The Macmillan Company, 1964.

HART, A. TINDAL. *The Country Priest in English History.* London: Phoenix House, 1959. [2]

HARTMANN, GEORGE W. "The Relative Social Prestige of Representative Medical Specialties," *Journal of Applied Psychology,* 20:659–663, December 1936. [13]

HARTMANN, HEINZ. *Education for Business Leadership: The Role* of the German Hochschulen. Paris: Organization for European Economic Co-operation, 1955. [4]

HASKINS, CHARLES H. The Rise of Universities. New York: Holt, Rinehart and Winston, Inc., 1923. [2]

HATHAWAY, STARKE R. "A Study of Human Behavior: The Clinical Psychologist," American Psychologist, 13:257–265, June 1958. [4]

HAVEMAN, ERNEST, AND PATRICIA S. WEST. They Went to College. New York: Harcourt, Brace, & World, Inc., 1952. [4]

HAWKES, ROBERT W. "The Role of the Psychiatric Administrator," Administrative Science Quarterly, 6:89–106, June 1961. [12]

HAZARD, JOHN N. Settling Disputes in Soviet Society. New York: Columbia University Press, 1960.

HAZELTINE, H. D. "Legal Profession and Legal Education: Ancient and Medieval," in Encyclopedia of the Social Sciences. New York: The Macmillan Company, 1933, Vol. 9, pp. 324–334. [2]

HEALY, EDWIN F. Medical Ethics. Chicago: Loyola University Press, 1956. [6]

HEERMANCE, EDGAR L. Codes of Ethics. Burlington, Vt.: Free Press Printing Co., 1924. [6]

———. The Ethics of Business. New York: Harper & Row, Publishers, 1926. [6]

HENDERSON, ALGO D. "Finding and Training Academic Administrators," Public Administration Review, 20:17–22, Winter 1960. [4]

HENDERSON, L. J. "Physician and Patient as a Social System," New England Journal of Medicine, 212:819–823, May 2, 1935. [5]

HILLER, E. T. Social Relations and Structures. New York: Harper & Row, Publishers, 1947, Chaps. 33–35 on the professions.

HILTNER, SEWARD. "Tension and Mutual Support Among the Helping Professions," Social Service Review, 31:377–389, December 1957. [10]

HODGE, ROBERT W., PAUL M. SIEGEL, AND PETER H. ROSSI. "Occupational Prestige in the United States, 1925–1963," American Journal of Sociology, 70:286–302, November 1964. [13]

HODGE, ROBERT W., DONALD J. TREIMAN, AND PETER H. ROSSI. "A Comparative Study of Occupational Prestige," in Reinhard Bendix and Seymour Martin Lipset (eds.), Class, Status, and Power, 2nd ed. New York: Free Press, 1966, pp. 309–321. [13]

HOFFMAN, LOIS. "How Do Good Doctors Get That Way?" in E.

Gartly Jaco (ed.), *Patients, Physicians and Illness*. New York: Free Press, 1958, pp. 365–381. [5]

HOFSTADTER, RICHARD, AND C. DEWITT HARDY. *The Development and Scope of Higher Education in the United States*. New York: Columbia University Press, 1952. [4]

HOFSTADTER, RICHARD, AND WILSON SMITH (eds.). *American Higher Education: A Documentary History*. Chicago: The University of Chicago Press, 1961. 2 vols. [2]

HOFSTETTER, H. W. *Optometry: Professional, Economic and Legal Aspects*. St. Louis, Mo.: C. V. Mosby Co., 1948.

HOLLINGSHEAD, AUGUST B. "Ingroup Membership and Academic Selection," *American Sociological Review*, 3:826–833, December 1938. [4]

HOLLIS, ERNEST V., AND ALICE L. TAYLOR. *Social Work Education in the United States*. New York: Council on Social Work Education, 1959. [4]

HOOKER, WORTHINGTON. *Physician and Patient; or a Practical View of the Mutual Duties, Relations, and Interests of the Medical Profession and the Community*. New York: Baker and Scribner, 1849. [5]

HOOVER, THEODORE J., AND JOHN C. L. FISH. *The Engineering Profession*, 2nd ed. Stanford, Calif.: Stanford University Press, 1950.

HOPKE, WILLIAM E. *The Encyclopedia of Careers and Vocational Guidance*. Garden City, N.Y.: Doubleday & Company, Inc., 1967. 2 vols.

HORSKY, CHARLES A. *The Washington Lawyer*. Boston: Little, Brown and Company, 1952.

HOWE, RUEL L. "A More Adequate Training for Ministers," in Paul B. Maves (ed.), *The Church and Mental Health*. New York: Charles Scribner's Sons, 1953, pp. 239–252. [4]

HOWER, RALPH M., AND CHARLES D. ORTH. *Managers and Scientists: Some Human Problems in Industrial Research Organizations*. Boston: Graduate School of Business Administration, Harvard University, 1963. [11]

HOWES, RAYMOND F. *Toward Better Preparation of College and University Administrators*. Washington, D.C.: Association for Higher Education, 1964. [4]

HUGHES, EDWARD. "The Professions in the Eighteenth Century," *The Durham University Journal*, 44:46–55, March 1952. [2]

HUGHES, EVERETT C. "Dilemmas and Contradictions of Status," *American Journal of Sociology*, 50:353–359, March 1945. [13]

———. "Education for a Profession," *Library Quarterly*, 31:336–343, October 1961. [4]

———. "The Making of a Physician: General Statement of Ideas and Problems," *Human Organization*, 14: 21–25, Fall 1956. [4]

———. *Men and Their Work*. New York: Free Press, 1958.

———. "Mistakes at Work," *Canadian Journal of Economics and Political Science*, 17:320–327, August 1951. [6]

———. "Professions," *Daedalus*, 92:655–668, Fall 1963. Reprinted in Kenneth S. Lynn (ed.), *The Professions in America*. Boston: Houghton Mifflin Company, 1965. [1]

———. "The Professions in Society," *Canadian Journal of Economics and Political Science*, 26:54–61, February 1960. [1, 14]

———. "Stress and Strain in Professional Education," *Harvard Educational Review*, 29:319–329, Fall 1959. [4]

———. "The Study of Occupations," in Robert K. Merton and others (eds.), *Sociology Today: Problems and Prospects*. New York: Basic Books, Inc., 1959, Chap. 20, pp. 442–458.

HUGHES, EVERETT C., AND OTHERS. *Twenty Thousand Nurses Tell Their Story*. Philadelphia, Pa.: J. B. Lippincott Company, 1958.

HUNTINGTON, MARY JEAN. "The Development of a Professional Self-Image," in Robert K. Merton and others (eds.), *The Student Physician*. Cambridge, Mass.: The Commonwealth Fund, 1957, pp. 179–187. [6]

———. "Sociology of Professions, 1945–55," in Hans L. Zetterberg (ed.), *Sociology in the United States of America*. Paris: UNESCO, 1956, pp. 87–93. [1]

HUNTINGTON, SAMUEL P. "Power, Expertise and the Military Profession," *Daedalus*, 92:785–807, Fall 1963. Reprinted in Kenneth S. Lynn (ed.), *The Professions in America*. Boston: Houghton Mifflin Company, 1965.

———. *The Soldier and the State*. Cambridge, Mass.: The Belknapp Press of Harvard University Press, 1957.

HURST, JAMES W. *The Growth of American Law*. Boston: Little, Brown and Company, 1950. [2]

HUTCHINS, EDWIN B. "The Study of Applicants, 1961–1962," *Journal of Medical Education*, 38:707–717, September 1963. [4]

———. "The Study of Applicants, 1962–1963," *Journal of Medical Education*, 38:999–1003, December 1963. [4]

HUTCHINS, EDWIN B., JUDITH REITMAN, AND DOROTHY KLAUB. "Minorities, Manpower and Medicine," *Journal of Medical Education*, 42:809–821, September 1967.

HUTCHINS, ROBERT M. "The Administrator," *Journal of Higher Education,* 17:395–407, November 1946. [12]

HYDE, DAVID R., AND PAYSON WOLFF. "The American Medical Association: Power, Purpose, and Politics in Organized Medicine," *Yale Law Journal,* 63:938–1022, May 1954. [9]

IMSE, THOMAS P. *The Professionalization of Business Management.* New York: Vantage Press, 1962. [3]

INKELES, ALEX. "Social Stratification and Mobility in the Soviet Union: 1940–1950," *American Sociological Review,* 15:465–479, August 1950.

INKELES, ALEX, AND PETER H. ROSSI. "National Comparisons of Occupational Prestige," *American Journal of Sociology,* 61:329–339, January 1956.

INTERNATIONAL LABOUR OFFICE. *Employment and Conditions of Work of Nurses.* Geneva: La Tribune de Genève, 1960.

IVANOV, NIKOLAY. "The Training of Soviet Engineers," in George L. Kline (ed.), *Soviet Education.* New York: Columbia University Press, 1957. [4]

JACO, E. GARTLY (ed.). *Patients, Physicians and Illness.* New York: Free Press, 1958.

JAHODA, MARIE. "A Social Psychologist Views Nursing as a Profession," *American Journal of Nursing,* 61:52–59, July 1961.

JAMES, JEAN M. "The Social Role of the Priest," *American Catholic Sociological Review,* 16:94–103, June 1955. [13]

JANOWITZ, MORRIS (ed.). *The New Military.* New York: Russell Sage Foundation, 1964.

——. *The Professional Soldier: A Social and Political Portrait.* New York: Free Press, 1960.

——. *Sociology and the Military Establishment,* rev. ed. New York: Russell Sage Foundation, 1965.

JELLIFFE, D. B. "Cultural Variation and the Practical Pediatrician," in E. Gartly Jaco (ed.), *Patients, Physicians and Illness.* New York: Free Press, 1958, pp. 397–405. [5]

JENKINS, DANIEL. *The Educated Society.* London: Faber and Faber, Ltd., 1966, especially pp. 83–96 on "the use of power by the educated," and Chap. III (pp. 97–143), "The Academic Community as a School of Maturity." [6, 14]

——. *The Protestant Ministry.* London: Faber and Faber, Ltd., 1958.

JENKINSON, HILARY. *The English Archivist: A New Profession.* London, H. K. Lewis, 1948. [3, 7]

JOHNSON, CHARLES S. *The Negro College Graduate.* Chapel Hill, N.C.: University of North Carolina Press, 1938.

JOHNSON, DAVIS G., AND EDWIN B. HUTCHINS. "Doctor or Dropout," *The Journal of Medical Education,* Vol. 41, No. 12, entire issue, December 1966. [4]

JOHNSON, ELMER H. "The Professional in Correction: Status and Prospects," *Social Forces,* 40:168–176, December 1961. [3]

JOHNSTONE, QUINTIN, AND DAN HOPSON, JR. *Lawyers and Their Work: An Analysis of the Legal Profession in the United States and England.* Indianapolis, Ind.: The Bobbs-Merrill Company, Inc., 1967. Includes extensive references.

JUDD, ROBERT P. "The Newspaper Reporter in a Suburban City," *Journalism Quarterly,* 38:35–42, Winter 1961.

JUDKINS, CALVERT J. *Trade and Professional Associations of the United States.* Washington, D.C.: U.S. Department of Commerce, 1942. [6]

KADUSHIN, CHARLES. "Social Distance Between Client and Professional," *American Journal of Sociology,* 67:517–531, March 1962. [5]

KAHN, ALFRED J. *Issues in American Social Work.* New York: Columbia University Press, 1959.

KANDEL, I. L. *Professional Aptitude Tests in Medicine, Law, and Engineering.* New York: Teacher's College, Columbia University Press, 1940.

KAPLAN, NORMAN. "Research Administration and the Administrator: U.S.S.R. and U.S.," *Administrative Science Quarterly,* 6:51–72, June 1961. [12]

———. "The Role of the Research Administrator," *Administrative Science Quarterly,* 4:20–42, June 1959. [12]

KELSALL, R. K. *Higher Civil Servants in Britain.* London: Routledge and Kegan Paul, Ltd., 1955, especially Chap. 10, "The Nature of the Profession."

———. "The Social Origins of Higher Civil Servants in Great Britain, Now and in the Past," in *Transactions of the Second World Congress of Sociology.* London: International Sociological Association, 1954, Vol. II, pp. 131–142. [4]

KELSALL, R. K., AND OTHERS. "The New Middle Class in the Power Structure of Great Britain," in *Transactions of the Third World Congress of Sociology.* London: International Sociological Association, 1956, Vol. III, pp. 320–329. [13]

KENDALL, KATHERINE A. "Social Work Education: A Responsibility of the Total Profession," *Social Casework*, 34:17–23, January 1953. [4]

KENDALL, PATRICIA L. "Impact of Training Programs on the Young Physician's Attitudes and Experiences," *The Journal of the American Medical Association*, 176:992–997, June 24, 1961. [4]

———. *The Relationship Between Medical Educators and Medical Practitioners: Sources of Strain and Occasions for Cooperation.* Evanston, Ill.: Association of American Medical Colleges, 1962. [7]

KENDALL, PATRICIA L., AND ROBERT K. MERTON. "Medical Education as a Social Process," in E. Gartly Jaco (ed.), *Patients, Physicians and Illness*. New York: Free Press, 1958, pp. 321–350. [4]

KENDALL, PATRICIA L., AND HANAN C. SELVIN. "Tendencies Toward Specialization in Medical Training," in Robert K. Merton and others (eds.), *The Student Physician*. Cambridge, Mass.: The Commonwealth Fund, 1957, pp. 153–174. [7]

KEPHART, WILLIAM M. "Status After Death," *American Sociological Review*, 15:635–643, October 1950. Practices of funeral directors.

KERCKHOFF, RICHARD K. "The Profession of Marriage Counseling as Viewed by Members of Four Allied Professions: A Study in the Sociology of Occupations," *Marriage and Family Living*, 15:340–344, November 1953. [7]

KERSHAW, JOSEPH A., AND ROLAND N. MCKEAN. *Teacher Shortages and Salary Schedules*. New York: McGraw-Hill, Inc., 1962.

KIBRE, PEARL. *Scholarly Privileges in the Middle Ages: The Rights, Privileges, and Immunities of Scholars and Universities at Bologna, Padua, Paris, and Oxford*. Cambridge, Mass.: Mediaeval Academy of America, 1962. [2]

KIDD, J. ROBY. "Continuing Education in the Professions," in University of British Columbia, *Symposium on Continuing Education in the Professions*. Vancouver: University of British Columbia, 1962, pp. 17–31. [4]

KING, STANLEY H. *Perceptions of Illness and Medical Practice*. New York: Russell Sage Foundation, 1962. [5]

KITCHEN, HELEN (ed.). *The Educated African*. New York: Frederick A. Praeger, 1962.

KOERNER, JAMES D. *The Miseducation of American Teachers*. Boston: Houghton Mifflin Company, 1963. [4]

KOOS, EARL LOMON. *The Sociology of the Patient*. New York: McGraw-Hill, Inc., 1950. [5]

KORNAUSER, WILLIAM. *Scientists in Industry*. Berkeley: University of California Press, 1962. Chap. I, "Strains Between Professions and Organizations" includes a brief discussion of the criteria of professionalism. [1, 11]

KOROL, ALEXANDER G. *Soviet Education for Science and Technology*. Boston and New York: Massachusetts Institute of Technology and John Wiley & Sons, Inc., 1957. [4]

KRAMER, CHARLES. *The Negligent Doctor*. New York: Crown Publishers, 1968. [5]

KRIESBERG, LOUIS. "The Bases of Occupational Prestige: The Case of Dentists," *American Sociological Review*, 27:238–244, April 1962. [8, 13]

KUIPER, G. "The Recruitment of the Learned Professions in the Netherlands," in *Transactions of the Third World Congress of Sociology*. London: International Sociological Association, 1956, Vol. III, pp. 230–238. [4]

KURTZ, RUSSELL H. (ed.). *The Public Assistance Worker: His Responsibility to the Applicant, the Community and Himself*. New York: Russell Sage Foundation, 1938. [5, 14]

KUTNER, BERNARD. "Surgeons and Their Patients: A Study in Social Perceptions," in E. Gartly Jaco (ed.), *Patients, Physicians and Illness*. New York: Free Press, 1958, pp. 384–397. [5]

LABEDZ, LEOPOLD. "The Structure of the Soviet Intelligentsia," *Daedalus*, 89:503–519, Summer 1960.

LACHENAL, PAUL. "The Organized Bar in Switzerland," *American Bar Association Journal*, 39:109–169, February 1953. [9]

LADINSKY, JACK. "Careers of Lawyers, Law Practice and Legal Institutions," *American Sociological Review*, 28:47–54, February 1961.

LAMBERT, WALLACE E., AND OTTO KLINEBERG. "Cultural Comparisons of Boys' Occupational Aspirations," *British Journal of Social and Clinical Psychology*, 3:56–65, February 1964. [4]

LANCOUR, HAROLD. "The Librarian's Search for Status," *Library Quarterly*, 31:369–381, October 1961. [13]

LANDSBERGER, HENRY A. "Interaction Process Analysis of Professional Behavior: A Study of Labor Mediators in Twelve Labor-Management Disputes," *American Sociological Review*, 20:566–575, October 1955. [5]

LAREY, JOHN L. (ed.). *The Accounting Profession*. New York: American Institute of Certified Public Accountants, 1962.

LASKI, HAROLD J. "The Decline of the Professions," *Harper's Magazine*, 171:676–685, November 1935. [2]

LEFEBVRE, GUSTAVE. *Essai sur la Médicine Egyptienne à l' Epoque Pharonique*. Paris: Presses Universitaires de France, 1956. [2]

LEGA, CARLO. *La Libera Professione*. Milano: Giuffré, 1950.

LEIGH, ROBERT D. *The Public Library in the United States*. New York: Columbia University Press, 1950, especially Chap. 10, "Library Personnel and Training."

LEPAULLE, PIERRE G. "Law Practice in France," *Columbia Law Review*, 50:945–958, November 1950.

LESSA, WILLIAM A., AND EVON Z. VOGT (eds.). *Reader in Comparative Religion*, 2nd ed. New York: Harper & Row, Publishers, 1965, Chap. 10, "Shamans and Priests."

LEVINE, DAVID L. "Teacher-Counselor: Role and Qualifications," *Marriage and Family Living*, 15:313–315, November 1953. [5]

LEVINSON, HARRY. "The Psychologist in Industry," *Harvard Business Review*, 37:93–99, September–October 1959. [11]

LEWIN, BERTRAM D., AND HELEN ROSS. *Psychoanalytic Education in the United States*. New York: W. W. Norton & Company, Inc., 1960. [4]

LEWIS, GORDON F., AND C. ARNOLD ANDERSON. "Social Origins and Social Mobility of Businessmen in an American City," in *Transactions of the Third World Congress of Sociology*. London: International Sociological Association, 1956, Vol. III, pp. 253–266. [4]

LEWIS, ROY, AND ANGUS MAUDE. *The English Middle Classes*. New York: Alfred A. Knopf, Inc., 1950, especially Chap. 9, "The Professions."

———. *Professional People*. London: Phoenix House Ltd., 1952.

Library Quarterly, The, Vol. 31, No. 4, October 1961. Articles on Professionalization of the Occupation, History, Education, Specialization, and Organization.

LIEBERMAN, MYRON. "The Disorganization Man," *School and Society*, 86:165–167, April 12, 1958. A critique of the American Association of University Professors. [9]

———. *Education as a Profession*. Englewood Cliffs, N.J.: Prentice-Hall, Inc., 1956.

LIEBERSON, STANLEY. "Ethnic Groups and the Practice of Medicine," *American Sociological Review*, 23:542–549, October 1958.

LIGHTMAN, J. B. "Welfare and the Profession of Social Work Vis-à-Vis In-Service and Volunteer Training," *Indian Journal of Social Work*, 24:27–34, April 1963. [4]

LINDSEY, ALMONT. *Socialized Medicine in England and Wales: The National Health Service.* Chapel Hill: University of North Carolina Press, 1962.

LIPSET, SEYMOUR M., AND REINHARD BENDIX. "Social Mobility and Occupational Career Patterns," *American Journal of Sociology,* 57:366–374, January 1952; and 57:494–504, March 1952. [4]

LLEWELLYN, KARL N., AND E. ADAMSON HOEBEL. *The Cheyenne Way.* Norman: University of Oklahoma Press, 1941. Legal institutions of the Cheyenne. [2]

LLOYD-JONES, ESTHER, AND MARY V. HOLMAN. "Why People Become Teachers," in Lindley J. Stiles (ed.), *The Teacher's Role in American Society.* New York: Harper & Row, Publishers, 1957, pp. 235–246. [4]

LORTIE, DAN C. "Anesthesia: From Nurse's Work to Medical Specialty," in E. Gartly Jaco (ed.), *Patients, Physicians and Illness.* New York: Free Press, 1958, pp. 405–412. [7]

————. "Laymen to Lawmen: Law School, Careers, and Professional Socialization," *Harvard Educational Review,* 29:352–369, Fall 1959. [4]

LOWE, C. MARSHALL. "Value Orientations: An Ethical Dilemma," *American Psychologist,* 14:687–693, November 1959. [6]

LOWELL, A. LAWRENCE. "The Profession of Business," *Harvard Business Review,* 1:129–131, January 1923.

LUDLUM, ROBERT P. "Academic Freedom and Tenure: A History," *Antioch Review,* 10:3–34, Spring 1950. [11]

LUND, FRED B. *Greek Medicine.* New York: Paul B. Hoeber, 1936. [2]

LUND, THOMAS G. "The Legal Profession in England and Wales," *Journal of the American Judicature Society,* 35:134–145, February 1952.

LUNDBERG, FERDINAND. "The Legal Profession: A Social Phenomenon," *Harper's Magazine,* 178:1–14, December 1938.

LURIE, MELVIN. "Professors, Physicians, and Unionism," *American Association of University Professors Bulletin,* 48:272–276, Autumn 1962. [9]

LUXON, NORVAL NEIL. *The Accrediting Program of the American Council on Education for Journalism.* Chattanooga, Tenn.: Southern Newspapers Publishers Association, 1952. [6]

LYNN, KENNETH S., AND THE EDITORS OF *Daedalus* (eds.). *The Professions in America.* Boston: Houghton Mifflin Company, 1965.

MACE, DAVID R. "What Is a Marriage Counselor?", *Marriage and Family Living*, 16:135–138, May 1954.

MACGREGOR, FRANCES COOKE. *Social Science in Nursing.* New York: John Wiley & Sons, Inc., 1965.

———. *Social Science in Nursing: Applications for the Improvement of Patient Care.* New York: Russell Sage Foundation, 1960. [4]

MACHLUP, FRITZ. *The Production and Distribution of Knowledge in the United States.* Princeton, N.J.: Princeton University Press, 1962.

MACIVER, ROBERT M. "Social Significance of Professional Ethics," *Annals of the American Academy of Political and Social Science,* 237:118–124, January 1955. [14]

MACK, RAYMOND W. "Occupational Determinateness: A Problem and Hypothesis in Role Theory," *Social Forces,* 35:20–25, October 1956.

MADDOCK, CHARLES S. "The Corporation Law Department," *Harvard Business Review,* 30:119–136, March–April 1952.

———. "Present and Future Role of House Counsel," in University of Chicago, Law School, *Conference on the Profession of Law and Legal Education,* Conference Series No. 11, December 4, 1952. Chicago: published by the Law School, pp. 11–22. [11]

MADDOX, JOHN LEE. *The Medicine Man: A Sociological Study of the Character and Evolution of Shamanism.* New York: The Macmillan Company, 1923. [2]

MADSEN, WILLIAM. "Shamanism in Mexico," *Southwestern Journal of Anthropology,* 11:48–58, Spring 1955. [2]

MANGAT-RAI, C. RAJINDER. "Engineering Education in India," *The Educational Record,* 42:231–241, July 1961. [4]

MANIS, JEROME G. "A Quantitative Note on the Academic Role," *American Sociological Review,* 16:837–839, December 1951.

MANSON, T. W. *The Church's Ministry.* Philadelphia, Pa.: The Westminster Press, 1948.

MARCSON, SIMON. "Decision-Making in a University Physics Department," *American Behavioral Scientist,* 6:37–39, December 1962.

———. *The Scientist in American Industry.* Princeton, N.J.: Industrial Relations Section, Princeton University, 1960. [11]

MARGULIES, HAROLD. "The Structure of Medical Education in Pakistan," *Journal of Medical Education,* 38:752–759, September 1963. [4]

MARSHALL, T. H. *Class, Citizenship, and Social Development*. Garden City, N.Y.: Doubleday & Company, Inc., 1964, Chap. VI, "The Recent History of Professionalism in Relation to Social Structure and Social Policy." [3]

MARTIN, T. D. "The Profession Looks at Itself." *Annals of the American Academy of Political and Social Science*, 265:151–159, September 1949. Relates to teaching.

MARTIN, WILLIAM. "Preferences for Types of Patients," in Robert K. Merton and others (eds.), *The Student Physician*. Cambridge, Mass.: The Commonwealth Fund, 1957, pp. 189–205. [5]

MASLAND, JOHN W., AND LAURENCE I. RADWAY. *Soldiers and Scholars: Military Education and National Policy*. Princeton, N.J.: Princeton University Press, 1957. [4]

MASON, WARD S., AND NEAL GROSS. "Intra-Occupational Prestige Differentiation: The School Superintendency," *American Sociological Review*, 20:326–331, June 1955. [8]

MATTFELD, JACQUELYN, AND CAROL VAN AKEN (eds.). *Women and the Scientific Professions*. Cambridge, Mass.: The M.I.T. Press, 1965.

MATTHEWS, JOSEPH J. "The Profession of War Correspondence," *Journalism Quarterly*, 33:23–34, Winter 1956.

MAUKSCH, HANS O. "Becoming a Nurse: A Selective View," *Annals of the American Academy of Political and Social Science*, 346:88–98, March 1963. [4]

MCCAWLEY, ALFRED L. *Professional Engineering Registration Laws*. Jefferson City, Mo.: Trustee Publication Fund, 1954. [6]

MCCLUGGAGE, ROBERT W. *A History of the American Dental Association*. Chicago: American Dental Association, 1959. [9]

MCCORCLE, THOMAS. "Chiropractic: A Deviant Theory of Disease and Treatment in Contemporary Western Culture," *Human Organization*, 20:20–23, Spring 1961. [7, 10]

MCCORMACK, THELMA H. "The Druggists' Dilemma: Problems of a Marginal Occupation," *American Journal of Sociology*, 61:308–315, January 1956. [7, 10]

MCEWEN, WILLIAM J. "Position Conflict and Professional Orientation in a Research Organization," *Administrative Science Quarterly*, 1:208–224, September 1956. [11]

MCGLOTHLIN, WILLIAM J. "The Accommodation of Specialization," *Library Quarterly*, 31:356–364, October 1961. [7]

———. *Patterns of Professional Education*. New York: G. P. Putnam's Sons, 1960. [4]

MCGRATH, EARL J. *Liberal Education in the Professions.* New York: Bureau of Publications, Teachers' College, Columbia University, 1959. [4]

———. "Professional Curricula in Liberal Arts Colleges," *School and Society,* 87:188–191, April 25, 1959. [4]

MCLAUGHLIN, ROBERT W. *Architect: Creating Man's Environment.* New York: The Macmillan Company, 1962.

MEANS, JAMES HOWARD. "Homo Medicus Americanus," *Daedalus,* 92: 701–723, Fall 1963. Reprinted in Kenneth S. Lynn (ed.), *The Professions in America.* Boston: Houghton Mifflin Company, 1965.

MELTON, MARLI SCHENCK. "Health Manpower and Negro Health: The Negro Physician," *Journal of Medical Education,* 43:788–814, July 1968.

MENDENHALL, DOROTHY MABEL. *Midwifery in Denmark.* Washington, D.C.: Government Printing Office, 1929.

MENZEL, HERBERT. "Innovation, Integration, and Marginality: A Survey of Physicians," *American Sociological Review,* 25:704–713, October 1960. [7]

MERTON, ROBERT K. "The Functions of the Professional Association," *American Journal of Nursing,* 58:50–54, January 1958. [9]

———. "The Search for Professional Status: Sources, Costs, and Consequences," *American Journal of Nursing,* 60:662–664, May 1960. [3]

———. *Social Theory and Social Structure,* rev. ed. New York: Free Press, 1957, Chap. VII, "Role of the Intellectual in Public Bureaucracy." [11]

———. "Some Preliminaries to a Sociology of Medical Education," in Robert K. Merton and others (eds.), *The Student Physician.* Cambridge, Mass.: The Commonwealth Fund, 1957, pp. 3–79. [4]

———. *Some Thoughts on the Professions in American Society.* Brown University Papers, No. 37, June 6, 1960. [1]

MERTON, ROBERT K., AND ELINOR BARBER. "Sociological Ambivalence," in Edward A. Tiryakian (ed.), *Sociological Theory, Values, and Sociocultural Change.* New York: Free Press, 1963, pp. 91–120. Primarily concerned with professional-client relations. [5]

MERTON, ROBERT K., GEORGE READER, AND PATRICIA L. KENDALL (eds.). *The Student Physician: Introductory Studies in the Sociology of Medical Education.* Cambridge, Mass.: Harvard University Press for The Commonwealth Fund, 1957. [4]

MERTON, ROBERT K., AND OTHERS. "Socialization: A Terminological Note," in Robert K. Merton and others (eds.), *The Student Physi-*

cian. Cambridge, Mass.: The Commonwealth Fund, 1957, pp. 287–293, Appendix A. [4]

————. "Studies in the Sociology of Medical Education," *Journal of Medical Education,* 31:552–564, August 1956. [4]

METCALF, HENRY C. (ed.). *Business Management as a Profession.* Chicago: A. W. Shaw Company, 1927.

MEYER, HENRY J. "Professionalization and Social Work," in Alfred J. Kahn (ed.), *Issues in American Social Work.* New York: Columbia University Press, 1959, pp. 319–340. [3]

MIKHAILOV, ALEXANDER A. "The Organization of Scientific Work in the U.S.S.R.," *American Review of the Soviet Union,* 8:26–35, March 1947.

MILLER, GEORGE A. "Professionals in Bureaucracy: Alienation Among Industrial Scientists and Engineers," *American Sociological Review,* 32:755–768, October 1967. [11]

MILLER, NORMAN P. "Professional Education," *Annals of the American Academy of Political and Social Science,* 313:58–67, September 1957. [4]

MILLER, SAMUEL H. "The Tangle of Ethics," *Harvard Business Review,* 38:59–62, January–February 1960. Ethical problems in industry. [6]

MILLERSON, GEOFFREY. *The Qualifying Associations: A Study in Professionalization.* London: Routledge and Kegan Paul, Ltd., 1964. Historical and statistical analysis of associations in England and Wales. Appendix I lists all such associations, year founded, year exam introduced, membership grades, size, and journals published. [3, 6]

MILLS, C. WRIGHT. *White Collar: The American Middle Classes.* New York: Oxford University Press, 1951, especially Chap. 6, "Old Professions and New Skills," pp. 112–141.

MILLS, LAWRENCE W. *The Osteopathic Profession and Its Colleges.* Chicago: American Osteopathic Association, 1959.

MISRA, B. B. *The Indian Middle Classes: Their Growth in Modern Times.* London: Oxford University Press, 1961, especially Chaps. 7 and 11.

MITFORD, JESSICA. *The American Way of Death.* New York: Simon and Schuster, Inc., 1963. Critical discussion of funeral directors and "the burial business."

MONTAGUE, JOEL B., AND BERNARD PUSTILNIK. "Prestige Ranking of Occupations in an American City with Reference to Hall's and

Jones' Study," *British Journal of Sociology*, 5:154–160, June 1954. [13]

MOORE, WALTER WILLIAM. "The Preparation of the Modern Minister," in John R. Mott (ed.), *The Claims and Opportunities of the Christian Ministry*. New York: YMCA Press, 1911, pp. 60–83. [4]

MOORE, WILBERT E. "Changes in Occupational Structures," in Neil J. Smelser and Seymour Martin Lipset (eds.), *Social Structure and Social Mobility in Economic Development*. Chicago: Aldine Publishing Company, 1966, pp. 194–212. [2]

————. *The Conduct of the Corporation*. New York: Random House, Inc., 1962. Chap. XIII, "Two-Faced Experts" discusses representational functions of corporate staffs; Chap. XVIII, "The Advice Market," concerns external consultants to corporate managements. [5, 11]

————. "Economic and Professional Institutions," in Neil J. Smelser (ed.), *Sociology: An Introduction*. New York: John Wiley & Sons, Inc., 1967, Chap. 5, pp. 273–328.

————. "Notes for a General Theory of Labor Organization," *Industrial and Labor Relations Review*, 13:387–397, April 1960.

MORE, DOUGLAS M. "The Dental Student," *Journal of the American College of Dentists*, 28:1–93, March 1961. [4]

————. "A Note on Occupational Origins of Health Service Professions," *American Sociological Review*, 25:403–404, June 1960. [4]

MORE, DOUGLAS M., AND NATHAN KOHN, JR. "Some Motives for Entering Dentistry," *American Journal of Sociology*, 66:48–53, July 1960. [4]

MORRIS, CHARLES N. "Career Patterns of Teachers," in Lindley J. Stiles (ed.), *The Teacher's Role in American Society*. New York: Harper & Row, Publishers, 1957, pp. 247–263. [11]

MORRIS, RICHARD T., AND RAYMOND J. MURPHY. "The Situs Dimension in Occupational Structure," *American Sociological Review*, 24:231–239, April 1959. [13]

MORISON, ROBERT S. "The Importance of Being Earnest: The Physician's Role and Image," *The Graduate Journal*, 7:151–165, December 1965. [5]

MORSE, WILLIAM R. *Chinese Medicine*. New York: Paul B. Hoeber, 1934. Historical. [2]

MOWRER, O. HOBART. "Payment or Repayment? The Problem of Private Practice," *American Psychologist*, 18:577–580, September 1963. [5]

MOYNIHAN, DANIEL P. "The Professionalization of Reform," *The Public Interest*, 1:6–16, Fall 1965. [3]

MUELLER, FREDERICK F., AND HUGH HARTSHORNE. *Ethical Dilemmas of Ministers*. New York: Charles Scribner's Sons, 1937. [6]

MUELLER-DIETZ, HEINZ. *Medical Education in the Soviet Union*. Berlin: Prof. Dr. Max Brandt, 1958. [4]

NAEGELE, KASPAR D. "Clergymen, Teachers and Psychiatrists: A Study in Roles and Socialization," *Canadian Journal of Economics and Political Science*, 22:46–62, February 1956.

NATIONAL ACADEMY OF SCIENCES–NATIONAL RESEARCH COUNCIL. *Scientific and Technical Societies in the United States and Canada*. Published periodically by the Academy, Washington, D.C. Officers, publications, membership, medals and awards, addresses, membership requirements, of 1800 national organizations listed. [6]

NATIONAL EDUCATION ASSOCIATION. *Profile of the School Superintendent*. Washington, D.C.: American Association of School Administrators, 1960.

NATIONAL RESEARCH COUNCIL, OFFICE OF SCIENTIFIC PERSONNEL. *Doctorate Production in United States Universities 1920–1962: With Baccalaureate Origins of Doctorates in Science, Arts and Professions*. Washington, D.C.: National Academy of Sciences, 1963. [4]

NATIONAL SOCIETY FOR THE STUDY OF EDUCATION, COMMITTEE ON EDUCATION FOR THE PROFESSIONS. *Education for the Professions*. Chicago: The Society, 1962. [4]

NEW, PETER K. "The Osteopathic Student: A Study in Dilemma," in E. Gartly Jaco (ed.), *Patients, Physicians and Illness*. New York: Free Press, 1958, pp. 413–421. [4]

NEWCOMB, THEODORE M. "On 'The Certification of Academic Professions': An Exchange," *American Sociological Review*. 24:95–96, February 1959. [6]

NEW YORK LIFE INSURANCE COMPANY, CAREER INFORMATION SERVICE. *Guide to Career Information: A Bibliography of Recent Occupational Literature*. New York: Harper & Row, Publishers, 1957.

NICHOLSON, LOWELL S. *The Law Schools of the United States*. Baltimore: The Lord Baltimore Press, 1958. [4]

NIEBUHR, H. RICHARD, AND OTHERS. *The Advancement of Theological Education*. New York: Harper & Row, Publishers, 1957. [4]

NIEBUHR, H. RICHARD, AND DANIEL D. WILLIAMS (eds.). *The Minis-*

try in Historical Perspective. New York: Harper & Row, Publishers, 1956. [2]

NIGHTINGALE, FLORENCE. *Notes on Nursing: What It Is, and What It Is Not*. New York: D. Appleton and Company, 1860.

NORDAL, JÓHANNES. "The Recruitment of the Professions in Iceland," in *Transactions of the Second World Congress of Sociology*. London: International Sociological Association, 1954, Vol. II, pp. 153–165. [4]

NORTH, CECIL C., AND PAUL K. HATT. "Jobs and Occupations: A Popular Evaluation," in Logan Wilson and William L. Kolb (eds.), *Sociological Analysis*. New York: Harcourt, Brace & World, Inc., 1949, pp. 464–474. [13]

NORTHRUP, HERBERT R. *Unionization of Professional Engineers and Chemists*. New York: Industrial Relations Counselors, 1946. [9]

NUNBERG, HERMAN. "Psychological Interrelations Between Physician and Patient," *The Psychoanalytic Review*. 25:297–308, July 1938. [5]

NUNNALLY, JUM, AND JOHN M. KITTROSS. "Public Attitudes Toward Mental Health Professions," *American Psychologist*, 13:589–594, October 1958. [13]

O'DONOVAN, THOMAS R., AND ARTHUR X. DEEGAN. "Some Career Determinants of Church Executives," *Sociology and Social Research*, 48:58–68, October 1963. [4]

OLENCKI, MARGARET. "Range of Patient Contacts in the Comprehensive Care and Teaching Program," in Robert K. Merton and others (eds.), *The Student Physician*. Cambridge, Mass.: The Commonwealth Fund, 1957, pp. 271–284. [5]

OPINION RESEARCH CORPORATION. *Engineering Professionalism in Industry*. Princeton, N.J.: Opinion Research Corporation, 1960. [9]

OPLER, MARVIN K. "Industrial Societies and the Changing Roles of Doctors," *Journal of Occupational Medicine*, 4:237–241, May 1962.

ORLEANS, LEO A. *Professional Manpower and Education in Communist China*. Washington, D.C.: Government Printing Office, 1961.

ORNSTEIN, MARTHA. *The Role of Scientific Societies in the Seventeenth Century*. Chicago: University of Chicago Press, 1928. [2]

ORZACK, LOUIS H. "Work as a 'Central Life Interest' of Professionals," in Erwin O. Smigel (ed.), *Work and Leisure*. New Haven, Conn.: College and University Press, 1963, pp. 73–84. [6]

ORZACK, LOUIS H., AND JOHN R. UGLUM. "Sociological Perspectives of the Profession of Optometry," *American Journal of Optometry and Archives of American Academy of Optometry.* 35:407–424, August 1958.

OSLER, WILLIAM. *The Evolution of Modern Medicine.* New Haven, Conn.: Yale University Press, 1921. [2]

OSTER, GERALD. "Scientific Research in the U.S.S.R.: Organization and Planning," *Annals of the American Academy of Political and Social Science,* 263:134–139, May 1949. [9]

PARSONS, TALCOTT. "Illness and the Role of the Physician: A Sociological Perspective," *American Journal of Orthopsychiatry,* 21:452–460, July 1951. [5]

———. "Mental Illness and 'Spiritual Malaise': The Role of the Psychiatrist and of the Minister of Religion," in Talcott Parsons, *Social Structure and Personality.* New York: Free Press, 1964, pp. 292–324. [5]

———. "Professional Training and the Role of the Professions in American Society," in National Science Foundation, *Scientific Manpower 1958.* Washington, D.C.: National Science Foundation, 1959, pp. 80–87. [4]

———. "Professions," in David L. Sills (ed.), *International Encyclopedia of the Social Sciences.* New York: Free Press, 1968, Vol. 12, pp. 536–547.

———. "The Professions and Social Structure," in Talcott Parsons, *Essays in Sociological Theory,* 2nd ed. New York: Free Press, 1954, pp. 34–49.

———. "Remarks on Education and the Professions," *International Journal of Ethics,* 47:365–369, April 1937. [4]

———. "Service," in *Encyclopedia of the Social Sciences.* New York: The Macmillan Company, 1933, Vol. 13, pp. 672–694.

———. *Social Structure and Personality.* New York: Free Press, 1964, Chap. 12, "Some Theoretical Considerations Bearing on the Field of Medical Sociology," pp. 325–328.

———. *The Social System.* New York: Free Press, 1951, especially Chap. 10, "Social Structure and Dynamic Process: The Case of Modern Medical Practice," pp. 428–479.

———. "A Sociologist Views the Legal Profession," in University of Chicago Law School, *Conference on the Profession of Law and Legal Education.* Chicago: University of Chicago Law School, Conference Series No. 11, pp. 49–63, December 4, 1952.

———. "Some Trends of Change in American Society: Their

Bearing on Medical Education," in Talcott Parsons, *Structure and Process in Modern Societies*. New York: Free Press, 1960, Chap. 9, pp. 280–294. [4]

PARSONS, TALCOTT, AND RENÉE FOX. "Illness, Therapy, and the Modern Urban Family," *Journal of Social Issues*, 8:31–44, 1952. [5]

PATTERSON, C. H. "Counseling and/or Psychotherapy," *American Psychologist*, 18:667–669, October 1963. [7]

PAYNE, GEORGE L. *Britain's Scientific and Technological Manpower*. Stanford, Calif.: Stanford University Press, 1960.

PEARLIN, LEONARD I. "Alienation from Work: A Study of Nursing Personnel," *American Sociological Review*, 27:314–326, June 1962. [11]

PELZ, DONALD C. "Interaction and Attitudes Between Scientists and Auxiliary Staff: I. Viewpoint of Staff; II. Viewpoint of Scientists," *Administrative Science Quarterly*, 4:321–336, 410–425, June 1959 and March 1960. [10]

———. "Motivation of the Engineering and Research Specialist," *General Management Series*. New York: American Management Association, No. 186, January 1957. [11]

PENNELL, MARYLAND Y., AND PAULA A. STEWART. *State Licensing of Health Occupations*, U.S. Public Health Service, Publication No. 1758. Washington, D.C.: Government Printing Office, 1968. [6]

PERLOFF, HARVEY S. *Education for Planning: City, State and Regional*. Baltimore, Md.: The Johns Hopkins Press, 1957. [4]

PERROTT, GEORGE ST. J., AND OTHERS. *Education for the Health Services*. Albany, Williams Press, Inc., 1948. [4]

PERRY, CYRUS C. "A Code of Ethics for Public School Teachers," *Annals of the American Academy of Political and Social Science*, 297:76–82, January 1955. [6]

PERUCCI, ROBERT. "The Significance of Intra-Occupational Mobility: Some Methodological and Theoretical Notes Together with a Case Study of Engineers," *American Sociological Review*, 26:874–883, December 1961. [4]

PETUCHOWSKI, JAKOB J. "The Modern Rabbi," *Commentary*, 35:153–158, February 1963.

PHELPS, CHARLES E. "Women in American Medicine," *Journal of Medical Education*, 43:916–924, August 1968.

PHILLIPS, ORIEL, AND PHILBRICK MCCOY. *Conduct of Judges and*

Lawyers: A Study of Professional Ethics, Discipline and Disbarment. Los Angeles: Parker and Co., 1952. [6]

PIERSON, FRANK C., AND OTHERS. *The Education of American Businessmen.* New York: McGraw-Hill, Inc., 1959. [4]

POLANSKY, NORMAN A. "The Professional Identity in Social Work," in Alfred J. Kahn (ed.), *Issues in American Social Work.* New York: Columbia University Press, 1959, pp. 293–318. [6]

PORTER, CHARLES O. "Surveying the Legal Profession," *Journal of the American Judicature Society,* 32:134–142, February 1949.

POUND, ROSCOE. *The Lawyer from Antiquity to Modern Times: With Particular Reference to the Development of Bar Associations in the United States.* St. Paul, Minn.: West Publishing Co., 1953. [2]

———. "The Legal Profession in America," *Notre Dame Lawyer,* 19:334–353, June 1944.

———. "The Professions in the Society of Today," *New York Medicine,* 5:21–26, 45–46, October 1949. [14]

———. "What Is a Profession? The Rise of the Legal Profession in Antiquity," *Notre Dame Lawyer,* 19:204–205, March 1944. [1, 2]

PRANDY, KENNETH. *Professional Employees: A Study of Scientists and Engineers.* London: Faber and Faber, Ltd., 1965.

PRATT, LOIS, AND OTHERS. "Physicians' Views on the Level of Information Among Patients," in E. Gartly Jaco (ed.), *Patients, Physicians and Illness.* New York: Free Press, 1958, pp. 222–229. [5]

QUINNEY, EARL R. "Occupational Structure and Criminal Behavior: Prescription Violation by Retail Pharmacists," *Social Problems,* 11:179–185, Fall 1963. [5]

RADIN, MAX. "Legal Profession and Legal Education. Modern Legal Education," in *Encyclopedia of the Social Sciences.* New York: The Macmillan Company, 1933, Vol. 9, pp. 334–340. [4]

RASHDALL, HASTINGS. *The Universities of Europe in the Middle Ages.* Oxford: The Clarendon Press, 1895. 2 vols. [2]

RAY, OLIVER A. "The Imperial Russian Officer," *Political Science Quarterly,* 76:576–592, December 1961.

READER, W. J. *Professional Men.* New York: Basic Books, Inc., 1966. The rise of the professional classes in nineteenth-century England. [2]

RECORD, WILSON. "Some Reflections on Bureaucratic Trends in Sociological Research," *American Sociological Review,* 25:411–414, June 1960. [11]

REIF, F. "The Competitive World of the Pure Scientist," *Science,* 134:1957–1962, December 1961. [8]

REISS, ALBERT J., JR. "Occupational Mobility of Professional Workers," *American Sociological Review,* 20:693–700, December 1955. [4]

REISS, ALBERT J., JR., AND OTHERS. *Occupations and Social Status.* New York: Free Press, 1961. [13]

REISSMAN, LEONARD. "Life Careers, Power and the Professions: The Retired Army General," *American Sociological Review,* 21: 215–221, April 1956.

REISSMAN, LEONARD, AND OTHERS. "The Motivation and Socialization of Medical Students," *Journal of Health and Human Behavior,* 1:174–182, Fall 1960. [4]

REITZES, DIETRICH C. *Negroes and Medicine.* Cambridge, Mass.: Harvard University Press, 1958.

RETTIG, SOLOMON, AND OTHERS. "Status Overestimation, Objective Status, and Job Satisfaction Among Professions," *American Sociological Review,* 23:75–81, February 1958. [8, 13]

RICHARDSON, G. A., AND OTHERS. *The Education of Teachers in England, France, and U.S.A.* Paris: UNESCO, 1953. [4]

RIESMAN, DAVID. "Toward an Anthropological Science of Law and the Legal Profession," *American Journal of Sociology,* 57:121–135, September 1951.

RILEY, JOHN W., JR., AND OTHERS. *The Student Looks at his Teacher.* New Brunswick, N.J.: Rutgers University Press, 1950. [5]

RIVERS, W. H. R. *Medicine, Magic and Religion.* London: Kegan Paul, Trench, Trubner and Co., Ltd., 1924. [2]

RIVLIN, ALICE M. *Critical Issues in the Development of Vocational Education.* Washington, D.C.: The Brookings Institution, 1966. [4]

ROADY, THOMAS G., AND WILLIAM R. ANDERSEN (eds.). *Professional Negligence.* Nashville, Tenn.: Vanderbilt University Press, 1960. [5]

ROBERTSON, STEWART, AND GEORGE F. MOTT. "Journalism as a Vocation," in George F. Mott (ed.), *New Survey of Journalism.* New York: Barnes and Noble, Inc., 1950, pp. 11–19.

ROBINSON, VICTOR. *The Story of Medicine.* New York: Tudor Publishing Company, 1931.

———. *White Caps: The Story of Nursing.* Philadelphia, Pa.: J. B. Lippincott Company, 1946. Historical and comparative. [2]

ROBSON, ROBERT. *The Attorney in Eighteenth Century England.* New York: Cambridge University Press, 1959. [2]

RODEHAVER, MYLES W. "Ministers on the Move: A Study of Social Mobility in Church Leadership," *Rural Sociology,* 13:400–410, December 1948. [11]

RODEHAVER, MYLES W., AND LUKE M. SMITH. "Migration and Occupational Structure: The Clergy," *Social Forces,* 29:416–421, May 1951. [4]

ROE, ANNE. *The Making of a Scientist.* New York: Dodd, Mead & Company, 1952. [4]

———. *The Psychology of Occupations.* New York: John Wiley & Sons, Inc., 1956.

ROGOFF, NATALIE. "The Decision to Study Medicine," in Robert K. Merton and others (eds.), *The Student Physician.* Cambridge, Mass.: The Commonwealth Fund, 1957, pp. 109–129. [4]

ROOK, ARTHUR. "Medical Education and the English Universities Before 1800," *Journal of Medical Education,* 38:638–643, August 1963. [2]

ROSEN, GEORGE. *Fee and Fee Bills: Some Economic Aspects of Medical Practice in Nineteenth Century America.* Baltimore, Md.: The Johns Hopkins Press, 1946. [5]

———. *A History of Public Health.* New York: MD Publications, Inc., 1958.

ROSENBERG, HERBERT H., AND LUTHER W. STRINGHAM. "Manpower for Medical Research," in U.S. Department of Health, Education, and Welfare, *New Directions in Health, Education, and Welfare.* Washington, D.C.: Government Printing Office, 1963, pp. 136–145.

ROSENBERG, MORRIS, AND OTHERS. *Occupations and Values.* New York: Free Press, 1957. [4]

ROSS, JAMES STIRLING. *The National Health Service in Great Britain.* London: Oxford University Press, 1952.

ROSSIANIN, IVAN. "Teachers' Colleges in the Soviet Union," in George L. Kline (ed.), *Soviet Education.* New York: Columbia University Press, 1957, pp. 79–93.

ROTH, JULIUS A. "Ritual and Magic in the Control of Contagion," in E. Gartly Jaco (ed.), *Patients, Physicians and Illness.* New York: Free Press, 1958, pp. 229–234. [2]

RUESCHEMEYER, DIETRICH. "Doctors and Lawyers: A Comment on the Theory of the Professions," *The Canadian Review of Sociology and Anthropology,* 1:17–30, February 1964. [1]

RUHE, C. H. WILLIAM. "A Survey of Activities of Medical Schools in the Field of Continuing Medical Education," *Journal of Medical Education,* 38:820–828, October 1963. [4]

RUSHING, WILLIAM A. *The Psychiatric Professions: Power, Conflict and Adaptation in a Psychiatric Hospital Staff.* Chapel Hill, N.C.: The University of North Carolina Press, 1964. [7, 10]

RUTHERFORD, M. LOUISE. *The Influence of the American Bar Association on Public Opinion and Legislation.* Philadelphia, Pa.: University of Pennsylvania, 1937. [9]

SADTLER, B. "The Education of Ministers by Private Tutors, Before the Establishment of Theological Seminaries," *The Lutheran Church Review,* 12:167–183, April 1894. [4]

SALZ, ARTHUR. "Occupation," in *Encyclopedia of the Social Sciences.* New York: The Macmillan Company, 1933, Vol. 11, pp. 424–435.

———. "Specialization," in *Encyclopedia of the Social Sciences.* New York: The Macmillan Company, 1933, Vol. 14, pp. 279–285.

SANAZARD, PAUL J., AND EDWIN B. HUTCHINS. "The Origin and Rationale of the Medical College Admission Test," *Journal of Medical Education,* 38:1044–1050, December 1963.

SARAPATA, ADAM, AND WLODZIMIERZ WESOLOWSKI. "The Evaluation of Occupations by Warsaw Inhabitants," *American Journal of Sociology,* 66:581–591, May 1961. [13]

SCHMID, CALVIN F., AND MILDRED GIBLIN. "Needs and Standards in Training Sociologists," *Sociology and Social Research,* 39:296–306, May–June 1955. [4]

SCHROEDER, W. WIDICK. "Lay Expectations of the Ministerial Role," *Journal for the Scientific Study of Religion,* 2:217–227, Spring 1963. [5]

SCHWARTZ, BENJAMIN. "The Intelligentsia in Communist China: A Tentative Comparison," *Daedalus,* 89:604–621, Summer 1960.

SCHWARTZ, MORRIS S., AND OTHERS. *The Nurse and the Mental Patient: A Study in Interpersonal Relations.* New York: Russell Sage Foundation, 1956. [5]

SCHWARTZ, RICHARD D., AND JAMES C. MILLER. "Legal Evolution and Societal Complexity," *American Journal of Sociology,* 70:159–169, September 1964. [2]

SCHWEINBERG, ERIC F. *Law Training in Continental Europe: Its Principles and Public Function.* New York: Russell Sage Foundation, 1945. [4]

SCOTT, RICHARD, AND EDMUND VOLKART (eds.). *Medical Care:*

Readings in the Sociology of Medical Institutions. New York: John Wiley & Sons, Inc., 1966.

SEEMAN, MELVIN. "Role Conflict and Ambivalence in Leadership," *American Sociological Review,* 18:373–380, August 1953. [12]

SEEMAN, MELVIN, AND JOHN W. EVANS. "Apprenticeship and Attitude Change," *American Journal of Sociology,* 67: 365–378, January 1962. [4]

SEGAL, BERNARD E. "Nurses and Patients: Time, Place, and Distance," *Social Problems,* 9:257–264, Winter 1962. [5]

SEN, P. K. "The Present Position of Medical Education in India," *Journal of Medical Education,* 38:577–583, July 1963. [4]

SHAPIRO, CAROL S., AND OTHERS. "Careers of Women Physicians: A Survey of Women Graduates from Seven Medical Schools, 1945–1951," *Journal of Medical Education,* 43:1033–1040, October 1968.

SHARAF, MYRON R., AND DANIEL J. LEVINSON. "The Quest for Omnipotence in Professional Training: The Case of the Psychiatric Resident," *Psychiatry,* 27:135–149, May 1964. [4]

SHEATS, PAUL H. "The Role of University Extension in Liberalizing Continuing Education of Professionals," in University of British Columbia, *Symposium on Continuing Education in the Professions.* Vancouver: University of British Columbia, 1962, pp. 41–54. [4]

SHERMAN, MORTON. *Professional Careers in Science and Technology.* New York: The Scarecrow Press, Inc., 1963. [4]

SHEWMAKER, WILLIAM O. "The Training of the Protestant Ministry in the United States of America Before the Establishment of Theological Seminaries," *Papers of the American Society of Church History,* 6:73–202, 1921, 2nd series. [4]

SHIH, CH'ENG-CHIH. *The Status of Science and Education in Communist China and a Comparison with that in U.S.S.R.* Hong Kong: Union Research Institute, 1962. [4]

SHIH, CHUNG. *Higher Education in Communist China.* Kowloon, Hong Kong: The Union Research Institute, 1953. [4]

SHIMKIN, D. "Scientific Personnel in the U.S.S.R.," *Science,* 116: 512–513, November 1952. [4]

SHRYOCK, RICHARD H. "The Academic Profession in the United States," *American Association of University Professors Bulletin,* 38:32–70, Spring 1952. Historical, including the growth of the Association.

———. *The Development of Modern Medicine.* New York: Alfred A. Knopf, Inc., 1947. [2]

———. *Medical Licensing in America, 1650–1965.* Baltimore, Md.: Johns Hopkins University Press, 1967. [6]

———. *Medicine and Society in America, 1660–1860.* New York: New York University Press, 1960. [2]

———. *Medicine in America: Historical Essays.* Baltimore, Md.: Johns Hopkins University Press, 1966. [2]

SHUVAL, JUDITH. "Ethnic Stereotyping in Israeli Medical Bureaucracies," *Sociology and Social Research,* 46:455–465, July 1962.

SIBLEY, ELBRIDGE. *The Education of Sociologists in the United States.* New York: Russell Sage Foundation, 1963. [4]

SIGERIST, HENRY E. *A History of Medicine,* Vol. I, *Primitive and Archaic Medicine.* New York: Oxford University Press, 1951. [2]

———. *Medicine and Health in the Soviet Union.* New York: The Citadel Press, 1947.

SIMMEL, ERNEST. "The 'Doctor-Game,' Illness, and the Profession of Medicine," *International Journal of Psychoanalysis,* 7:470–483, 1926. [5]

SIMMONS, LEO W., AND HAROLD G. WOLFF. *Social Science in Medicine.* New York: Russell Sage Foundation, 1954. [7]

SKLARE, MARSHALL. *Conservative Judaism.* New York: Free Press, 1955, Chap. 6, "The Conservative Rabbi," pp. 159–198.

SLAMECKA, VLADIMIR. *Science in East Germany.* New York: Columbia University Press, 1963.

SLOCUM, WALTER L. *Occupational Careers.* Chicago: Aldine Publishing Company, 1966.

SMALL, LEONARD. "Toward Professional Clinical Psychology," *American Psychologist,* 18:558–562, September 1963. [3]

SMIGEL, ERWIN O. "The Impact of Recruitment on the Organization of the Large Law Firm," *American Sociological Review,* 25:56–66, February 1960. [11]

———. "Trends in Occupational Sociology in the United States: A Survey of Postwar Research," *American Sociological Review,* 19:398–404, August 1954.

———. *The Wall Street Lawyer: Professional Organization Man?* New York: Free Press, 1964.

SMITH, DAN T. "Education for Administration," *Harvard Business Review,* 23:360–371, Spring 1945. [4]

SMITH, HARVEY L. "Contingencies of Professional Differentiation," *American Journal of Sociology*, 63:410–414, January 1958. [7]

———. "Psychiatry in Medicine: Intra- or Interprofessional Relationships?" *American Journal of Sociology*, 63:285–296, November 1957. [7]

SMITH, HENRY. "Accountancy in the Modern State," *Political Quarterly*, 18: 116–122, April–June 1947.

SMITH, JAMES OTIS, AND GIDEON SJOBERG. "Origins and Career Patterns of Leading Protestant Clergymen," *Social Forces*, 39:290–296, May 1961. [4]

SMITH, LUKE M. "The Clergy: Authority Structure, Ideology, Migration," *American Sociological Review*, 18:242–248, June 1953.

SMYTH, FRANCIS SCOTT. "Health and Medicine in Indonesia," *Journal of Medical Education*, 38:693–696, August 1963.

SOEMARDI, SOELAEMAN. "Some Aspects of the Social Origin of Indonesian Political Decision Makers," in *Transactions of the Third World Congress of Sociology*. London: International Sociological Association, 1956, Vol. III, pp. 338–348. [4]

SOMERS, ANNE RAMSAY. "Conflict, Accommodation and Progress: Some Socioeconomic Observations on Medical Education and the Practising Profession," *Journal of Medical Education*, 38:466–478, June 1963. Conflict between the American Association of Medical Colleges and the American Medical Association. [9]

SOMERS, HERMAN M., AND ANNE R. SOMERS. *Doctors, Patients, and Health Insurance: The Organization and Financing of Medical Care*. Washington, D.C.: The Brookings Institution, 1961. [5]

SONI, B. D. "Sociological Analysis of Legal Profession: A Study of Mechanisms in Lawyer-Client Relationship," *Journal of Social Sciences*, 1:63–70, January 1958. [5]

SPENCER, HERBERT. *The Principles of Sociology*. New York: D. Appleton and Company, 1896, Vol. II–3, Part VII, pp. 179–324, "Professional Institutions." [2]

SPERRY, WILLARD L. *The Ethical Basis of Medical Care*. New York: Paul B. Hoeber, Inc., 1950. [14]

STANDLEE, MARY. *The Great Pulse: Japanese Midwifery and Obstetrics Through the Ages*. Rutland, Vt.: Chas. E. Tuttle Co., 1959. [2]

STANLEY, C. MAXWELL. *The Consulting Engineer*. New York: John Wiley & Sons, Inc., 1961.

STERN, BERNHARD J. *American Medical Practice.* New York: The Commonwealth Fund, 1945.

———. *Medicine in Industry.* New York: The Commonwealth Fund, 1946. [5]

———. "The Specialist and the General Practitioner," in E. Gartly Jaco (ed.), *Patients, Physicians and Illness.* New York: Free Press, 1958, pp. 352–360. [7]

STIGLER, GEORGE J. *Employment and Compensation in Education.* New York: National Bureau of Economic Research, Occasional Paper No. 33, 1950.

STINETT, T. M. "The Accreditation and Professionalization of Teaching," *Journal of Teacher Education,* 3:30–39, March 1952. [3]

STOKE, HAROLD W. *The American College President.* New York: Harper & Row, Publishers, 1959. [12]

STONE, ERIC. *Medicine Among the American Indians.* New York: P. B. Hoeber, Inc., 1932. [2]

STORER, NORMAN W. "The Coming Changes in American Science," *Science,* 142:464–467, October 1963. [7]

———. *The Social System of Science.* New York: Holt, Rinehart and Winston, Inc., 1966.

STOREY, ROBERT G. *Professional Leadership.* Claremont, Calif.: Associated Colleges at Claremont, 1958. The lawyer's responsibility to the client and the public. [5, 14]

STRAUSS, ANSELM L., AND OTHERS. *The Professional Scientist: A Study of American Chemists.* Chicago: Aldine Publishing Company, 1962.

STRAUSS, GEORGE. "Professionalism and Occupational Associations," *Industrial Relations,* 2:7–31, May 1963. [9]

STREETER, BURNETT H. *The Primitive Church: Studied with Special Reference to the Origins of the Christian Ministry.* New York: The Macmillan Company, 1929. [2]

SUSSMAN, MARVIN B. "Occupational Sociology and Rehabilitation," in Marvin B. Sussman (ed.), *Sociology and Rehabilitation.* Washington, D.C.: American Sociological Association, n.d.—app. 1965, Chap. 10. See especially pp. 181–189 on a scale of professionalism. [1]

SUSSMAN, MARVIN B., AND OTHERS. *Professional Associations and Memberships in Rehabilitation Counseling.* Cleveland: Western Reserve University, 1965, Working Paper No. 2. [9]

SWAINE, ROBERT T. "Impact of Big Business on the Profession,"

American Bar Association Journal, 35:89–92, 168–171, February 1949.

SWEET, WILLIAM W. "The Rise of Theological Schools in America," *Church History,* 6:260–273, September 1937. [2]

TAEUSCH, CARL F. *Professional and Business Ethics.* New York: Holt, Rinehart and Winston, Inc., 1926. [6]

TAFT, RONALD. "The Social Grading of Occupations in Australia," *British Journal of Sociology,* 4:181–188, June 1953. [13]

TAWNEY, R. H. "Industry as a Profession," in R. H. Tawney (ed.), *The Acquisitive Society.* New York: Harcourt, Brace & World, Inc., 1920, pp. 91–122. [1]

TAYLOR, LEE. *Occupational Sociology.* New York: Oxford University Press, 1968.

TAYLOR, LEE, AND ROLAND J. PELLEGRIN. "Professionalization: Its Functions and Dysfunctions for the Life Insurance Occupation," *Social Forces,* 38:110–114, December 1959. [3]

TEAD, ORDWAY. "Faculty-Administration Relationships in the Colleges of New York: Ten-Year Appraisal," *American Association of University Professors Bulletin,* 34:67–78, March 1948. [11]

———. "The Place and Functions of the Faculty in College Government," *American Association of University Professors Bulletin,* 25:163–168, April 1939. [12]

TEITSWORTH, CLARK S. "Growing Role of the Company Economist," *Harvard Business Review,* 37:97–104, January–February 1959. [11]

TELLER, W. *The Office of a Bishop.* London: Darton, Longman, and Todd, 1962.

TERRIEN, FREDERIC W. "Who Thinks What About Educators?" *American Journal of Sociology,* 59:150–158, September 1953. [13]

TERRIS, MILTON, AND MARY MONK. "Changes in Physicians' Careers: Relation of Time After Graduation to Specialization," in E. Gartly Jaco (ed.), *Patients, Physicians and Illness.* New York: Free Press, 1958, pp. 361–365. [7]

THIELENS, WAGNER. "Some Comparisons of Entrants to Medical and Law School," in Robert K. Merton and others (eds.), *The Student Physician.* Cambridge, Mass.: The Commonwealth Fund, 1957, pp. 131–152. [4]

THOMAS, EDWIN J. "Role Conceptions and Organizational Size," *American Sociological Review,* 24:30–37, February 1959. [11]

THOMAS, H. ORISHE JOLIMI. "The Changing Pattern of Medical

Education in Nigeria," *Journal of Medical Education,* 38:1011–1015, December 1963. [4]

THOMAS, WILLIAM I. "The Relation of the Medicine Man to the Origin of the Professional Occupations," in University of Chicago *The Decennial Publications.* Chicago: University of Chicago Press, 1903, First Series, Vol. 4, pp. 239–256. [2]

THOMPSON, CHARLES H. "Some Critical Aspects of the Problem of Higher and Professional Education for Negroes," *Journal of Negro Education,* 14:509–526, Fall 1945.

THOMPSON, CHARLES J. S. *The Mystery and Art of the Apothecary.* London: The Bodley Head, Ltd., 1929. The history of the apothecary from Babylonia to the 18th century. [2]

THOMPSON, DANIEL C. *The Negro Leadership Class.* Englewood Cliffs, N.J.: Prentice-Hall, Inc., 1963.

THOMPSON, DONNA. *Professional Solidarity Among the Teachers of England.* New York: Columbia University Press, 1927. [6]

THORNER, ISIDOR. "Nursing: The Functional Significance of an Institutional Pattern," *American Sociological Review,* 20:531–538, October 1955. Aspects of the patient-nurse relationship are discussed, using Parsons' *pattern* variables. [5]

———. "Pharmacy: The Functional Significance of an Institutional Pattern," *Social Forces,* 20:321–328, March 1942. [5]

T'IEN, H. Y. "A Profile of the Australian Academic Profession," *Australian Quarterly,* 32:66–74, March 1960.

TIRYAKIAN, EDWARD A. "The Prestige Evaluation of Occupations in an Underdeveloped Country: The Philippines," *American Journal of Sociology,* 63:390–399, January 1958. [13]

TITMUSS, RICHARD M. *Essays on the Welfare State.* London: Allen and Unwin, 1958. Chaps. 8–10 deal with aspects of the National Health Service in England.

TROPP, ASHER. "Factors Affecting the Status of the School Teacher in England and Wales," in *Transactions of the Second World Congress of Sociology.* London: International Sociological Association, 1954, Vol. II, pp. 166–174. [13]

———. *The School Teachers: The Growth of the Teaching Profession in England and Wales from 1800 to the Present Day.* London: William Heinemann, Ltd., 1957. [2]

TROW, MARTIN. "Some Implications of the Social Origins of Engineers," in National Science Foundation, *Scientific Manpower 1958.* Washington, D.C.: National Science Foundation, 1959, pp. 67–74. [4]

TRYON, ROBERT C. "Psychology in Flux: The Academic, Professional Bipolarity," *American Psychologist*, 18:134–143, March 1963. [7]

TURKEVICH, JOHN. "The Soviet's Scientific Elite," *Saturday Review*, 39:60–62, March 24, 1956.

ULMER, SIDNEY S. "Public Office in the Social Background of Supreme Court Justices," *American Journal of Economics and Sociology*, 21:57–68, January 1962. [4]

UNDERWOOD, E. ASHWORTH (ed.). *A History of the Worshipful Society of Apothecaries of London, Vol. I, 1617–1815.* London: Oxford University Press, 1963. [2]

UNESCO, *Teachers' Associations.* Paris: UNESCO, 1961. [9]

U.S. BUREAU OF THE CENSUS. *U.S. Census of Population, 1960; Subject Reports: Characteristics of Professional Workers,* Final Report, PC(2)–7E. Washington, D.C.: Government Printing Office, 1964.

———. *Wages in the U.S.S.R., 1950–1966: Health Services.* Washington, D.C.: U.S. Department of Commerce, April 1968.

U.S. OFFICE OF EDUCATION. *Accreditation in Higher Education.* Washington, D.C.: U.S. Department of Health, Education, and Welfare, 1959. Historical and statistical treatment of accreditation by state, regional and professional agencies. [6]

———. *Education for the Professions.* Washington, D.C.: Government Printing Office, 1955.

U.S. PUBLIC HEALTH SERVICE, NATIONAL CENTER FOR HEALTH STATISTICS. *Health Resources Statistics: Health Manpower and Health Facilities, 1968.* Washington, D.C.: Government Printing Office, 1968.

———. *The Licensing of Health Occupations.* Washington, D.C.: Government Printing Office, 1968. [6]

VANDERBILT, ARTHUR T. *A Report on Prelegal Education.* New York: New York University School of Law, 1944. [4]

VAN DER KROEF, JUSTUS M. "The Cult of the Doctor: An Indonesian Variant," *Journal of Educational Sociology*, 32:389–391, April 1959. [2]

VEBLEN, THORSTEN. *The Higher Learning in America: A Memorandum on the Conduct of Universities by Business Men.* New York: B. W. Huebsch, 1918. [4]

VINTER, ROBERT D. "The Social Structure of Service," in Alfred J. Kahn (ed.), *Issues in American Social Work.* New York: Columbia University Press, 1959, pp. 242–269.

VOLLMER, HOWARD M., AND DONALD L. MILLS. "Nuclear Technology and the Professionalization of Labor," *American Journal of Sociology*, 67:690–696, May 1962. [3]

———. *Professionalization*. Englewood Cliffs, N.J.: Prentice-Hall, Inc., 1966. [3]

VON FERBER, CHRISTIAN. "The Social Background of German University and College Professors Since 1864," in *Transactions of the Third World Congress of Sociology*. London: International Sociological Association, 1956, Vol. III, pp. 239–244. [4]

WAGNER, H. A. "Principles of Professional Conduct in Engineering," *Annals of the American Academy of Political and Social Science*, 297:46–58, January 1955. [6]

WALKER, HELEN E. *The Negro in the Medical Profession*. Charlottesville, Va.: University of Virginia, Phelps Stokes Fellowship Papers, No. 18, 1949.

WALLER, WILLARD. *The Sociology of Teaching*. New York: John Wiley & Sons, Inc., 1932. [5]

WALTON, RICHARD E. *The Impact of the Professional Engineering Union*. Boston: Harvard Business School, 1961. [9]

WARDWELL, WALTER I. "Limited, Marginal, and Quasi-Practitioners," in Howard E. Freeman and others (eds.), *Handbook of Medical Sociology*. Englewood Cliffs, N.J.: Prentice-Hall, Inc., 1963, pp. 213–239. [10]

———. "A Marginal Professional Role: The Chiropractor," in E. Gartly Jaco (ed.), *Patients, Physicians and Illness*. New York: Free Press, 1958, pp. 421–433. [7]

———. "The Reduction of Strain in a Marginal Social Role," *American Journal of Sociology*, 61:16–25, July 1955. The chiropractor. [7]

———. "Social Integration, Bureaucratization and the Professions," *Social Forces*, 33:356–359, May 1955. [11]

WARDWELL, WALTER I., AND ARTHUR L. WOOD. "The Extra-Professional Role of the Lawyer," *American Journal of Sociology*, 61:304–307, January 1956. [13, 14]

WARKOV, SEYMOUR. *Lawyers in the Making*. Chicago: Aldine Publishing Company, 1965. [4]

WATSON, GOODWIN. "Moral Issues in Psychotherapy," *American Psychologist*, 13:574–576, October 1958. [5, 14]

WATSON, T. *The Principles of Medical Ethics of the American Medical Association*. Chicago: American Medical Association, 1953. [6]

WATTENBERG, WILLIAM, AND ROBERT J. HAVIGHURST. "The American Teacher—Then and Now," in Lindley J. Stiles (ed.), *The Teacher's Role in American Society*. New York: Harper & Row, Publishers, 1957, pp. 3–12.

WEBB, SIDNEY, AND BEATRICE WEBB (eds.). "Special Supplement on Professional Associations," *New Statesman*, Vol. IX, Parts I and II, April 21 and 28, 1917.

WEBER, MAX. "Science as a Vocation," in H. H. Gerth and C. Wright Mills (eds.), *From Max Weber: Essays in Sociology*. New York: Oxford University Press, 1958, pp. 129–179.

WESLEY, EDGAR B. *NEA: The First Hundred Years*. New York: Harper & Row, Publishers, 1957. The history and structure of the National Education Association. [9]

WEST, S. STEWART. "Class Origins of Scientists," *Sociometry*, 24: 251–269, September 1961. [4]

WETTER, GUSTAV. "Ideology and Science in the Soviet Union: Recent Developments," *Daedalus*, 89:581–603, Summer 1960.

WILENSKY, HAROLD L. *Intellectuals in Labor Unions: Organizational Pressures on Professional Roles*. New York: Free Press, 1956. [11]

———. "Orderly Careers and Social Participation: The Impact of Work History on Social Integration in the Middle Mass," *American Sociological Review*, 26:521–539, August 1961.

———. *Organizational Intelligence: Knowledge and Policy in Government and Industry*. New York: Basic Books, Inc., 1967. [11]

———. "The Professionalization of Everyone?" *American Journal of Sociology*, 70:137–158, September 1964. [1, 3]

———. "The Uneven Distribution of Leisure: The Impact of Economic Growth on 'Free Time,' " *Social Problems*, 9:32–56, Summer 1961.

———. "Work as a Social Problem," in Howard S. Becker (ed.), *Social Problems: A Modern Approach*. New York: John Wiley & Sons, Inc., 1966, Chap. 3, pp. 117–166. Discusses differential occupational commitment and alienation from work. [1]

WILENSKY, HAROLD L., AND CHARLES N. LEBEAUX. *Industrial Society and Social Welfare*. New York: Russell Sage Foundation, 1958, especially Chap. XI, "The Emergence of a Social Work Profession." [3]

WILLIAMS, GEORGE. *Some of My Best Friends Are Professors*. New York: Abelard-Schuman Limited, 1958.

WILLIAMS, JOSEPHINE J. "Patients and Prejudice: Law Attitudes

Toward Women Physicians," *American Journal of Sociology,* 51:
283–287, January 1946. [5]

WILSON, BRYAN R. "The Pentecostalist Minister: Role Conflicts
and Status Contradictions," *American Journal of Sociology,* 64:
494–504, March 1959. [8]

———. "The Teacher's Role: A Sociological Analysis," *British
Journal of Sociology,* 13:15–32, March 1962.

WILSON, EUGENE H. "The Preparation and Use of the Professional
Staff," *The Library Quarterly,* 31:104–114, January 1961. [4]

WILSON, KENNETH M. *Of Time and the Doctorate, Report of an
Inquiry into the Duration of Doctoral Study.* Atlanta, Ga.: Southern Regional Education Board, 1965. [4]

WILSON, LOGAN. *The Academic Man: A Study in the Sociology of
a Profession.* New York: Oxford University Press, 1942.

———. "Disjunctive Process in the Academic Milieu," in Edward
A. Tiryakian (ed.), *Sociological Theory, Values, and Sociocultural
Change.* New York: Free Press, 1963, pp. 283–294. Faculty-administration conflicts, particularly from the point of view of the academic administrator. [12]

WILSON, WOODROW. "The Minister and the Community," in John R.
Mott (ed.), *The Claims and Opportunities of the Christian Ministry.* New York: YMCA Press, 1911, pp. 108–120. [14]

WINGER, HOWARD W. "Aspects of Librarianship: A Trace Work of
History," *Library Quarterly,* 31:321–335, October 1961. Historical
survey since ancient times. [2]

WINTERS, GLENN R. *Bar Association Organization and Activities.*
Ann Arbor, Mich.: Survey of the Legal Profession, 1954. [9]

———. "The Contribution of Professional Organizations to Stabil-
ity and Change Through Law," *Vanderbilt Law Review,* 17:265–
272, December 1963.

WITTLIN, ALMA S. "The Teacher," *Daedalus,* 92:745–763, Fall 1963.
Reprinted in Kenneth S. Lynn (ed.), *The Professions in America.*
Boston: Houghton Mifflin Company, 1965.

WOLFLE, DAEL. *America's Resources of Specialized Talent.* New
York: Harper & Row, Publishers, 1954.

WOOD, ARTHUR L. "Informal Relations in the Practice of Criminal
Law," *American Journal of Sociology,* 62:48–55, July 1956. [5]

———. "Professional Ethics Among Criminal Lawyers," *Social
Problems,* 7:70–83, Summer 1959. [6]

WOOD, FRANCIS. "Medical Education in America Before 1900,"
Journal of Medical Education, 38:631–637, August 1963. [2]

WOODSON, CARTER GODWIN. *The Negro Professional Man and the Community.* Washington, D.C.: The Association for the Study of Negro Life and History, Inc., 1934.

WOOTON, BARBARA. "The Image of the Social Worker," *British Journal of Sociology,* 11:373–384, December 1960. [13]

WYLE, FREDERICK. "The Soviet Lawyer: An Occupational Profile," in Alex Inkeles and Kent Geiger (eds.), *Soviet Society.* Boston: Houghton Mifflin Company, 1961, pp. 210–218.

YEAGER, WAYNE, AND OTHERS. "The Mental Health Worker: A New Public Health Professional," *American Journal of Public Health,* 52:1625–1630, October 1962. [3]

YOUNG, DONALD. "Sociology and the Practicing Professions," *American Sociological Review,* 20:641–648, December 1955. A call for cooperation with practitioners of social work, law, and the health services. [10]

————. "Universities and Cooperation Among Metropolitan Professions," in Robert M. Fisher (ed.), *The Metropolis in Modern Life.* New York: Doubleday & Company, Inc., 1955, pp. 289–303. [10]

ZAPOLEON, MARGUERITE W. "Women in the Professions," *Journal of Social Issues,* 6:13–24, 1950.

ZINBERG, NORMAN E. "Psychiatry: A Professional Dilemma," *Daedalus,* 92:808–823, Fall 1963. Reprinted in Kenneth S. Lynn (ed.), *The Professions in America.* Boston: Houghton Mifflin Company, 1965. Discussion of the acceptance of psychiatry in the United States. [13]

ZNANIECKI, FLORIAN. *The Social Role of the Man of Knowledge.* New York: Columbia University Press, 1940. [14]

ZUCKERMAN, HARRIET. "Nobel Laureates in Science: Patterns of Productivity, Collaboration, and Authorship," *American Sociological Review,* 32:391–403, June 1967. [8]

ZYTOWSKI, DONALD G. (ed.), *Vocational Behavior: Readings in Theory and Research.* New York: Holt, Rinehart and Winston, Inc., 1968.

Index